CONSOLING GHOSTS

CONSOLING GHOSTS

Stories of Medicine and Mourning from Southeast Asians in Exile

Jean M. Langford

University of Minnesota Press

Minneapolis

London

Contents

Note on Transliteration

Hmong, Kmhmu, Lao, and Khmer words have been romanized according to the most common spellings in scholarly texts consulted or, in the absence of textual references, according to the suggestions of my bilingual research associates. I apologize for any resulting inconsistencies in transliteration styles.

Introduction **Afterlives**

IMAGINE THIS WORK AS CIRCLING RESTLESSLY around two ethnographic conversations—one that was regretted, another that was refused. In 1999 one of my research associates and I spoke several times with a middle-aged Lao couple, Major Samsuthi and his wife Bouakhay.[1] While writing my doctoral thesis on an entirely different topic, I'd been hired by the research unit of a hospital to talk to Lao, Khmer, Kmhmu, and Hmong emigrants about death.[2] Unable to ask them directly for stories of the deaths they had known, I asked them instead for the stories of their lives. Like many others, Major Samsuthi and his wife were generous with their stories, which retraced years of war, reeducation camp, and escape from Laos across the Mekong River, intermixed with reminiscences of schooling, marriage, Buddhist practice, healings, soul-callings, funeral rites, and migration to the United States. Our last conversation took place in their living room, where we sat on the carpet in a semicircle around the miniature tape recorder supplied by the hospital, that social scientific prosthetic that promises to transform stories into information, as if sounds and pauses etched on vinyl ribbon (or these days inscribed in binary code) might supplement the gaps and lapses in listeners' comprehension. After dinner we sipped chrysanthemum tea, discussing its virtues for dispelling heat.

We had made plans to talk to the couple's grown children also, but a week later we heard that Major Samsuthi and his wife had suffered nightmares and insomnia following our final visit. Their children were angry that their parents had been disturbed by our conversations and understandably declined to speak with us. Thinking over that last evening, I assumed that the couple's nightmares had repeated the terrors of being rowed across the Mekong under gunfire or waiting in a Thai relocation camp where the soldiers sometimes robbed refugees at gunpoint. But no: they had dreamed, we learned, of the deaths by liver cancer of their first spouses in U.S. hospitals.

1

This book, then, contemplates a palimpsest of nightmares through which this family and others are haunted not only by the violence of Southeast Asian war zones, but also by more subtle violations within the institutions that manage death in North America. I ask how memories of a loved one's death in a U.S. hospital might come to be as powerfully disturbing as memories of crossing borders under rifle fire or near starvation in a prison or reeducation camp. At times the temporalities of these two sets of memories slip into simultaneity through the insistent if dreamlike (or literally dreamed) presence of the dead. For the dead, as anyone who has grieved knows, do not appear only in memories, safely ensconced in the past, but also erupt into the present with a physical, if oneiric, force.

As James Siegel has shown for Java, "productive" spirits of the dead appear in dreams as vitally embodied, and even nicely dressed. Such dreams are, he argues, forms of mourning that "efface" the transformation at death of living body into corpse, allowing the "mutilated" body to be forgotten (2006, 121–22). Dreams of contented spirits with intact bodies are not nightmares, then, but more benign visitations. When Douang, a Lao counselor, tried to articulate why grief was more prolonged in the United States than in Laos, he mused, "In Laos, people talk about their dreams. . . . People ask you, 'Have you had any dreams about your husband? Did he come and tell you the lottery number?' And you laugh together." Nightmares, on the other hand, repeat the death itself, remaining preoccupied with an image of the corpse or the manner of death. During nightmares of the war in Laos, for instance, Hmong men report encountering the decomposing bodies of deceased family members (Mouanoutoua 2003, 217–18). Significantly, the Khmer word *khmoc* can refer either to a corpse or to a malevolent ghost (E. Davis 2009, 76). Whatever images of the dead dominated Major Samsuthi's or Bouakhay's nightmares, they were evidently not benevolent spirits imparting lottery numbers, but more likely cancer-ravaged spirits lying in hospital beds.

Just before dinner, Bouakhay had spoken of her first husband's last conscious moments. After refusing surgery, he agreed to enter the hospital for chemotherapy.

> They could not get the needle in the vein for the chemotherapy. And he moved too much. He was kind of struggling. So they gave him an injection, and after that he went into a coma and never recovered. And then on the fourth day after he was hospitalized he died. . . . I am not very happy with that injection, because after he received that injection he could not talk. For two days he did not talk. He became just like unconscious. He could

open his eyes, but he could not talk. . . . That doctor who took care of my husband, he does not work there any more. I don't know, maybe he had a problem with the hospital after giving that injection to my husband. There is still a question in my mind, but I know that my husband was sick, so I just let it go.

Later in the evening, someone told a story about a boy in Laos who contracted malaria. The family consulted a local *moh phi* (spirit doctor) who pierced the boy's skin with a sharpened stick, demanding that the spirit who was troubling him return to the forest. The cure failed, and everyone agreed that such shamanic treatments are very frightening. Only later did I register the uncanny homology between the doctor's needle and the *moh phi*'s stick, both ineffective, both arousing uneasiness. In Bouakhay's image of her first husband's body after the injection, the body is less mutilated (in Siegel's terms) than medicalized, or rather it is mutilated in a specifically medical way. When asked to generalize her impressions of U.S. medicine, Bouakhay, like many emigrants, assured me that hospitals here are very good: there are lots of drugs and procedures available, unlike in Laos. Medicine's violence is not manifest in responses to ethnographic questions, but rather is uncannily referenced in stories of appearances of the dead.

As far as I know, the couple's nightmares were the only occasion on which the dead temporarily shut down my fieldwork, displacing the disciplinary surveillance of interviews with a literally haunted silence. In retrospect, however, this displacement of conversation by nightmares was simply one of the starker moments of fieldwork when my attention to emigrants' lives was forcefully redirected toward the dead. Emigrants' stories often referred and deferred me to the dead: their needs, their discomfort, their authority, their power. The recurring appearances of spirits in emigrants' narratives obliquely registered the institutionalized exclusion or neglect of the souls and bodies of the dying and the dead. Souls are driven out of hospitalized patients by clinical talk of death, leaving the patients listless and depressed. Spirits of those who died in violence or whose bodily remains were lost return to haunt the living with bloodied limbs and muddy faces. Dead whose gravesites were disturbed or whose funeral rites were incomplete induce illness in living relatives. Guardian spirits of villages regretfully admit that they can hardly be expected to rescue the living when they themselves must flee because of war or a political crackdown on specters of all kinds. To take account of these phantom protagonists is not so much to identify a field of cultural difference based on spirit beliefs as to confront the histories through which spirits become critical players (cf.

Ong 1987; Morris 2000, 2002; Keyes 2002; Taussig 1987; Mueggler 2001; Kwon 2008).

By evoking the possibility of haunting, emigrants call spirits as witnesses to violations of the dead in wartime Asia that resonate with similar violations within U.S. institutions. Rather than read such violations of the dead as metaphorical of violence against the living, I understand them as metonymic of a pervasive tendency within thanatopolitical regimes (in which I include war and state terror alongside medicine and mortuary science) to foreclose social interchange between living and dead. While Giorgio Agamben coined the term "thanatopolitics" to refer to those moments when biopolitics— Michel Foucault's (1990) term for the management of life in modern societies—results in a decision about death (Agamben 1998, 122, 148), I use it here to highlight the way that everyday biopolitics, as deployed in a number of settings, involves determinations about the relative value of particular lives, the relative permissibility of particular deaths, and an implicit governance of the traffic between living and dead. In this formulation, thanatopolitics is resonant with Mbembe's idea of necropolitics, in that it draws attention to the institutionalized dispensability of racialized peoples and the reduction of the dead within specific regimes of violence to "empty, meaningless corporealities" (2003, 35). However, thanatopolitics, as I invoke it here, expands on necropolitics to consider the implications of such regimes of violence for the social existence of the dead, and to force a recognition, as Stuart Murray suggests, of the "co-belonging" of the living and the dead (2008, 206).

To interpret a terror of contemporary management of death as simply the displacement of a memory of more violent deaths in Southeast Asia would reproduce a security that there is no reason for dread within the cleanly impartial ethos of a modern hospital. Yet nightmares such as those of Major Samsuthi and his wife suggest the uncanny presences that attend the medical and mortuary governance of life and death. The violence registered by nightmares and hauntings is not only the remembered and embodied violence of war or state terror but also the structural violence of minoritization and poverty. One of the sites where this violence is most acutely felt is in professional regulation of the end of life, which in denying the social presence of the dead may impel them, in their desperation, to harass the living. Stories of hauntings and potential hauntings gesture to an embodied testimony of the dead that questions business as usual in the halls of thanatopolitics and within the institutionalized mourning of personal and collective loss.

A Matter of Life and Death

MRS. TRAN: You have to realize this is a difficult decision. This is a life-and-death decision. He's saying if we leave everything, she'll die slower. If we remove everything, she'll die faster.

. . . .

SOCIAL WORKER (working hard to show respect for the way the family perceives the situation): I know, culturally, your family needs to come to a decision.

MRS. TRAN: Not even culturally—this is life and death. (Kaufman 2005, 172)

A matter of life and death. I take Mrs. Tran's succinct statement as a compass for my consideration of the stories in this book. Despite what might be the temptation to read these stories as parables of cultural difference, I suggest they be read as parables of life and death. Emigrant storytellers and their dead and dying protagonists suggest ways to face death, conduct relationships with the dead and the dying, and address the effects of violence that continue to reverberate in bodies and social worlds. They invite dialogue on ethics, care for the dying, and afterlives. Not reducible to examples of cultural belief or symptoms of historical trauma, these stories enact vernacular theorizations of death, not as locally specific perspectives, but as possibilities for modes of engagement with death and with the dead. They offer philosophical interventions into questions of materiality, subjectivity, mourning, bioethics, and the socialities of living and dead.

When I was hired to conduct the research from which this book eventually emerged, ethnicity had already been established as the primary variable. The central concern of the people with whom I spoke, however, was not so much ethnically marked worldviews as the ethics of life and death. In the context of his work with Thai Buddhists, Alan Klima notes that Buddhist theories can hardly be placed in dialogue with academic theories as long as each is envisioned as belonging to a mutually exclusive cultural world. Culture, he observes, "is a favored form for readmitting alterity into liberal discourse on that discourse's own terms" (2002, 20). In the chapters to follow, I trace the theories of death, memory, violence, and mourning that are implicit and explicit in emigrants' stories in order to place them in dialogue with other theories both latent and overt in medical and mortuary management of death and in scholarly accounts of biopower. This book is therefore not so much an ethnography of particular communities as a meditation on forms of engagement with death and the dead that are precluded or marginalized by thanato-political institutions, and on the power of ghosts to derail certain versions of biopolitical theory. The conversations, incidents, poetry, and memoirs consulted here are not located in culturally defined places, but rather in the condition of displacement itself, which is infused with the presence of the dead. The chapters to follow are not organized by ethnicity or focused on ethnographic description for two reasons: first, to avoid flattening and reifying "complex persons" (A. Gordon 1997) into cultural representatives; and second, to discourage a reading that would explain away critical perspectives on thanatopolitics as the result of cosmologies relevant only to specific social worlds. The choice makes for a sometimes difficult text, shifting rapidly from one story to another, one country to another, one ritual to another. Underlying this polyphony, however, is a pervasive intention: to question normative bioethics and mourning, and to imagine otherwise.

To consider the storytellers quoted in this book as cotheorists of death means to resist casting them not only as cultural representatives, but also as suffering refugees or struggling immigrants—categories that would reduce them to targets of disciplinary social service agendas (cf. Gómez-Barris and Gray 2010, 4). In the pages to follow I refer to storytellers as emigrants, not only to call attention to the drag of the past (rather than the frequently false promises for the future), but also to steer away from a sociological designation toward one that, through its literary associations, might carry more depth, more gravitas.[3] It is noteworthy that the term "emigrant" tends to be most often used for those of European descent. The displacement of Europeans is seldom represented simply as victimization but is almost always intertwined (in literature or social theory) with powers of philosophical and social reflection. The emigrant is imagined as one who inhabits exile in a way that interrupts a teleological narrative of assimilation.[4] If the immigrant or refugee is often a figure of abjection, the emigrant is a contemplative and ethical subject, reflecting on memory and loss, time and place, life and death.[5]

The Kmhmu, Hmong, Lao, and Khmer emigrants cited in this book are linked to one another, not only through political exile and overlapping repertoires of cultural practice, but more specifically through their involvement within a particular postcolonial theater of war and its aftermaths. Their perspectives on death are shaped by unique subject positions in relation to histories that they partly share with other North Americans. Both emigrants from Laos and Cambodia and other U.S. residents remember American wars in Southeast Asia that involved chemical defoliation, bombed-out villages, military-driven boom economies, and a blossoming of new technologies, but they remember these wars from crucially different vantage points.[6] Both have undergone the increasing hegemony of biomedicine, but from vastly different circumstances of access. It is little wonder, perhaps, that the medical management of death is mnemonically linked, for both emigrants and a wider U.S. public (though in very different ways), to the military management of death in Southeast Asia. Historical vantage points are critical here, because relations with death and the dead are inevitably influenced by differing exposure to death-postponing or death-dealing technologies; differing patterns of risk for violent or sedated death; localized experiences of the connection among death, violence, and medicine; and specific politics of grief. If emigrants' perspectives on death have been shaped by specific histories, no less have more prevalent U.S. perspectives. In chapter 3, for instance, I suggest that dominant North American standards for end-of-life care might partly be traced to widespread ambivalence about the increasingly powerful technologies deployed to intervene in courses of life and death.

When emigrants' approaches to death, dying, and the dead are explained through recourse to cultural difference, they become easier to dismiss, requiring liberal lip service while remaining external to ethical discussion. There are times, of course, when emigrants themselves mobilize the concept of culture, invoking unique customs related to death in order to effectively navigate medical or mortuary protocols. In doing so they appeal to the liberalism of their listeners with an awareness that liberalism, rather than empathy, parity, or collaborative exploration, is what is on offer. The multiculturalist commitment of modern liberalism, however, may evaporate in the face of more deeply rooted investments or at "moments of serious difference, difference that matters" (Povinelli 2006, 162; cf. Povinelli 2002). In chapter 4 I introduce a doctor at a hospital ethics meeting who emphasized the need to resist any temptation of cultural liberalism in the face of the refusal of an African family to tell their father his terminal prognosis. For him the incitement to cultural sensitivity easily fell before the principle of patient autonomy. Only if he were able to "share thought" (Lowe 2006) with this family about life, death, and afterlives might the questionable value of cultural relativism open out into a current of existential possibility. The logic of his bioethical position, based as it was in a forced choice between what Elizabeth Povinelli (2006) outlines as the autology of personal freedom and the genealogy of cultural legacy, did not allow for any such cosmological cross-pollination.

In Laos, rural Kmhmu celebrated the New Year after the rice harvest. They dug up the sweet potatoes and taro and offered them in a feast to the ancestors, notifying them that the year was done. Around the same time they also fed sweet potatoes, taro, and peanuts to the "waste spirits" *(róoy yáap)*, a group of dead—including stillborn babies and those who died by violence or accidents—who had not been given full funeral rites. The meal ensured that *róoy yáap* would not haunt the barns and deplete the rice stores (Lindell et al. 1982, 120–22). For those primarily Christian Kmhmu who have emigrated to the United States, on the other hand, the New Year is observed by what one woman, Kampheang, described to me as a "cultural celebration only." In a New Year festivity held in a U.S. city in 1999, Kmhmu and friends gathered in the chilly concrete basement of a Catholic church that many of them attended, stamping the snow off their shoes, greeting one another with smiles and handshakes. Plates of food were laid out on long tables, and crepe paper ribbons were looped on the walls and ceiling. A platter holding a cooked chicken, rice, flowers, candles, and other offerings stood next to a long-necked ceramic jar of rice wine at the front of the room. During *súu hrmàal*, the soul calling, everyone clustered around the jar, those who were closest placing their hands on its surface while knowledgeable older men recited a prayer for health and happiness. Those who could not reach the jar directly touched someone in front of them, so that everyone present was physically connected to the rice wine. Afterward, we all waited our turn to sip rice wine from the jar through a long straw. Then we circulated through the crowd with handfuls of white strings, brushing each other's wrists three times with a string before tying it on and offering blessings for the coming year. When forearms were crowded with strings, the food was served and beers and sodas were handed around. We settled down in metal folding chairs for an evening of speeches emphasizing the importance of maintaining Kmhmu traditions; rice-planting and harvest dances in which women (some dressed as men) mimed the gendered activities of sowing and reaping; and sword dances, in which older men waved curved swords around their bodies in graceful circles. In Laos, non-Christian Kmhmu would have sung specific songs integral to the agricultural cycle for the feeding of the ancestors and waste spirits (Lindell et al. 1982), but here the genre of songs performed (known as *trnèem*) were simply for entertainment. Similarly, sword dances that might once have engaged spirits,[7] now celebrate Kmhmu culture.[8] In contrast to the Kmhmu New Year in Laos, which ensured prosperity, the event in the church basement seemed to largely serve up cultural distinctiveness and pride.[9] Yet even here, the good fortune generated by *súu hrmàal* was transmitted as a material substance through the chain of bodies to everyone present. Even among these (mostly) Christian converts, the white strings were understood to fasten souls more closely to bodies.

While modern liberalism with its commitment to religious freedom allows the staging of a minority religious tradition in a civic space such as a church basement, it is less able to acknowledge the extent to which such a rite might enact not just a set of cultural beliefs, but also a theory of life and death. For emigrants themselves, culture is a term that is inherently charged with a sense of loss. Indeed it is arguable that culture, in its anthropological sense, is always already imagined to be at risk.[10] The ever-present loss of culture can have the effect of masking other losses, of specific and heterogeneous practices and relations (cf. Pemberton 1994) such as relations with the dead. While it might be tempting to understand an ongoing attention to the dead or to place-specific spirits as primarily symptomatic of cultural loss, a figure of cultural loss is just as apt to be a displacement of an insistent need to address the dead. Just as modern revivals of ritual in Southeast Asia mark their increasing confinement to a domain of representation (Morris 2000, 9), so rituals of racialized groups in diaspora, or of Christian converts, may collapse speci-ficities into a sphere of cultural celebration wherein the purpose of a feast (e.g., gift exchange with spirits) may disappear into its symbolic meaning (to affirm Kmhmu culture).

In such ways minoritization exerts its force. While minority status is famil-iar to Kmhmu and Hmong, who were already minorities in Laos, it is less so for Lao and Khmer, who enjoyed majority status in their respective countries.[11] Sodoeung, a Khmer health-care worker, recalled one physician who told a Khmer family "You are welcome to perform your ceremony [for an extension of life] in the chapel," even though that meant that the focal point of the cer-emony, the patient herself, hooked up to machines in the intensive care unit (ICU), would be absent. Under the rule of the symbolic, the chant would be just as meaningful offered in the Christian chapel away from the patient's body. Yet, as I discuss in chapter 6, care for the spirits of the dead and the dying exceeds this symbolic logic, insisting on a material response to specific crises of violence, illness, or death. Within such care, relationships with the dead or the dying are not so much expressions of religious identity as techniques for sustaining ongoing relationships of reciprocity and need. Within the com-partment of religion made available by a modern civil order, on the other hand, relationships with spirits of the living or the dead are reconfigured as symbolic interactions in order to be rendered intelligible to a liberal respect for freedom of worship.

When emigrants do not engage a liberal language of majority and minor-ity cultures, they sometimes invoke instead a language of host and guest or giver and recipient. "Here we are guests," as one Lao man put it, ". . . the good guest will keep his mouth shut and be respectful" (quoted in Proudfoot 1990, 86). Yet beneath the seeming resignation to that "suspension of social and political rights" that anthropologists note "comes with the guest status" (Can-dea and Da Col 2012, S5; cf. Pitt-Rivers 2012, 512–14), the unarticulated subtext is the responsibility, not only of the guest, but of the host. As another Lao man observed, "Few men here act to me as an equal friend. . . . In my country we always treat the American person very well. Special things to eat when they come to our house. We are always glad to know them" (quoted in Proudfoot 1990, 155). The lack of hospitality is made starker when contrasted to the invitations broadcast by Radio Free America in the mid-1970s, advertising money and jobs for those who would renounce communism. The failure of hospitality is similarly intensified for Hmong and Kmhmu by memories of the promises made by CIA operatives of material assistance and new homes in exchange for their military service. One Hmong man, who became a soldier in the covert war at the age of thirteen, and who suffers nightmares of war, often feeling suffocated by *dab tsog*, a malevolent spirit who may appear as a decaying body, told a psychologist that he was angry that the U.S. government never recognized his contribution to the war or offered him veteran benefits. "He feels many promises have been broken" (Culhane-Pera et al. 2003, 207).

What is critical to note here is that even if a discourse of "rights" has made a place for itself within anthropological accounts of hospitality, the language of host and guest, unlike a juridical understanding of rights, invokes a social ethos that encompasses both living and dead (cf. Ladwig 2012).[12] For emigrants note that the dead also must be shown hospitality, at a series of mourning rites spaced out over months and years, as well as on the New Year, and during annual festivals of the dead. Speaking of the last meal offered to the dead (*ju plig*, after which the soul is sent to be reborn), one Hmong elder, Pao Chang, told me: "We call the soul back to repay him, to celebrate like at a birthday, to relieve him of his duty, that he worked so hard on earth. It's the last food we feed him since he was human." The comparison with a birthday celebration serves simultaneously to familiarize Hmong death practices and to outline their pragmatic logic. This universalizing gesture refuses culture as a minority ghetto, making instead a coevalist move (Fabian 1983) to locate Hmong rites in the same world as contemporary North American birthdays. The comparison demonstrates a self-reflection that is engaged less in a declaration of belief than in the questioning of exotic distance. Here Pao Chang sidesteps the pedagogical frame by which he would be identified as an ethnic minority lost in a fantasy world of spirits (cf. Bhabha 1990; Chakrabarty 2000). His remark is a reminder that what is at stake is not so much the preservation of minority cultures as a crucial sociality of living and dead that is founded on hospitality and reciprocal care. Within this sociality, he suggests, death is analogous to birth in inaugurating a new existence for the deceased and a new mode of interaction with him that is both physical and phantasmal.

Relating to the Dead

I am walking by his side across an expanse of grass. His body is transparent, watery. His eyes question mine. I love you, I say. He waves his hand dismissively, then searches my face again, and finally evaporates slowly, mist in sunlight.

This dream encounter with my own dead father is informed by a specific cultural longing for authentic love, a longing that becomes meaningful within a history where love can be either rote or genuine, conventional or inwardly felt. It is this authentic love, the elusive figure of so many European and North American novels, that is conjured in the dream, rather than, say, a habitual love of daily physical caretaking and concern.[13] In this dream, it seems, only a love marked emphatically as true and interior has the power to console the ghost, resolving the uneasy debt to a father with whom my relationship in life was characterized more by exchanges of bodily care and money than by expressions of inner feeling. The dream serves as a reminder that interactions with the dead are not exotic remnants of premodern worldviews, but common, if minimally institutionalized, events of contemporary Euroamerican life. But the dream also suggests that Euroamerican encounters with the dead are apt to be structured by particular forms of subjectivity and visions of eschatology, which, I will suggest, underlie techniques of managing and mourning death in medical and mortuary institutions.

Love is no less central to relationships with the dead in the dreams and waking lives of those emigrants whose stories drive this book. In those relationships, however, authenticity is not the primary demand of that love. Rather these storytellers are concerned with whether the love is steady, persistent, visible; whether it is empathic, loyal, and manifest in meticulous physical care; whether it is generous and attentive; whether it meets the particular responsibilities of kin or friend that prevail between a specific living person and the deceased. At a Lao *wat* (Buddhist temple) I visited in 1998 on the outskirts of a U.S. city, there were several small houses the size of dollhouses, intricately constructed out of wood. Some were elaborately detailed with staircases, windows, doors, pitched roofs, and ornate architectural features. I was told that families had obtained permission from the *wat* to build these residences for dead relatives, and that sometimes the ashes of the dead were placed inside. When I returned to the *wat* a few years later, hoping to take photos of those houses, or similar ones, I found that the old *wat* had been replaced with a splendid new one, its doorway guarded by carved dragons, painted in yellow, red, green, and gold, their scaly bodies thrust into the parking lot, wooden tongues lashing from their mouths. I spoke with another monk, who, in the absence of the cleverly constructed houses for the dead, now removed, showed me gifts piled five feet deep along an interior wall of the *wat* offered for the dead. There were blue plastic laundry baskets crammed with housewares, a four-poster bed frame decorated with a tinseled canopy, pillows in clear plastic sheathes, wicker baskets, colanders, stainless steel pots and pans (some still in their boxes, others unwrapped and gleaming), the whole adorned with bouquets of plastic roses, streamers of gold and silver paper, and strings of colored glass beads. I took some photos and, before leaving, made my own offering of paper currency and received the monk's blessing, while kneeling before a life-size golden Buddha seated in a lotus asana.

Dead such as those who were invited to occupy those small houses, and who might make use of the ethereal transpositions of plastic laundry baskets, require from their mourners not so much interior feeling as material nurturance. The dead may be offended by how their remains are handled or uncomfortable in their graves. They may be hungry or thirsty. They may crave cigarettes, be distressed at their nakedness, or require money or visas to cross to the world of the ancestors. They demand not simply a verbal communication of feelings, but physical company, shared meals, and household goods. They need not just to be let go, as in the current advice of death experts to families of the dying, but also, sometimes, to be offered detailed directions about how and where to go, how (sometimes) to find their way across oceans and through forests or negotiate the tangle of afterlife bureaucracies and border guards. In the chapters to follow, this materiality of posthumous existence is contrasted with the covertly Christian (largely Protestant) eschatologies that structure the treatment of dead bodies in hospitals and funeral homes as empty corpses devoid of social presence and shape the consideration of souls as immaterial phantoms without physical needs.

For to understand the dead in emigrant stories is not to counterpose a world in which spirits are real against a world of scientific rationality, in which only bodies are factual. U.S. institutions such as hospitals and funeral homes, not to mention popular media, are as possessed (unofficially) by the uncanny (cf. V. Nelson 2001) as emigrant communities are possessed of a modern reason. Hospitals are no doubt disciplinary spaces that separate bodies into individual cases to be compared and classified in relation to certain norms (Foucault 1973), but they are also uncanny spaces teeming with ghostly residues, the traces of souls housed by or departing from these bodies. For Freud (1955b), experiences of the uncanny—which he traces to remnants of animism underlying modern rationality—are especially evoked in relation to death and the dead. As both bastions of rationality and sites of death, North

American hospitals are prime locations for uncanny eruptions.[14] If much has been written of the forms of bodiliness reinforced by medical hospitals (e.g., Foucault 1973; Armstrong 1987a), less attention has been paid to the medicalization of the soul. Hovering in the hallways of hospitals, morgues, and funeral homes, these medicalized souls confer intuitive sense, I will argue, on practices such as the communication of terminal prognosis, autopsy, organ harvesting, embalming, and cosmetic reconstructions of corpses. The institutionalization of such practices relies on a conception of subjectivity that shapes not only how contemporary Euroamericans inhabit our bodies, but also how we imagine or most recently used to imagine our souls. One of the undertakings of this book is to explore the shadows of secular science for these implicit eschatological presumptions. Not only is the hospital "a historically religious institution that reshapes practices of death and suffering," as physician and anthropologist Barry Saunders has observed (2008, 8; cf. Naraindas 2008), but it is an institution that often suppresses its own religious commitments, disguising them in techno-ethical protocols of decision making.

Medical management of death serves to institutionalize the division between body and soul, and matter and spirit, infusing end-of-life care with Euroamerican theological presumptions, which support both an inward soul-searching before death and specific bodily dispositions after death. In chapter 4, for instance, I note that the practice of "truth-telling" or disclosure of a terminal prognosis presumes an interiority and sovereignty of the modern subject that is essentially theological. A pastoral strain in medical management of death manifests in a prescriptive emphasis on medico-moral preparations for death, wherein a good death is one in which the dying person self-consciously faces and grieves their death in advance. Latent Christian theology shapes not only the premortem introspection that posits a reflexive inner soul but also a postmortem divestment that presumes that the soul has radically departed, leaving the corpse an inert piece of flesh, to be personalized at select moments for the emotional benefit of the mourners. The invisibility of such latent theology can be sustained only by projecting religiosity on those who endorse other ontologies, while retaining for itself a mask of secular science. Emigrants' stories force these Christian presumptions into visibility by jostling against them, proposing an alternative ethos of death rooted in other cosmological imaginaries. Stories of spirits who are shocked out of their bodies by a terminal prognosis as retold in chapter 4, as well as funeral songs that explicitly encourage the deceased to confront their deaths as discussed in chapter 5, suggest understandings of body and spirit, and of materiality and language, that render an inner confrontation of death in advance superfluous or even dangerous.

Death rites that explicitly provision the body for the journey into death, as I explore in chapters 6 and 7, implicitly question the presumption of a radical rupture between body and soul at death and the understanding of the corpse as possessing a merely symbolic relation to the social person. While an institutionalized separation between matter and spirit tends to encourage mourning practices that emphasize memorialization over material exchange, emigrants often continue to seek out rituals that offer a bodily and sensory intimacy with death and the dead. They cite the possibility of haunting that may result from incomplete or sterile ceremonies that fail to assist the dead in concrete ways. This enforced incompleteness of mourning helps to make intelligible the alienation of spirits in the United States. In chapter 2, I consider emigrants' accounts of topological spirits who are newly excluded from U.S. social worlds, yet manifest in bodily ways, especially illness, often necessitating a renewed connection with ancestral landscapes. The alienation of spirits of place in U.S. society prefigures the alienation of spirits of the ill on hospital wards and the alienation of spirits of the dead in morgues and mortuaries as discussed in chapters 6 and 7. When viewed through this alienation, U.S. death practices are more readily understood as a locus of emigrant nightmares. The management of death in hospitals, funeral homes, crematoria, and cemeteries effectively invalidates the social existence of the dead in ways that echo violations of the dead during wartime.

Immanent Pasts

The reverberations between a thanatopolitics of hospitals, morgues, and mortuaries and a thanatopolitics of war zones and refugee camps ensure that the ghost stories animating this book suggest not only different possibilities for encountering the dead but also different possibilities for encountering the past events that we know as history. For ghost stories are told and retold in a world that is organized not only by disciplinary templates for the most significant events in human (or animal) lives, but also by neocolonial wars, political exile, and racialized regimes of vulnerability. Specifically, these stories are shadowed by the covert war in Laos, the Khmer Rouge regime in Cambodia, and the displacement of hundreds of thousands of people to reeducation or refugee camps, and then to the United States and other countries. These events are the direct consequences of U.S. military involvement in Southeast Asia from the 1950s through 1975. Emigrants' stories are in conversation not only with the eschatological visions that haunt modern hospitals and funeral homes, then, but also with medicalized interpretations of the embodied effects of witnessing or experiencing violence and with the public management of historical memory. Even as emigrants' stories speak to death and the dead, they simultaneously address questions of power, violence, and the entanglement of the past in the present.

Emigrants' memories of covert war in Laos and Cambodia—the loss of families and communities, homelessness, flight, political exile, and finally acceptance into the impoverished margins of a U.S. populace—compose a concatenation of deaths, marginal lives, and death-in-lives driven by a violence that has been, at different times and places, both bloody and structural. Given this violence the prevalence of spirits in emigrants' stories is easily read as a symptom of trauma. Not surprisingly, for instance, the Hmong man mentioned above who suffered from nightmares of suffocating spirits was diagnosed with post-traumatic stress disorder (PTSD) and depression (Culhane-Pera et al. 2003, 208). If social science is apt to consign spirits to a realm of cultural belief, medicine is apt to consign them to a realm of psychic disturbance, a strategy made available by a certain version of Freudian theory which, as Avery Gordon observes, "rid itself of all vestiges of animism by making all the spirits or the hauntings come from the unconscious" (1997, 48). How might we make sense of the ghostly figures in emigrants' memories without either "anthropologizing" (Chakrabarty 2000) or psychologizing them, that is, without reducing them to signs of cultural belief or psychic symbols of trauma? As Gordon notes, spirits are social figures who seize our attention with their restlessness in the wake of violent pasts. Yet whereas for Gordon, ghosts are literary traces of slavery, paramilitary terror, or gendered violence, in this book ghosts are ethnographic figures, slamming doors, cracking branches, causing illness, and demanding clothes and cigarettes.

When my own father died, the hospice nurse arrived within the hour to declare the death. She took off his pajamas and covered him with a thin sheet. An hour later two men from a local funeral home came to take the body to cold storage until it could be delivered to the medical school. (My father, taking my mother's lead, had gifted his body to science. It was his way of following her, twenty-six years later, to the weedy gravesite beneath the pines in the medical school cemetery.) We watched carefully, declining to leave the room, as the undertakers zipped my father into a clear plastic body bag. Later that week we cleaned out his bedroom closet and dresser. Some time later my father appeared to my brother in a dream, demanding "What did you do with my clothes?" In another scene of the dream they tended my father's beehives together. How startlingly similar this dream was to those I heard from Lao or Khmer, in which a deceased relative appears in a dream, asking for clothing. My brother's dream seemed symptomatic of his distress in the wake of seeing our father's naked body placed in a plastic bag, and later clearing the house of our father's clothes. He responded not so much to the dream itself as to the anxiety it indexed by caring for my father's apiary with the help of a local bee-keeper until the land was sold and the beehives moved to other fields. Elderly Lao and Khmer who dream such dreams, on the other hand, commonly inter-pret them as visitations from the dead. The dreamers respond by offering cloth-ing to the dead, often through monks at the Buddhist *wat*. One deceased woman I heard about continually appeared to her family, requesting her favorite out-fit. Finally they brought the outfit to her gravesite, and the next day she appeared in a dream wearing it. For my brother, the oneiric appearance of a dead parent can perhaps be called a symptom, but can the same be said for the Lao and Khmer?

If not, we are left to consider what is at stake in apprehending a ghost as a social figure in reciprocal relationship with the living rather than as a symp-tom of trauma. Much contemporary discussion of mourning, both personal and collective, is driven by a narrative of the healing of trauma through prac-tices of testimony, wherein terrifying relivings are replaced by coherent nar-rative (Caruth 1996; Laub 1992). Yet the ghosts in emigrants' stories suggest a different possibility of addressing the violence of a past that remains imma-nent in the present: through material encounters with the dead. Spirits may linger in a prolonged melancholy (Freud 1955a; Hertz 1960) due to the dis-avowal of their social existence through extremes of violence or everyday practices of thanatopolitics. Like the ghosts of Vietnamese dead who were dislocated during the American war (Kwon 2008), the ghosts in emigrants' stories are most active when violence and displacement have interrupted the sociality of living and dead, requiring the dead to intervene in distinctive ways to restore that sociality.

Seemingly magical practices designed to calm restless spirits may also work, therefore, as material strategies for addressing a violence erupting from the past but continuously reinstated in the present (cf. Mueggler 2001). In this violence, memories of recent events and distant events are overlaid, the struc-tural violence of poverty and minoritization interleaved with the violence of war and terror. Engagements with the dead ranging from dream conversa-tions to shamanic negotiations, or from community feasts to material manip-ulations of the remains, address a diffuse field of violence that attends the restless spirits of the dead. As I argue in chapter 1, a narrative of the haunting effects of "bad death"—anthropology's term for a sudden, violent death that is especially difficult for the living to mourn—wherein memories of extreme violence in the past are intermingled with dread of violence in the present, offers an alternative to a narrative of trauma. Emigrants may be haunted not only by the deaths they witnessed, or sometimes caused, but also by the deaths they nearly died, their own deaths that hovered before them, taunting and imminent. If healing of trauma often works by trying to unravel terror's grasp on the imagination, healing the haunting of bad death works rather by confronting terror on its own phantasmal terms, through magically mediated encounters with the dead. While a psychodynamic treatment of post-traumatic effects attempts to reintegrate a violent past into the sufferer's personal history, negotiations with the dead attempt rather to confront the immanence (and we could as well say imminence) of violence in the present.

When transposed beyond the psychic to the social, traumatology's emphasis on healing through verbal witnessing results in a psychodynamic narrative of the healing of historical violence through a public discourse in which the dead are evoked through monuments, eulogy, and collective testimony. Arguably, the emphasis on memorializing the dead as a means of addressing or redressing past injustice is the liberal political elaboration of a dominant Protestant mourning style, in which deliberate memories of the dead as living persons displace material care for the dead as dead (both remains and spirits). If the dead in such a narrative often serve as stand-ins for historical events—the Holocaust, the Vietnam War, the AIDS epidemic, or 9/11—the dead in the stories told by Lao, Khmer, Hmong, and Kmhmu emigrants suggest another semiotic spin whereby history might be viewed as a stand-in for the dead, insofar as it abstracts spectral relations from concrete interchanges to vague legacies. Here the dead work less as symbols of historical injustice than as participants in violated socialities of living and dead in the present. "Historical knowledge," Stuart McLean has written, "is founded on the silencing and sublation of other ways of knowing, including communion with spirits and the dead" (2004, 11, 17). Attending to the dead means evoking a past that is less an object of historical narrative than a "force to be viscerally reexperienced in the present" (144). In haunting, the alterity of the dead interferes with any easy invocations of their memory. The stories of haunting retold here suggest what it might mean to shift from reiterative references to absence—what the dead would have wanted or would have done (cf. Gilbert 2006)—to viscerally wrestling with a contemporaneous presence. Without a subjunctive mood to supplement and thereby secure chronological sequence, haunting unfolds in knotty temporalities where present and past collapse, past erupting within the present, present enveloping the past. When emigrant storytellers defer to the authority of the dead in questions of violence, medicine, or mourning, they are not so much invoking the perspectives of once living persons, but rather summoning ghosts as atemporal witnesses.

Death's Authority

For Walter Benjamin, stories are linked to death in that a person's "real life—and this is the stuff that stories are made of—first assumes transmissible form at the moment of his death." At the heart of story is "that authority which even the poorest wretch in dying possesses for the living around him" (1968, 94). In recent history, Benjamin suggests, stories have conceded this authority to sciences of information. In accordance with this argument it would seem that the storytelling authority of the dying has been replaced over the last century by the authority of experts on death. Information about death has proliferated in the form of statistics, certificates, psychological profiles, obituaries, autopsy records, bereavement studies, and, most recently, self-help and motivational literature on grief and the acceptance of mortality. Death and dying have been subject to increasing professionalization, annotated with a paper trail of procedures, ethics, definitions, and instructive memoirs. The proliferation of discourse suggests efforts to control and familiarize an event that nonetheless remains a radical alterity (cf. Serin 2012).

For death itself is an ontological question mark. Even if popular authors as well as scholars (myself included) refer to death as if it were a known event, it can perhaps only be that for the already dead. In this book, the task is to contemplate conflicting imaginations and ethics of death—places where thanatological ideas and practices snag and catch in productive friction (Tsing 2005)—while not forgetting how far death itself evades description (cf. Derrida 1993). While death appears to mark an ambiguous passage between animate and inanimate, embodiment and disembodiment, matter still growing and matter in decay, such dyads are far from ontologically secure.[15] Death is elusive in a specific, circular way in that it is precisely that which defies ontological presence or definition. Death, Siegel writes, is one of several ideas that "institute the social in the place where otherwise we recognize nothing" (2006, 8). For who is the social subject who undergoes death? Can the same subject be living in one moment and dead in another? The only imaginable epistemology with which to grasp a subject who undergoes death seems to be an impossible one that leaps toward a perspective of the dead, allowing itself to be haunted by those who are no longer living. That is why encounters with the dead, while they can yield no information as such, are critical to this study. Rather than write *about* death as if it were a knowable entity, I prefer to take my cue from the emigrants who shared their tales with me and write *to* death and the dead, as unknowable figures in the shadows (Spivak 1988; cf. Serin 2012), seeking not so much to re-present certain scenes and thoughts of death as to respond to them.

For Benjamin violent death was further connected with storytelling through the idea that modern warfare is a destroyer of stories:

> Was it not noticeable at the end of the war that men returned from the battle-field grown silent—not richer, but poorer in communicable experience? . . . For never has experience been contradicted more thoroughly than strategic experience by tactical warfare, economic experience by inflation, bodily experience by mechanical warfare, moral experience by those in power. (1968, 84)

Does he refer here to the way that technological warfare works to negate personal skill, courage, and heroism? Or is he thinking of the reports of dead infantry in World War I who were used as fire cover? As one survivor wrote in a letter home, "You hide behind someone who's been killed. . . . You don't bury them. What's the use? Another shell would dig them up" (Fernand Léger quoted in Gilbert 2006, 151). The stories of war survivors, including those consulted for this book, build themselves around silences, omissions, and chasms. Consider, for instance, the story of Lt. Phanha, a Kmhmu lieutenant working with the CIA, who was no longer sure of the location of the village for the dead in a landscape that had been remapped by military campaigns; or the stories of Lao who feel both alive and dead in the United States, invisible to and unacknowledged by others; or the comment of one Hmong man who would only say of the war in Laos, "It's the past. Leave it alone." It is better, sometimes, not to tamper with the burial grounds. Yet, despite the gaps, stories persist, twisting around the unspoken, scar tissue over wounds. If stories have passed away, as Benjamin suggested, they nonetheless continue to return in fragmented and inconclusive afterlives. With the increasing incommunicability of experience, Benjamin continued, we have no counsel either for ourselves or for others (1968, 86). Yet counsel, he wrote, is less an answer to a question than a gesture toward the continued unfolding of a story. In the discontinuous scraps of stories in this book, there are hints of counsel, if only the enigmatic counsel of the dead. For the stories recounted in these pages refer not just to the authority of the dying, but even more critically to the authority of the dead.

To invoke the authority of the dead involves acknowledging that, although stories may pack along information, it is not their center of gravity (cf. Benjamin 1968, 89). Listening for the dead involves remaining "attentive to what is elusive, fantastic, contingent and often barely there" (A. Gordon 1997, 26).

It is crucial, in this listening, to allow stories to retain their extraneity, contradiction, density, and detail, to acknowledge how far they evade any one reading and confront us with intimations edgy and unspoken. Stories have the capacity to discomfort, unsettle, hint at hidden realities, and mock semiotic certainty. "There is more to the history re-membered in . . . just talk than any master narrative can tell us," Kathleen Stewart observes (1996, 106–7). Never entirely finished or consistent, stories invite further stories or alternative versions, scattering out from multiple vantage points, carrying resonance that exceeds the representational value that seems to govern their terms of exchange. Stories are crosshatched with allusions too numerous and overlaid to track, repeating previously heard or told stories, each story borrowing on yet exceeding available repertoires and genres of stories (Steedly 1993, 135). Within this book, then, stories are offered not as empirical evidence, but rather as the imprecise traces of "absent presences" that are pivotal in the "making of social worlds" (cf. Gray and Gómez-Barris 2010, xv).

To conceive of these re-membered fragments (in this book, fragments blasted apart by war and state-sponsored terrorism, and gathered together as the material remains of the dead) as only supplemental history would be to lose sight of what they might help us understand, not only about the shape of events in this world, but about the shape of events spilling beyond this world that nonetheless pull on its historical tides with an insistent gravity. Such an approach would overlook the deeply conflicted enterprise of bearing witness. As Hoon Song suggests,

> To bear witness is the opposite of laying claim to the lucidity of representational knowledge. . . . We instinctively expect a credible witness to be struck with a certain inability, and impossibility of clear vision and speech. . . . Hence witnessing involves a reversal: disempowerment and impossibility transform into empowerment and possibility. (2010, 121)

In that sense the dead are the quintessential witnesses, as I suggest in chapter 1, struck dumb by a profound impossibility of speech that underwrites a literally unanswerable authority. The stories retold here often partake of magical realism, staggering like dreams between vagueness and startling detail, moving through a time that is both inside and outside of history, rendered incoherent by both terror and miracles, moving among human, nonhuman, and parahuman realms. While the "intelligence of earlier centuries," Benjamin wrote, "was inclined to borrow from the miraculous, it is indispensable for information to sound plausible" (1968, 89). The stories retold in this book require that we bypass plausibility in pursuit of the haunting powers of the telling, forgoing the "psychological shading" that would divert story into data (Benjamin 1968, 91). As Macarena Gómez-Barris and Herman Gray write, "cacaphonies, incoherences, assemblages, translations, appearances, and hauntings" are not simply phenomena that elude "orderly social categories," but "methodological necessities" (2010, 4).

Yet the stories in this book are not easily freed from complicity with projects of data collection. In the telling and retelling of stories, Benjamin noted, "traces of the storyteller cling to the story the way the handprints of the potter cling to the clay vessel" (1968, 92). Yet other handprints are found on stories as well. The route that emigrants' memories travel in order to enter public discourse is one that zigzags from one linguistic register to another, paying dues along the way to governmentalist disciplines and to ricocheting regimes of imagination. Some of the stories in the pages that follow were told to me in English; others were told through an interpreter. Yet the voices in this book are doubled and hybrid in more than a linguistic sense. None of the stories appearing in the chapters to follow are transparent translations of thought or experience. For Friedrich Kittler, the very concept of translation, as part of a Romantic discourse network of the nineteenth century, belongs to a hermeneutics that attempts to reproduce an authorial voice with which the reader can empathize (1990, 265). He suggests the alternative term "transposition" to convey the transference of messages from one medium to another. Transposition calls attention to the way that each new discursive strategy, no less than each new language, reshapes and reorients what is said. The biopolitical endeavor of gathering information about ethnicity, health, and religious practice inevitably leaves its stamp on the stories told here, which have been to varying degrees previously heard and handled by psychiatrists, counselors, social workers, physicians, nurses, Christian sponsors of refugees, interpreters, and ethnographers, all of us pressing on them our diverse bureaucratic, medical, and scholarly concerns. In the initial phase of the fieldwork that motivated this book, the emigrants and I were paid to talk with one another, often in small beige cubicles or conference rooms in community centers or clinics, sometimes in living rooms and around kitchen tables. It is necessary to stay alert to the ways that the elicitation of stories inevitably risked resemblance to other biopolitical interviews from psychiatric assessments to immigration questionnaires, and from prisoner interrogations to social work evaluations. It is no less essential to notice that social workers, funeral home staff, medical professionals, and Christian sponsors, not to mention Pathet Lao soldiers, Khmer Rouge cadres, CIA agents, and countless dead hover near these stories as the absent interlocutors to whom they are partly addressed (cf. Langford 2002).

To listen against the governmentalist grain is to question the categories that would frame these stories simply in terms of symptoms of trauma, supplements to official history, or signs of ethnicity. It is to listen less for what stories mean than for what they evoke through their poetic tactility, their rhythmic repetition, their invitation to relive, to imagine, to engage viscerally with memories not one's own. Counterintuitively, the intention of retelling stories here is not exactly to disentangle certain themes (violence, medicine, mourning) from accounts of chanting mantras, hiding in the jungle, keeping vigil by a hospital bed, or laboring to build a dam. Rather the intention is to follow such themes into a tangled terrain, grappling with them there in the mess of the story (cf. Law 2004). When a Lao lieutenant describes eating strange, bad-tasting leaves and cutting mud off his shoes with his knife, as he walks through the forest after escaping from prison camp, the materiality and heterogeneity of the tale resist being boiled down to abstractions of cultural practice or historical experience. The power of such stories may lie less in a distilled meaning than in an affective density that spills outside of any one illustrative project.

Why tell ethnographic stories at all, Klima asks, unless there is an obligation, unless stories offer and return some ineffable gift (2002, 243). Analysis seems an insufficient gift for the story of someone's life or death, or for a story of being suspended between life and death. While information sometimes purports to be its own reward, a provisionally final word, its value a product of its truth, stories move in a gift cycle, participating in a rolling and gathering of thoughts that is subject to an unraveling, expending, and reweaving into other stories, other thoughts. The stories in this book have haunted me since I first heard them, not least because they are themselves haunted. In reshaping and responding to them, I make my own fumbling gift to the dead, risking the magical exercise of listening for their voices.

I also inevitably leave my own desires, dreams, memories, and fantasies tucked into the folds and wrinkles of this retelling. I am writing one draft of this introduction, for instance, following the sudden death of a long-time friend and one-time lover. At this moment, death registers as a physical pressure in my chest and a strange fragility in the surrounding air. The realm of death seems close, intimate, jostling invisibly against this world where I sit writing, as if I could push my hand through a thin membrane to a place where the dead are engaged in shadowy projects of their own, throwing mute glances my way.

The sensations of my own encounters with death are side stories here, lending me a visceral though far from adequate orientation for other terrains of sorrow. In a psychoanalytic sense, there is an inevitable countertransference involved in listening, as a researcher, to others' stories of loss. As George Devereux (1967) pointed out years ago, a researcher's affective responses to what she studies necessarily shape her interpretation. The trick, for Devereux, is to resist the defense mechanism of pretensions to objectivity and draw on countertransference for insight. When, in these pages, I refer to my own encounters with death or the dead, I do so partly as an exploration of the historical positions and soteriological presumptions that underwrite dominant North American approaches to death, and partly as a reminder that even as the emigrants whose stories form the heart of this book are not only storytellers and mourners but also theorists of death, so I am not only an ethnographer, but also a mourner, dreamer, and teller of tales.

The Howling Dead

I didn't know you'd cremated me
until I couldn't find the little finger
of my left hand. I wailed for hours
and wanted to see you once and for all.

I came to pay you a visit,
wading backward like vapors
on a calm afternoon in April, and saw
many familiar faces with lips welded

by the military–industrial complex.
And when I arrived at your door,
which I used to pass through freely,
I was horrified by crosses on the threshold.

O, my love!
You induce in me everlasting sorrow.
Henceforth my world is different.
Henceforth I will live in the trees.

Listen to my howl through the winds,
look at my sorrows through the gray skies,
feel my tears through the rains,
O, my incomparable love!

—U Sam Oeur

Chapter 1   Violent Traces

LIEUTENANT SOMSY AND I SAT ON A BENCH in the lobby of the community center, waiting for our interpreter. Over a series of meetings he had been telling us the story of his life, especially his years as a soldier with the Royal Lao Army. During our previous conversation, he had described his nightmares.

> I dream I am in a meadow fighting. . . . I was with two other soldiers, and the shells fell on us in the foxhole. A friend of mine got cut in the hand. One person got hit in the leg. I helped my friend with a broken leg. The guy who got hurt on the hand also helped me, helped the other guy with the broken leg. Jumped from a cliff. Saw the water down there was very small because I had nowhere to go. I jumped from high to water, but I got into the water. I got into the water very deep, because I jumped from very high. I almost did not get back up to the surface of the water. So sometimes when we talk about the past, at night, I usually dream about it. Sometimes people make really big noise at home. So I would dream like I got shelled by mortars or big cannons from somewhere, then I would wake up. I have tried to forget many times. I just cannot.

Remembering this, I asked him whether he had had any nightmares in the interval since our last conversation. He replied that he had dreamed he was being shot at and suddenly realized he'd forgotten his "buddha," the protective amulet he wore around his neck during battles.[1]

Memories of violence are violent themselves, shot through with repetitive terror, so immersive it can be difficult to surface. The memories are material and embodied as much as storied, partaking as much of the phantasmal as of the real. In particular, for Lt. Somsy and other emigrants, they are the memories of death and survival during the U.S.-sponsored wars in Laos and Cambodia and their aftermaths, memories that are embodied in recurrent nightmares, spirit encounters, soul loss, haunting, and relations with the dead. All of these form the terrain of violent memories, which might better be termed traces, insofar as they are less narrative representations than sensate impressions, through which the spectral infuses the everyday, the dead call out to the living, and the past inhabits the present. In medical contexts, such traces are swept into the diagnostic category of post-traumatic stress. While this diagnosis prevents terrifying memories from being discounted, it also allows their horror to be contained in a clinical narrative driven by a specific temporal logic, which would relegate violence to the past. Even nonmedical theorizations of trauma bear the marks of this medical frame insofar as they understand violent memories as chaotic recurrence that fails to cohere into linear storyline.

In order to acknowledge the viscerality of these violent traces, their shadowy uncertainties, their scents and sensations, their tendency to elude articulation, and yet also to question the psychodynamic model that would assimilate them to forms of failed testimony, we might rethink the violence of memory as an aftermath to bad death, that is, to death by violence that results in haunting. This haunting is less an interior state than a relationship both with the dead and with an ambience of terror surrounding violent death. It is also an aftershock in which the tremors of violent histories are kept rolling by a structural violence in the present. In the context of social science and international justice, the effects of violent histories are most often addressed through a narrative of reconciliation in which repressed memories are healed in the telling. But the storytellers consulted here suggest a different and perhaps riskier intervention, in which the phantasmal and bodily effects of violence are addressed through equally phantasmal and bodily rituals to intervene in haunting.

These rites involve an active engagement with the dead that problematizes the psychoanalytic division between mourning and melancholy that often inflects contemporary understandings of the grieving of historical loss. The psychic choice between mourning and melancholy is organized around an assumption that the living, in order to be healthy, must free themselves from their relationship, or as Freud would have it their libidinal attachment, to the dead or the irretrievably lost (1955a, 244–45). Later analyses by Freud and others have complicated this assumption, suggesting that the ego itself is founded on a melancholic internalization of what is lost. In this perspective, melancholy inheres in identity, as an "archaeological reminder" as Judith Butler puts it, "of unresolved grief" (1997b, 133).[2] In Butler's reading of the later Freud, to let go of the lost one means not to relinquish her altogether but to internalize her as part of oneself.[3] The line between mourning and melancholy then becomes blurred as every loss invokes a melancholy at the heart of the self. In her astounding study of the melancholic structure of race, Anne Anlin Cheng shows how social oppression may derive its power from mimicking (and infiltrating) such psychic processes of self-making (2001, 27). She illuminates both the melancholy of democratic majorities who fail to mourn the racist violence on which our societies are founded, and the melancholy of racialized minorities who struggle between an ambivalent internalization of dominant social ideals and the deep sadness of denied subjectivity. Similarly, for David Eng (2002), melancholia is less pathology than a way to sustain a relationship with certain irresolvable losses, keeping history open for renegotiation.

Psychodynamic approaches to recovery from trauma, however, still implicitly rest on an assumption that mourning must be freed from its melancholic entanglements. These strategies of recovery involve the replacement of inchoate nightmares and hauntings—in which death and often the dead are immanent in the present—with narratives in which the encounter with death and the dead is relocated to the past. Meanwhile the stories of survivors of the covert war in Laos and the Khmer Rouge regime in Cambodia suggest a different possibility for mourning both the dead and the ambient bad death that attends violent memories. This possibility involves an ongoing and material engagement with the dead that is evocative of a lifelong mourning essential to the welfare of both living and dead. This engagement with the dead is less a matter of consigning the dead to narrative memories than of feasting or negotiating or even wrestling with them on their own ghostly turf. Such mourning mediates not just memories but spirits, remains, and objects, in practices designed not only to console the living but, just as importantly, to console the dead.

Impossible Testimonies

A violent memory is not only a story of the past, then, but a potentially explosive minefield in the present. One Lao man, recalling his wife's death in a bomb raid, said, "Always I remember my wife burns . . . no one helps her . . . many nights she comes to my head . . . even here in the USA. I thought when I left Laos that would stay there" (quoted in Proudfoot 1990, 104). Some respond to the terrorizing power of such memories through a lapse into a silence. As one Lao woman said, "I [am] surprised you ask me to remember pain . . . my mouth is shut about that . . . come and eat with us . . . next time . . . do not ask questions" (quoted in Proudfoot 1990, 79).

Theorists of trauma often trace an inability to speak to a past too horrific to recall, or even to experience at the time (e.g., Caruth 1995a, 1995b, 1996).[4] Agamben has argued, rather, that disarticulation results from a desubjectification from which it's not possible to speak. Such an argument moves from the unrepresentability of the event itself to the inability to speak that the event has wrought in a human psyche. To work through the problematic of bearing witness to violence, Agamben draws on Emile Benveniste's observation that the subject referred to within discourse by the pronoun "I" can never coincide with the subject who speaks (Agamben 2002, 115–21). This is a problem for memory generally, of course: the one who remembers never merges with the one who lived through the remembered event. Agamben suggests that this problem is intensified for memories of the desubjectification endured as the inhabitant of a concentration camp, a war prisoner, a refugee, or a victim of state terror. Survivors struggle to bear witness to a violence through which they were stripped of the social and political existence that would enable them to testify. The resulting testimony is marked by an internal contradiction whereby the survivor is in perpetual tension with her own "bare life" that was stripped of speech (162). Agamben draws on Primo Levi's insight that one who records his memories of Auschwitz is not the "true" or "complete" witness (cited in Agamben 2002, 60, 120–21). Rather, the true witness would be the one who is not able, by reason of a decisive dehumanization (or death) from which she cannot return, to tell her story.[5] As Agamben puts it, "To speak, to bear witness, is thus to enter into a vertiginous movement in which something sinks to the bottom, wholly desubjectified and silenced, and something subjectified speaks without truly having anything to say of its own" (120).

In *If This is a Man* (later published as *Survival in Auschwitz*), Levi recounts a recurrent dream in which he is with family and friends, telling stories of the concentration camp.

> They are all listening to me and it is this very story that I am telling: the [train] whistle of three notes, the hard bed, my neighbour [sharing my bunk] whom I would like to move, but whom I am afraid to wake as he is stronger than me. I also speak diffusely of our hunger and of the lice-control, and of the Kapo who hit me on the nose and then sent me to wash myself as I was bleeding. It is an intense pleasure, physical, inexpressible, to be at home, among friendly people and to have so many things to recount: but I cannot help noticing that my listeners speak confusedly of other things among themselves, as if I was not there. My sister looks at me, gets up and goes away without a word. (1993, 60)

He goes on to describe how he awoke in anguish and remembered that he had dreamed this same dream many times since coming to Auschwitz and that nearly everyone else there also dreamed some version of this dream. He asks, "Why is the pain of every day translated so constantly into our dreams, in the ever-repeated scene of the unlistened-to-story?" (60). Similarly Robert Antelme writes how he and other concentration camp survivors labored to tell their stories to their liberators: "No sooner would we begin to tell our story than we would be choking over it. And then, even to us, what we had to tell would start to seem *unimaginable*" (cited in Wall 2005, 32). Thomas Wall suggests that what Antelme and others choked on was "their very capacity for articulation" (32). They had become like the "muselmann," the xenophobic name used in the camps for the unresponsive and inarticulate victim who exists on the borderline of the human and the inhuman, no longer able to feel, converse, or care. As one Holocaust survivor said, "now that I remember those things, I feel more horrible than I felt at the time. We were in such a state that all that mattered is to remain alive" (Langer 1991, 65).[6]

As I discuss more extensively later on, Agamben's analysis of such states of muteness tends to conflate desubjectification with dehumanization or with a condition of hovering at the threshold of life and death. This conflation posits a world where only living humans are imagined to possess subjectivity and the capacity for communication, and where the loss of these signifies a reduction to animal or inanimate status. This vision of desubjectification is of limited relevance in social worlds where nonhuman agents abound, and where humans and nonhumans, as well as living and dead, have the possibility to transmigrate into one another. Agamben's theory of the impossible, true witness of violence also appears to be organized from the sidelines by the hidden assumption—more centrally articulated in Cathy Caruth's work (1995a)—that resubjectification, if it were possible, would turn nightmare into testimony, even while retaining a sense of incomprehensibility. For both Caruth and Agamben desubjectification seems to refer offscreen to a resubjectifying process of witnessing that, for Agamben, seems to be irrecoverably missing and, for Caruth, can perhaps be created.

Yet Agamben's analysis does offer the suggestive insight that to speak of an experience of violence is to speak on behalf of one who is absent. If only the voice of those who have not returned (including one's former "selves") may truly testify, then a lapse into silence serves as an opening for the indistinct appearances of the dead.[7] These appearances raise the possibility of another form of engagement with violent memories, less testimony than an encounter with the dead. The lapse into silence might then be seen not as a subjective incapacity, but as a gesture that makes space for a more spectral voice. Veena Das observes that women who were subjected to sexual violence during the partition of British India were compelled by an idiom not of bearing witness, but rather of containing and digesting poisonous memories (2007, 54). These memories refused translation into speech, since they exceeded even the common words that women used to describe everyday dishonors at the hands of men. Such refusals of speech might suggest recourse to a more ritualized, embodied, and spirit-ed response to violent memories.

Lisa Yoneyama has written of Japanese atomic bomb survivors who feel compelled to speak on behalf of the dead (1999, 140–43). Yet alongside an urgency to speak for the dead, survivors of violence paradoxically may also need the dead to speak for *them*. If only those who have not returned (including perhaps one's former selves) may truly testify, then an inability or refusal to speak of memories, a lapse into disarticulation and silence, serves as an opening for that phantom voice, less testimony than haunting, that speaks from beyond and outside of history. Later in this book I listen for that voice in the stories of gift exchanges between the living and the dead. Here, I listen for it in stories of the practices that address bad death. Material relations with the dead, I suggest, sidestep the impossibility of testimony, replacing a focus on narration with a focus on bodily enactment. I am not arguing, however, that the bodily and spectral response to violent memories that I draw attention to here is safer or more assured of success than more narrative or memorializing responses. Dealing with the dead is always a gamble (cf. Klima 2002). Mourners may turn to ritual encounters with spirits more out of desperation than out of religious certainty. They may choose it less for its safety than for its daring, intuiting that the excessive irrationality of violence needs to be answered by an equally excessive irrationality of magical intervention.

The Immanence of Violence

It has become a familiar move to speak of violence as that which somehow exceeds the field of signification (e.g., Daniel 1996), not only for survivors but for social analysts as well. Pradeep Jeganathan (1997) notes that violence is represented through a trope of inarticulable horror precisely when it is found to be politically meaningless. It is this failure of political explanation that allows a category of violence as such (distinct from other categories located securely in political narratives, such as "imperialist aggression," "national liberation," or "revolution") to emerge as an object of description. In some anthropological studies this political incomprehensibility of violence has been displaced into culturalist explanations of ethnic or religious conflict.

In others it remains as a cipher, impassable, subverting theorization. Jegana-than observes that the emergence of violence as an object of investigation can be correlated with the delegitimization of various well-known political narratives. Yet even an event like the American War in Vietnam (which, in Jeganathan's argument, is not framed as incomprehensible violence insofar as it can be explained through several possible political logics ranging from neocolonialism to communist revolution) may later lose these ideo-logics, making way for a ghostlier commentary. As Heonik Kwon (2008) shows, the ghosts of dislocated war dead who appeared in the Vietnamese countryside in the 1990s and early 2000s were concerned not with political causes, but only with an excess of suffering. These ghosts, and the living who were haunted by them, talked back to a nationalist discourse that might attempt to enfold some dead in a narrative of political martyrdom, while forgetting others.

Moreover, a naked category of violence that relies on the dissolution of political justifications does not necessarily force a return to political analyses in which any reference to violence would again disappear apart from its link to specific ideologies. Jeganathan cautions, for instance, that he does not want to explain violence and thereby lose it from view by diverting attention to its "causes" (1999, 113). In that sense he seems to be in sympathy with the Viet-namese ghosts. He writes:

> Violence, I suggest, is only visible in the cusp of things, at the moment of its emergence as violation, before its renormalization and relegitimation. After it is well named and known, it carries only traces of its temporal past. It ceases to be a violation and fades from view, or remains only a "well-understood" legitimate force.
>
> This fleeting, shifting violence that concerns me is in the lived world, embedded in fields of recollection and anticipation, fields that move in both temporal directions, past and future. Each recollection of "violence" can also be a moment of anticipation of "violence" to come and, as such, forms the conditions of possibility of the emergence of "violence" in the lived world. (Jeganathan 2004, 70)

The compelling insight here is that violence recalled is at the same time vio-lence anticipated, even for those no longer living in war zones. This "fleeting, shifting" violence has the spectral quality of terror insofar as it is neither nor-malized within political (or cultural) logics nor, to return to Das's insight, describable within the everyday language of the social sphere. To realize that violence has been or can be unmoored from such political causes as democ-racy or self-determination is not to concede that it is therefore a horror that can only leave us speechless, and that must itself be viewed primarily as a cause of, for instance, survivors' fear and anguish (Jeganathan 1999).[8] Violence, for Jeganathan, is more diffuse, more simultaneously absent and present, than causative. It is both remembered and imminent; it is as likely to refer to an injury that did not happen, but might have, as to one that did. The possibility of violence, even retrospectively, is terrifying in its own right. As Salman Rushdie writes through the voice of a war photographer protagonist:

> In combat zones there is no structure, the form of things changes all the time. . . . When you emerge from such a space it stays with you, its otherness randomly imposes itself on the apparent stability of your peaceful hometown streets. What-if becomes the truth, you imagine buildings exploding in Gramercy Park, and you see craters appear in the middle of Washington Square, and women carrying shopping bags drop dead on Delancey Street, bee-stung by sniper fire. You take pictures of your small patch of Manhattan and ghost images begin to appear in them, negative phantoms of the distant dead. (1999, 420)

Holding this evanescent terror of violence in mind, along with its tendency to follow the living across continents, I want to turn to the figure of bad death, whose haunting effects offer another way of speaking about the field of intermingled remembrance and anticipation of violence. For many North Americans who have followed the public dialogue on medicalized death, bad death has, as I discuss in a later chapter, become nearly equivalent to "unnatural" death, a death that is "artificially" and agonizingly postponed through technological means. For Southeast Asian emigrants (and many other peoples in the world), on the other hand, bad death is more often an untimely death by violence. Those who died such deaths are particularly likely to become restless ghosts who fall outside the workings of Buddhist karma or routine exchanges with the ancestors. Like violence that exceeds the terms of the social, bad death is unrehabilitated by political meaning. It is a remainder, a dangerous incompleteness requiring magical intervention, a surplus of violence that catapults the dead out of any stable scheme of significance or system of reciprocity. Bad death is, like the corpses of war Elaine Scarry describes, not a bearer of national or cultural insignia:

> Though a moment before he was blown apart he himself had a national identity that was Chinese, British, American, or Russian, the exposed bones and lungs and blood do not now fall into the shape of five yellow stars on a red field, nor into the configuration of the union jack, nor the stars and stripes, nor the hammer and sickle; nor is there written there the first line of some

national hymn, though he might have, up to a moment ago, been steadily singing it. Only alive did he sign: that is, only alive did he determine the referential direction of his body, did he determine the ideas and beliefs that would be substantiated by his own embodied person and presence. (1985, 118)

Nadia Seremetakis has given bad death a contemporary twist by calling it death that is insufficiently mourned or "unwitnessed" (1991, 101). With this adjective she identifies a resonance between the haunting of bad death and the disarticulation associated with memories of extreme violence. The idea that bad death is unwitnessed, however, shifts the discussion into a psychodynamic or, alternately, political register, summoning images of a desired confessionalist testimony or worldly justice. Whereas Seremetakis suggests that sufficient mourning might require narrative witnessing, I ask whether sufficient mourning might involve an active engagement with the dead.

According to Lao, Kmhmu, Khmer, and Hmong interlocutors, the manner of death is crucial to the subsequent journey of the spirit (be it the Lao *winyan*, Kmhmu *hrmàal*, Khmer *praloeng*, or Hmong *plig*).[9] Those who die violent deaths have the power to haunt and so require special ritual intervention. Though Lao usually cremate bodies, they prefer (at least in Laos) to bury the bodies of those who died violently, in order to discourage them from lingering at the death site. As Lt. Somsy explained, "Because maybe you think this is not the time to die yet for that person . . . the spirit may wander around and then come back to the body. . . . If the body is burned and the spirit comes back, it cannot go back to its body so it will go around and then give people a hard time." Those who died by violence are still attached to the world of the living and frustrated in their efforts to return to it. The greatest peril of being haunted by such bereft spirits is to be pulled into bad death after them, suffering illness or accident or a sudden dispiritedness. Indeed, Das has suggested that those who have seen and suffered extreme violence may be considered to have undergone a bad death of their own (1996, 78–79). Certain stories told by emigrants from Laos and Cambodia evoke this living bad death.

In 1979 when Sodoeung was in her midteens she escaped from her Khmer Rouge work team and rejoined her family. Eventually they returned to the rural area where the Khmer Rouge had first taken them. There they fished and grew vegetables but had no rice, so Sodoeung set out for Thailand in order to buy rice for her family.[10] "My dad had given me a ruby and gold earring. I sold it so I could buy seven cans of rice. I cried. I said, 'That's my only earring.' [My family] didn't want me to sell it, but I had no choice." Eventually Sodoeung found her sister and brother-in-law in a Thai refugee camp.

My sister said to stay because someone else was going to bring food to my parents, but I said, "No, I don't think so." I couldn't sleep or eat. I just stayed for seven days and then I left. . . .

We had to walk at night from the border over a minefield. When I made my first trip to the border a lot of people stepped on the mines and they exploded, and they died on the way. But we could not walk on a different path. So I had to step over their bones and the clothes. . . .

On the way back we were robbed, but not me. I was always lucky. I was sitting with the whole group and a lot of them had a lot of things that they had bought. Some of them were bringing electronic stuff back home so they could sell it in Cambodia.[11] They brought it from Thailand. Some of them had bought watches. I just had rice. I was carrying rice, very heavy, and some food that my dad liked before the war. . . . At first I heard a wolf pack sound. Some of them thought it was a real wolf. But I knew, because I was in the jungle for three or four years, and I knew what wolves sounded like. And then we could hear them in the forest, stepping on the dead leaves. The sound is very scary at night. I told them, "It is not a real wolf." A couple of them knew about that. But the rest didn't know and they didn't care. They said, "Oh, we can shoo them back." . . .

I thought, "What am I going to do? This is all I have. If they take this I have nothing to take back home." So I picked up the rice. They robbed all of them. It was raining and muddy, very muddy in that place. I was stuck in mud, like a mud bar up to my knees. And I carried the rice, I put it on my head, and I had my backpack. . . . Everybody was crying. Women got raped. I was stuck but nobody saw me. I managed to get out of the mud and hide myself under a bushy tree, a very big tree. People believe that you should not go under a bushy tree at night because there are a lot of snakes and poisonous animals. But there was no place else to go. And I knew that I was stepping on a snake with both of my feet. Because the rice was so heavy and I carried it on both sides there was no way the snake could move. I was sitting there and because I was barefoot I could feel it. It must have been stuck there. For awhile, almost an hour, I just sat there shaking because of the gunshots and people crying. They could not help me. And I could not help them. I wondered, "When are they going to finish?" For a while I almost fell asleep under the tree. Then I saw a couple of them come out, and they said, "Oh, they are gone." Before I came out I planned to run so the snake wouldn't come after me. I knew where the head was. I could feel it. So I stepped aside with one leg, and then with the other. . . .

The people asked me, "Where were you?" And I said, "I was under that tree." "Was anybody else there?" "No. I was by myself." "You know what is under there?" They told me that somebody was hanging there. I didn't know.

I didn't look up. They kept telling me. They said, "Somebody hung himself there." I said, "That's okay. Forget it." A couple of them, older ones, told the man not to tell me because I was young and might be scared. But I wasn't scared because I'd seen so many dead already. It was no problem. I got out and they said, "How did you manage to keep these things still?" After that they shined a flashlight on my face. It was all muddy and they could not tell who I was.

By the time Sodoeung arrived home it was light. Her family had already heard reports of the landmine explosion.

People said the young girl and the older woman were killed. I left with an older woman in the village. And there was a young girl about sixteen or seventeen, and they told my mom. And my mom was sure that it was me. Everybody took some food to the temple and prayed for me. They thought that I was dead. So they did some ceremony. And when I got there, my face was muddy and they thought that it was my ghost coming back. So they sprayed rice on me. They threw rice on me and I said, "What for? I'm here, Mom. I'm here, Dad." The youngest one is always quicker than anybody else. She said, "Oh she's here. I thought she died." And then my elder sister said, "No, I don't think so. She's still here. If she had died she would never have come back. But how come her face is like that?" By this time my dad was not scared. My dad said, "It must be her. Help her carry her stuff." They cried and they said, "From now on you are not going anywhere. You stay. If we die, we die here."

Then three or four days later I decided to take my parents out across the border to the camp. Of course we passed a lot of minefields and shooting and terrible things.

What is startling in the last part of this story is not so much the possibility of seeing a ghost, but rather the misrecognition of a living person as a ghost. In those years in Cambodia bad death became an ordinary event: the person killed under the tree, the young woman dying in the explosion of the mine, the death that Sodoeung might have died. For Sodoeung herself, to step over and around dead bodies did not necessarily constitute an unspeakable horror. "I'd seen so many dead already. It was no problem." Her words suggest how difficult it can be to predict when a memory will become violent, poisonous, and difficult to voice. They also call to mind the lines of the Cambodian poet U Sam Oeur: "It was too late for me to be afraid of ghosts / I was a walking ghost myself" (1998, 107). For in crossing and recrossing the border between Laos and Thailand, Sodoeung skirted the border of death, living in a state of intensified vulnerability to wild animals, bandits, and landmines. Her journey at the edges of death led her family (though not she herself) to imagine her as not only dead, but also one of those dangerous dead who suffer a violent and untended death. Michael Taussig (1997) suggests that the dead become ghosts when the incompleteness of their lives forces them to spill over into afterlives of spectral continuance. The lives of soldiers or refugees might be thought to possess a radical form of incompleteness that makes them especially active spirits. Having stepped over death and hidden in its shadow, Sodoeung eventually had to convince her own family that she was not a ghost. They threw rice to fend off the troublesome spirit she must have become. The excessive violence of those years made hauntings by restless dead ubiquitous, expected, and eerily concrete. The ghost for whom she is mistaken is a physical ghost, abroad in the world of the living, with traces of earth on her face from a too hasty burial, a ghost who might feel the pelting of rice on her skin and turn away, or who might, on the other hand, take one of her family with her into death. The undercurrent of this story is the connection between bad death and the near death of survival that is void of any sense of safety. At a time when the countryside was crowded with dead bodies and hungry ghosts, the impending death known as survival was a relationship with the ambient bad death everywhere around.

Other stories are marked by a similar intimacy between bad death and imminent death, the condition of being killable in countless possible ways. Recalling his flight from Laos, the Kmhmu soldier Lt. Phanha said,

> While I was escaping I lost two of my kids. They just disappeared. I don't know if they died or not. I sent people back to try to get one of them, because he knew where to hide, but they couldn't find him. The other one, I don't know what happened. We went in the same boat and then suddenly he was missing. I think that because people wanted to kill me, they took my boys and hid them to get money from me. But I didn't have any more connections to get them back. I'm still waiting [twenty years later] to see if the boys will send me a letter or if whoever has them will send a letter. But I haven't received one, or heard anything from them.

For Lt. Phanha there is no actual death to mourn, only a probability of death, a fear of the deaths that might have or must have occurred, the broken lines of connection and communication through which his sons might have been, or might yet be, found. This loss of connections, for someone who had been a key aide to the CIA, is finalized in the Thai refugee camp to which he eventually made his way.

> At the camp a Thai leader who knew me from before wanted me to go back to Laos and spy on the Pathet Lao. So I stayed and helped them for two years.

Otherwise they would have tried to find somebody to kill me. I was afraid so I obeyed the order. If I had continued to stay in Thailand I know that I would have been killed because nobody liked me at all. I was everybody's enemy. . . . They forced my friend to buy and sell opium for them. Then after he finished they killed him. I would be the same if I hadn't come here. It was really terrible the way they killed people. They really showed us, let us see the killings.

As he was transformed from soldier to refugee by shifting U.S. policies, Lt. Phanha understood how a radical devaluation had overwhelmed his political affiliations. He was now "everybody's enemy." If once he had opposed the Pathet Lao by military alliance, he later opposed them only in order to escape death. In his comments one hears the bitter retrospective awareness that perhaps, after all, there is little difference between being exploited by cold war politics as a mercenary or as a refugee. Forced to witness the bad deaths of other refugees he was constantly reminded of his own dispensability, the arbitrariness of his own constantly imminent death. If he were killed post-1975 he would die not as a war hero, but as an expendable body, not for any ideology, but on someone's whim. He encounters his own death in the deaths of others: "they really showed us, let us see the killings."

When John Prachitham, another Kmhmu man, decided to leave Laos, his father said, "If you want to move, okay. But you will never come back. They will kill you if you do." After living in Thailand for a year, however, John went back for his family.

I got to the village. I knocked on the door. My mom said, "Who's that?" I said it was me. They didn't believe it. I told them again. My dad said, "I told you not to come back." I said, "Pack your clothing. Just your clothing. Don't say anything. Pack your clothing. We are going now." My younger brothers and sister were still asleep. Everybody woke up and packed. I had a friend who had a boat. I'd told him, "You have to wait here, okay?" It took me two hours to get to my village. I ran. When we got to the river it was almost morning, about four o'clock. It was still dark. I looked for my friend. He wasn't there. I said, "Oh, I have killed my family today." It was almost day already, what could I do? I took them back to the village. My mother was very sad. She said, "Why did you do this to us?" I said, "Don't do anything different. Just wake up and do what you do every morning." When I went back my friend said he could not cross the Mekong. The communists were traveling near the river. On the second night I brought them over.

The imminence of violent death is here too, in the certainty that one who leaves home will not return alive, in the incredulity that he has returned, in the sinking horror that one has, in an instant of misjudgment, murdered one's own family. John went on,

> I took them to [Thai] immigration. At immigration it was very, very danger-ous. They have different soldiers at immigration. These are not police and not security guards. They are like half soldiers, half police. Three of them came to the tent and my family was asleep. They pointed a gun at them and said, "Give us the money. Either give it to us or we will kill you." My dad had some money. I had taken some with me, and I left some with them to buy food. He gave them everything. The second night they came again and he said "I don't have any more." They said, "You have some. You have to give it to us." My dad was afraid. My mother woke up and started screaming, "You can kill us right now. You can kill my whole family. Don't kill him by himself, kill all of us." She kept on screaming, and other people in the camp woke up and the soldiers ran away.

Notice again the quality of sustained imminence that attends the violence of the "half soldiers" who appear in the night with license to kill. Here the refugee camp operates as that "apparently innocuous space . . . in which the normal order is *de facto* suspended and in which whether or not atrocities are com-mitted depends not on law but on the civility and ethical sense of the police who temporarily act as sovereign" (Agamben 1998, 174).

Notice too that in these stories the ambience of terror works through cer-tain material effects: the ghost's muddy face, the waking from sleep to a gun barrel, the sight of the killings. Sodoeung spoke once of a Buddhist *wat* that had been converted to a killing field by the Khmer Rouge. "They took a lot of people to that temple to kill. They buried them there. People told me that it was just like a ghost town in the temple. It was so quiet. When you stepped in some places you could feel that the ground was mushy. It was not really solid." Her description is striking for its tactility. The ghosts at this site make them-selves known not in dream appearances or the slamming of doors, as they might in the United States, but in the swampiness of the ground. The earth's sponginess suggests the presence of dead who are beyond the reach of civility. Not having made the transition to benevolent ancestors, their abandonment is manifest in their still decaying bodies. Such a material haunting demands equally material rites of protection.

Cleaning the Bones

Once, while detailing for me the care of Kmhmu dead, John Prachitham began to recall a day when a group of CIA-affiliated mercenaries and a group of

Pathet Lao converged separately on his village in search of food. In the ensuing fight one of the Pathet Lao died barely an arm's length from John's home.

> My dad's older brother grabbed me down to a low place. He saw and he didn't want me to see. He said, "Don't look, don't look." But I still saw it, so I was crying. He died with his gun and his knapsack; he died right there. After this happened everybody moved away. Later the whole village tried to move the body. They didn't just pull him, they took a rope and dragged him, because nobody wanted to grab him. Dying that way, he's a bad spirit. . . . Only the *móo du* [spirit medium], he put his spirit on him, because he had a [protector] spirit. . . . They buried it. They just made a hole. They just put it in. They didn't wrap it; they didn't put anything. However he was, just push him in there. Everybody was hurried and scared. When people died in the village by shooting or anything like that, the *móo du* used his power to protect the whole village. He made all the old men go with him and say some words. He walked around the village and put holy water all around it. That kept the bad spirit from coming into the village and bothering people.

Avoidance of contact with the body, sacralized water, powerful words: these are possible (though not always successful) ways to contain the effects of bad death, to keep from being haunted into a bad death of one's own. Unsettled spirits of the dead operate with an arbitrariness parallel to that of violence. They are uncontrollable, as likely to do harm as good, but just possibly susceptible to sacred water and incantations. The water and magical words are akin to the amulet that Lt. Somsy had forgotten to wear in his nightmare of combat. For the amulet is not simply a mnemonic device to evoke the Buddha's teaching on the mental transcendence of suffering, but a tactile link to the Buddha's power.

Writing of terror, Avery Gordon notes that the practice of "disappearance" employed by sundry South American police states (and also by the Khmer Rouge) exercises its control on the imagination (1997, 124). People submit not because of the rational content of a message that conveys the consequences of disobedience, but because of the way the message is delivered, through unseen but suspected tortures and murders. Because unpredictable violence works on the imagination, its terrorizing effects may continue for years afterward, even when the terrorized are living in new countries far from the death squads. While trauma, as noted above, is often addressed through efforts to replace a sense of immanent violence with a narrative of survival, the haunting that occurs in the wake of bad death is addressed rather by facing the immanent violence in all its ghostliness. Speaking of his work with

Lao emigrants, one physician, Dr. Stoltz, noted their unwillingness to speak of the violent past:

> One of the things that we hear from people is, "I don't want to talk about it." People will say literally, "That stuff is old and rotten. It just stinks. It makes me sick. I get sick when I talk about it, after I talk about it." So then Khamphan [Stoltz's interpreter] says, "Well, I know that it's old and rotten, but that's how we do our work here, because sometimes we help people dig up the bones, and then we help them clean them, and we help them put them back." Now he was doing that in a number of my cases. And he never interpreted [to me] what he was saying to the patients. [When I found out] I said, "How many years do you think you've used that kind of word picture to talk to people?" He said he didn't know, maybe three or five years. I thought to myself, "The guy's a genius." He conversationally knew how to just spontaneously tie himself right into the core of the terror and the awful stuff that somebody was trying to talk to him about. "That stuff makes me sick." And the striking thing about it is—we have asked some of the patients, but we don't do it on a routine basis—but my guess is that a percentage of the patients have actually done what he just said. Moving the dead from one place to another for example. Coming to the conclusion that they're in a bad place, or we put them in the wrong place.

While most of the Lao for whom Khamphan served as an interpreter would have preferred to cremate the dead (except in cases of bad death), they would also have been aware of a practice of burial followed by a later disinterment of the bones, as part of a repertoire of Southeast Asian death rites practiced by some Khmer and often by people of Vietnamese or Chinese descent. The cleaning of the bones for such mourners is pivotal in transforming the dead from dangerous spirits who may haunt the living to benevolent ancestors or beings ready for rebirth.

Khamphan's interpretation is powerful not just as a culturally comprehensible metaphor, but also as a bodily intervention in the material effects of bad death. It offers the counseling session to the patient as a ritual mediation of what haunts them, not simply disembodied memories, but actual dead. Memories of violence are mucky and stinking like decayed bodies. Simply telling stories is not enough to inhibit their effects. It is necessary to handle the bones of what is remembered, to strip them of flesh, to cleanse their odor, to burn them to ash or rebury them in new soil. When the expectation and experience of violence has become the pervasive atmosphere of daily life, the response to bad death, Das suggests, is less a matter of detaching oneself from the loss than of learning to "inhabit" a world saturated and changed by this loss. "Instead of the simplified images of healing that assume that [it involves] reliving a trauma or decathecting desire from the lost object and reinvesting it elsewhere, we need to think of healing as a kind of relationship with death" (1996, 78)—and, I would add, with the dead themselves. This relationship with the dead is enacted in physical gestures toward spirits who are palpably present to the senses.

Dr. Stoltz went on to speak of ritual healings devised by his patients themselves to transform their relationships with death and with the dead.

> See, you have to watch for the malignant effects of the memory. Part of the toolkit here has to do with the individual learning how to deal with it. If somebody starts having nightmares again, and there are unnamed dead, unknown dead coming into their dreams, and trying to get them to eat with them, or chasing them, the patients will often wake up and they'll pray. They'll use their ancestral shrine, they'll use joss, they'll make gifts for somebody, could be the unnamed dead, could be a grandmother who's a helper. But if they've gotten into a problem, where they did that, and sure enough the next night or the same night it's back again, I deal with it in a pretty concrete sense. This is not some kind of theoretical stuff. I'll actually make suggestions based on what they told me, about the content of the prayer. I see that as an act that has multiple meanings. It validates what they're doing. It encourages the activity. Whether I believe it or not isn't nearly as important as whether we can have a conversation about it, respecting it, manipulating it. I'm probably going beyond the bounds of what we're supposed to do in a Western sense because I'm being pretty invasive and saying "Why don't you do this?" Some of the patients—and I have a couple of them who are pretty strong-willed— come back and say, "You know the last time I was here you said I should do this, but that's not what I did. What I did was—" and then they describe a reconstruction of the whole thing. I see that as just totally positive because what's happening is that they're just rearranging the toolkit. The suggestion was made to alter it, to do something a little different, and how they do it isn't nearly as important, as—. My sense is that the likelihood that they're going to do something that'll work is pretty high. And I don't have to use drugs, change the meds. That's why I think that it's important to have a conversation within the contextual framework of how the patient sees the terror. There are a lot of things that go on in there, things that I don't even know are going on. I don't think it helps to be too cerebral about this stuff. If you need a shovel, you pick up a shovel and start digging.

Here an alternative language to the language of trauma emerges, a language of bad death that calls for an engagement with the very realm of the uncanny from which terror materializes. Simply eliciting memories may exacerbate their "malignant effect." Instead Dr. Stoltz "manipulates" patients to improvise with their own repertoire of practices for dealing with the disturbed spirits of the dead.[12]

Marita Sturken has written of the ways that North American veterans communicate with the dead at the Vietnam Memorial (1997, 64–65, 78). The communications portray the close relationship between confronting memories of violence and mourning the dead. Yet they also suggest that for some veterans, mourning involves an active engagement with phantoms. Veterans leave letters not just to other U.S. soldiers whose deaths they witnessed and whose names are engraved on the wall, but also sometimes to anonymous Vietnamese they killed whose names are nowhere inscribed on a national monument that, while remembering North American dead, is actively involved in forgetting Vietnamese dead. Lao, Khmer, Hmong, and Kmhmu dead seem to have been even more radically forgotten in U.S. public memory than the Vietnamese, absent even from the query "Where are the Vietnamese names?" (Sturken 1997, 83).[13]

While Southeast Asian veterans and civilians now living in the United States are not offered a state-sponsored site for healing encounters with the dead, they are, like U.S. veterans, offered the diagnosis of PTSD along with its assorted treatment techniques. In his far-reaching genealogy of this diagnostic category, Allan Young notes that, for a confluence of political and scientific reasons, the disorder came to be defined according to a mono-directional temporal arc originating in a single traumatic event in the past, usually involving extreme violence (1995, 118–42). Without the definitive etiology of such a violent event, PTSD might have dissolved into a multifactorial problem with several indeterminate causes and moments of inception. It also might have failed to crystallize into a service-related disorder for which the state (in the agency of the Veterans Administration) might assume some modicum of responsibility. The category of PTSD was invented, as Young shows, through the historical convergence of a nosological turn in mental health, with the publication of the third edition of the *Diagnostic and Statistical Manual of Mental Disorders (DSM-III)*, and the return of Vietnam veterans who reported nightmares, violent rage, or emotional numbness.[14] A political demand for compensation to the veterans along with a scientific demand for a disorder that did not contravene the laws of causality or the directionality of time's passage required that the trauma be caused by a single violent event in the past.

Clinicians may, in practice, acknowledge that time and causality seem to move in two directions, "from a significant event out to its symptoms (the

DSM conception of PTSD) and from a person's current psychological state back to the event, where it acquires a genealogy and a discrete set of meanings" (Young 1995, 135). They may also ask, in reference to the suspected relationship between a Vietnam memory and a childhood memory, "What is a metaphor of what?" with the understanding that a war trauma might swallow and intensify a childhood memory (161). For the most part, however, such temporal snarls are implicitly combed out into a coherent timeline in which PTSD, after its inception in a single event, becomes more or less symptomatic depending on preexisting anxieties or a lower threshold of tolerance for stress. To preserve the definition of the disorder, memories of violence that predate or postdate the etiological event are framed, through elegant argumentation, as effects of PTSD (137–41).

Haunting and the repertoire of responses through which its effects might be dispelled moves within other temporalities. PTSD in its strict clinical definition fails to grasp the diffuse and phantasmal intermingled memory and anticipation of immanent violence that drifts in the wake of bad death. An etiology of haunting, rather than being rooted in the past, shifts restlessly between past and present. Incidents of haunting often arise in the midst of present events that echo past violence. If a psychodynamic treatment of PTSD (which is perhaps even more frequently treated in the twenty-first century with cognitive, behavioral, or pharmaceutical approaches) attempts to reintegrate a traumatic past into the sufferer's personal history, negotiations with ghosts attempt rather to confront the violence immanent in the present. Even if the bad death that gives rise to haunting belongs to the past, the dead arguably belong to the here and now.

Dr. Stoltz went on to recount his clinical interaction with a Hmong *txiv neeb* (shaman) with a spiraling physical illness, who was troubled by the dead.

> If the patient is using a rich, non-Western contextual framework, why not use it? In fact, from my perspective, it's the only way to bail the boat. Let me tell you another story. This is a shaman in town. He's got a wife who's got what's viewed as hysterical blindness. Can't see, and all of the testing, extensive testing, suggests that she isn't really blind. There's a whole series of reports of people who've been victims of the war who have had this.[15] He's taken care of her for years. And now he's going deaf. His son was always with him, and one of the [case] workers who was interpreting for him, and they had to shout, because he could hardly hear. But it was very clear that sometimes he heard stuff that wasn't shouted. So I decided that this was a kind of folie à deux, that he'd gotten the same kind of sickness his wife had, only we'd better head it off at the pass.

A couple of [case] workers asked me to see him because they weren't making any headway. He wasn't taking care of himself; he was screaming at people. From being a very polite, interactive man, he had just gone off the deep end and was going to pieces. He had the whole family, the whole household in an uproar. Nobody knew what to do about it, including [the nurse practitioner] and me and everybody else. I decided, from my view of what was going on with this guy, that he had come to the conclusion that he was dying. He constantly had brothers and other people trying to get him to go with them. He had a bunch of stories about how they died. I had a sense that he felt like he was responsible in part for some stuff that happened to them.

We had to negotiate quite a while about this before I did what I did. The day that I challenged him, we sat down and I warned his son that we were going to do something that his son might find uncomfortable. The deal we made beforehand was that the case manager should be sure that the man knows that what he's saying is directly from me. It's not what the case manager wants to say, but it's what I'm saying. So I got bossy, manipulative as hell. I didn't know what else to do. I don't see how you can dance around the edges of what's going on with this guy who's convinced he's dying. He acknowledged that he thought he was dying. He predicted his own death. I told him that I didn't feel that he was dying. I told him that there was a significant chance that he'd made a mistake, that he wasn't going to die, and I didn't want to have this conversation five years from now, with him still unable to feed himself and clean himself. That he needed to go down this other path. So then we told him what he had to do about it, which was pretty simple stuff. He had to start taking a bath; he had to start feeding himself; he had to do a bunch of things that he wasn't doing. I said, "You're the only one that can take the shower for yourself. That's what you have to do." We got pretty plain.

And of course he had a whole long list, they had every ceremony done, and nothing was working. So we also gave him some instructions about what to do with [the dead], that he had to tell them to go away. That he had important things to do, that he was still a father, and he had to still look after his wife, and she was sick, and they shouldn't bother him. They should help him. I think if you use the shamanistic model, you have to be positively predictive. I'm not going to ask him, "Do you think you might get better if you did this?" [I said] "You'll probably have a dream or two—I don't know when this is going to happen, maybe next week, maybe six weeks from now—but I'll bet you you're going to have a dream where you're convinced that they're helping you. But you have to tell them to first. They don't know what's up with you, because I told you, you may have made a mistake here. You're not dying. You have to tell them, 'I'm not dying.'"

Now he's doing a whole bunch of stuff he wasn't: he's going out in the community, he comes in clean, he's taking care of himself. He still shouts at people, but the behavior has changed significantly. I don't know how much more it will change or what we can do about it.

He's on my list of shamans that I've treated. I've got a long list of those, a whole bunch. It's interesting. And one of the problems that people have if they've been engaged in traditional healing practices, they know that words and language and thoughts can kill or change reality, or that's the perception. So if that's happened in their own life, their own illness, how do you undo it?

Allan Young noted that in the PTSD clinic where he conducted fieldwork in the late 1980s recovery was construed as "making the past dead" (1995, 201), releasing patients from patterns of reenactment wherein they had tried impossibly to resolve past violence in the present. Dr. Stoltz's intervention with the *txiv neeb* works in an inverse way, resolving past violence by confronting the dead in the present. If, for Freud, healing from trauma required "recollection with affect" (Young 1995, 37), here it requires dealing with the dead. The treatment involves less a relation to memories than an encounter with spirits, less a psychic adjustment vis-à-vis images of the past than a pragmatic transformation of interactions with the dead.

It might be tempting to assimilate these spirits to the spectral figures that appear as metaphors in much writing on historical memory, as when, for instance, Dominick LaCapra writes of "putting the ghosts to rest" to gloss the process of effectively mourning historical loss (2001, 90). In such analyses active revenants signify a possession by and reenactment of traumatic memory that, due to a failure to "work through" the loss, devolves into a "melancholic feedback loop" (21). The engagement with ghosts in the wake of bad death, however, is melancholic only insofar as melancholia is an aspect of ongoing mourning, as suggested above. In this ghostly encounter the intent is not simply to drive the dead away, but to assist them to heal from their own traumatic deaths so that they become protective, rather than disturbing. The point is not to exorcise uncanny forces, but to harness their power. Moreover, the possibility remains of being haunted again, of being compelled to further negotiations with the dead—especially if they become forgotten or neglected—in a process of lifelong mourning.[16]

In her genealogy of trauma, Ruth Leys (2000) notes that from Freud to van der Kolk, the concept of trauma has been marked by an unresolved tension between, on the one hand, an idea of unrepresentable but imprinted horror that persists in the present, erupting in nightmares, flashbacks, and compulsive repetition (what she terms the mimetic aspect of "trauma"), and, on the other hand, a notion of a repressed memory that must and can be remembered, articulated, and cognitively grasped as the past by an autonomous subject. She traces the ways that the cure of trauma has consequently oscillated between abreactive emotional release, sometimes hypnotically or narcotically induced, and the generation of a narrative that, in representing the violent event, defuses its power. She links this tension to the technology of hypnotic suggestion, which hovers, in her narrative, as the sometimes hidden apparatus that shapes traumatic memory as the object of its knowledge. Indeed it was the practice of hypnosis itself, she argues, that suggested to early theorists the possibility of a memory being implanted in a patient's mind yet inaccessible to deliberate recall. The traumatic event itself is understood, in the mimetic paradigm, to work hypnotically (8).

Might this tension between inchoate, somatic, mimetic, suggestible memory, with its blurring of historical event and phantasm, on the one hand, and coherent, narrative memory, on the other, depend on a modern Christian vision of subjectivity? An ambivalent vacillation between mimetic repetition of trauma and antimimetic representation of trauma appears to be rooted in the figure of a subject who struggles out of a pathological (historically also glossed as primitive) identification with the world toward an autonomous spectatorship (cf. Romanyshyn 1989), and who similarly endeavors to shape overlapping waves and undertows of past, present, and future into a monolinear chronicity. To turn toward an etiology of haunting in the context of violent memories is to question not only a tacit knowledge that the dead do not return, but also an assumption that the mature self exercises her will over an external world from a secure mooring in a discrete present time. Dr. Stoltz recalled of one of his Khmer patients:

> This woman was taking care of her grandchildren, and one of her complaints was that she couldn't speak English well enough. She didn't feel like she was an adequate grandmother. She was always afraid that the kids were going to get in trouble. A couple of her grandchildren were already in gangs. She was a very worried, caring person, very anxious about this. So I'm like "Well you know you have a choice, you could go to ESL. I bet you could even have your grandchildren help with your language lessons. You could get better at it." [The interpreter] looked at me like, this isn't going to work. She said, "I can't say that in Khmer." I said, "Say what?" "I can't say that she has a choice." Well what she did was she said to this lady, "If you want to make merit for the next life in this life, you should go to ESL lessons. You know you have no control over this yourself. But you can make merit." To me she said, "You're always using words like that. And we always have to change them." I always forget

that this is a different pathway. There are a series of ways that this can be reconstructed.

According to Dr. Stoltz, this woman would be willing to take steps to alleviate her anxiety, to better care for her grandchildren and possibly even to avert their entry into gang violence, as long as these steps are framed not as an exercise of personal will, but as a way to make merit. For Lao and Khmer Buddhists making merit is intricately interwoven with caring for the dead, as well as for one's own posthumous future, as I elaborate later. In this interaction, then, the interpreter implicitly offers a way for the woman to improve not only her own afterlife, but also the afterlives of those already dead. Following the interpreter's lead, Dr. Stoltz enters into a narrative of merit, rather than pressuring the woman into a narrative of personal autonomy.

Spirits of violence are still restless in the United States, as memories of war and terror exacerbate and are exacerbated by the everyday violence of minoritization, poverty, and social fragmentation in the present.[17] The violent traces of a descent into marginal life are overlaid with experiences as racialized immigrants and public aid recipients. Emigrants speak of humiliations at the welfare office and a lower standard of care in the hospitals. One Lao man said of Adult and Family Services, "I will not go there. They have no respect for me. Believe me, they make me feel so small. They check every penny, expecting us to be lying. This is what the communists did when they took over our country. They counted every chicken. That's why I came here, to get away from that. So, what's the difference?" (quoted in Proudfoot 1990, 190). As Dr. Stoltz commented of his Southeast Asian patients:

> Sometimes the suffering they're having in this country is all we talk about. For example, kids out of control, a constant focus of discussion. Husbands out of control or drinking. Deaths in the family, infidelities, married to two women and having a hard time over that whole thing, and unwilling to admit that it's a polygamous relationship so you can't even talk about what the problem is. Kid in prison on drug charges. Don't want to tell anybody about that because they're embarrassed about it, but they're worried to death. I think they're right next to each other all the time. They're overlaid. The past and the present. If a patient has something go wrong now, a daughter or son has disappeared, and they don't know where they are, and they're gone for three days, and hanging around with kids that the patient doesn't trust, and the patient starts having nightmares of being chased by the Khmer Rouge, the nightmares are about what went on before, but what triggers it is current distress. It's amazing how many people live in the U.S. during the daytime and in Cambodia during the nighttime.

Psychiatrist J. D. Kinzie notes that Khmer memories of violence have been compounded in the United States "where they confronted a new culture, a new language, a limited social network, and precarious financial status . . . unemployment, an uncertain future, and continuing stress, usually without friends and in an unsympathetic environment" (1990, 348). If memories of gang warfare or drug busts or deaths in U.S. hospitals are not simply screen memories (Freud 1962) for losing children while fleeing through the jungle or witnessing summary executions, then how might we conceive the relationship between these differently located memories? Psychoanalyst Dori Laub suggests that more recent tragedies work as "the final corroboration of the defeat of [the sufferers'] powers to survive and rebuild" (1992, 65). This corroboration becomes evidence, in her analysis, that survivors "live not with memories of the past, but with an event that could not and did not proceed through to its completion, has no ending, attained no closure, and therefore, as far as its survivors are concerned, continues into the present and is current in every respect" (69). While this lack of closure might seem to resemble the intermingled anticipation and fear of violence evoked by Jeganathan, Laub understands it as a compulsive reenactment, akin to LaCapra's "melancholic feedback loop," from which the survivor cannot escape. She cites the testimony of Martin Gray, who witnessed the deaths of his family in Warsaw and Treblinka, and then years later the deaths of his second family in a fire in the south of France: "At that time too, I could save nothing but my naked life. . . . Their death has reopened all the graves. In those graves, my people, my parents, my siblings, my friends were coming back to life; my people, my family, died in them a second death" (quoted in Laub 1992, 66). From a psychodynamic standpoint, this reopening of the graves cannot but become symbolic of the unearthing of buried memories that must be, once and for all, confronted and grieved. Yet, from the standpoint of Dr. Stoltz's hybrid response to haunting, the reopening of graves has a more literal resonance. Lao, Khmer, Hmong, and Kmhmu have, among their repertoire of cures, the possibility of addressing the dead, rearranging their remains, offering them gifts, making a bid for their assistance in place of their haunting. This magical intervention is, as Morris has noted in another context, "anti-representational" (2000, 9), a matter not of quieting trauma with narrative accounts, but of altering the effects of bad death with specialized tools of spectral-material force. In this process, the repetition that "makes us ill" as Gilles Deleuze writes, "also heals . . . testifying in both cases to its [literally] 'demonic' power" (1994, 19).

Mrs. Sann is among those still tormented by her memories of life under the Khmer Rouge. The first time that my interpreter and I arrived at her Section 8 apartment she greeted us in flower-print blouse and bare feet. On a small shrine in the corner was a painted statue of Buddha, fresh flowers in a glass vase, and an incense holder. On a table was a photograph of her deceased husband in uniform. As she told her story she sometimes grew teary, and often we did too. Mrs. Sann was taking medications for insomnia, depression, mood swings, high blood pressure, and stomach trouble. Yet one of her greatest anxieties had to do not with her experiences in Cambodia, but with the sudden death of one of her daughters in the United States a few years before our conversations. She felt uncertain about the well-being of her daughter's spirit because, after making the decision to bury her, she discovered that she would not be able to disinter and clean her bones. The figure of melancholy in her story is not only Mrs. Sann herself, but her daughter as well, who, because of sudden death and inadequate burial, might be ambivalently torn between resentment and longing, unable to release herself from her attachment to the living. It is this extreme distress of the dead that makes them dangerous. Cheng insightfully observes that in Freud's description of melancholy it is not only the ego that becomes ghostly but also the ego's introjected object, whose "potential for subjectivity" Freud overlooks (Cheng 2001, 10). For Mrs. Sann, however, the subjectivity of her deceased daughter is not in question. Her own consolation and that of the dead are densely intertwined. Only if her dead child could cease her melancholy wandering would she herself have a chance of finding peace.

"Since my daughter passed away," she told us, "I have been thinking about all of this. People who are sad or depressed go to school or to a certain place and feel better. As for me, I don't. I keep thinking about all these things." Mrs. Sann is clearly aware that, like many Khmer emigrants, she suffers from *koucharang* (literally "thinking too much").[18] Khmer interpreters and caseworkers have been trained to translate such illness conditions into psychological terms. As Dr. Stoltz remarked:

> My sense was that as language intermediaries, and youngsters who were born right on the edge of the Pol Pot regime, or on the edge of Cambodia, in Thailand, and then got their brains scrubbed as MSWs, and then just picture them acting as a language intermediary to a Western-trained psychiatrist who has a whole lot of power that nurse practitioners and psychiatrists have, that case managers don't have. And they sit there, and "She says she's depressed." Well I learned a long time ago that none of our patients say that they're depressed. They don't use that word. So the case manager just made a diagnosis.

Khmer women who are asked about *koucharang* often link it to memories of wartime Cambodia. One woman told researchers, "My husband thinks too much about our three sons killed by Pol Pot. Then he gets *koucharang*," while another said, "All my children died during Pol Pot time. I think too much about death" (quoted in Frye and D'Avanzo 1994, 92). Khmer say one should speak "softly" and "sweetly" to the sufferers of *koucharang*, keeping them company, offering them "good thoughts," making them laugh, encouraging them to "forget [their] sad thoughts." As one woman said, "We give each other comfort when we think too much" (92–93; cf. North 1995, 229, 256). In early attempts to treat Khmer refugees, Kinzie noted that, with Khmer patients, the clinical interview to address post-traumatic stress simply intensified "intrusive thoughts." He added, "There was no catharsis or healing effect" (1990, 345). He concluded, "our usual means of dealing with these experiences— verbal interaction—seems inappropriate and strange to the Khmer" (349). Aihwa Ong tells the story of an educational "psychodrama" about PTSD shown to groups of Khmer women in San Diego in hope of "sparking a catharsis of their (assumed) suppressed feelings." Ong goes on to observe, "Some women claimed to be cured after watching the videotape," in that way avoiding "having to go to a clinic and be labeled as 'crazy'" (2003, 100). The women's inventive refusal of the call to catharsis in this incident is reminiscent of that of the Vietnam vets, in Young's (1995) account, who are angered by the directive to interact with a toy replica of the Vietnam Memorial wall as part of their treatment.

At times, as Dr. Stoltz's work, my own fieldwork, and numerous memoirs suggest,[19] Khmer emigrants may choose to tell stories of life under Pol Pot. In our conversations, although Mrs. Sann told her story willingly and with much repetition—the deaths witnessed, the children lost—she showed no signs of relief in the telling. The one time during our conversations when she became animated and smiling was when we watched together a video recording of her mother's disinterment and reburial ceremony.[20] On the screen a white string passed from the coffin through the line of monks to encircle the piles of food and gifts offered for her mother's spirit. "It's the way of sending goods to the person," Mrs. Sann said. She told us that after the body was exhumed the flesh was removed by two of her mother's nephews.[21] Afterward she herself helped to wash the bones.

> In that village they say that if you are a good person and you did not do anything bad to anyone or commit any sins, then, when they do the second burial, no one will smell anything. And that's what happened. Before we dug up

my mom's remains, I prayed, saying that I wanted to do the second burial for her, so please don't let her have any odor. And she didn't. A lot of people watched when we first dug up the remains. There were no flies, and the villagers were very happy and spoke a lot about it.

Mrs. Sann returned over and over in our conversations to her grief, sleeplessness, and sense of guilt, especially about the death of two daughters, one in the United States and another in Cambodia. Yet she seemed relaxed and happy as she narrated the videotape of her mother's second burial, including the memory of handling her bones, which clearly never evoked for her the piles of skulls or spongy earth of the killing fields. Here what intervened in *koucharang* was a replay of the material transformation of her mother from potential ghost into gracious ancestor. For a time Mrs. Sann could evade the haunting of her daughter's bad death in a video performance of her mother's clean bones.

Water Buffalo Cobra and the Prisoner of War

Work, work—hacking at trees, uprooting them,
    clearing bushes,
transplanting rice, no time to rest.
At noon, alone, as I cleared the canebrake,
a beautiful black cobra

opened his hood before me, displaying his power.
He thought I was his foe.
"He's beautiful, just like in the Indian movies!"
I exclaimed to myself while my knees knocked.

"O cobra! Your flesh and blood are truly
Buddha's flesh and blood.
I am just a prisoner of war,
but I am not your food.

You, cobra, are free,
and if my flesh is truly your blood,
plead my case with the spirits of this swamp
to lead me to Buddham, Dhammam, and Sangham."

The cobra stared at me with loving kindness
then lowered his head.
He slithered into the swamp to the south,
and I went back to my work of surviving.

—U Sam Oeur

Chapter 2 Displacements

THE COBRA IN OEUR'S POEM strikes a familiar motif. Like other nonhuman agents who appear in Southeast Asian literature, folktales, and memoirs about life under conditions of war and state-sponsored terror, Oeur's cobra is a figure of beauty, power, and imagined rescue as well as danger. The encounter is not simply an ethnographic reference to a rural lifestyle, where the land along with its creatures is animated by intelligence, sentience, and will. For the cosmopolitan prisoner of the poem, who has been forced at gunpoint into a rural work camp by the Khmer Rouge (as was Oeur himself), the cobra borrows some of its magical luster from Bollywood movies. That does not prevent the prisoner from addressing a fervent prayer to this magnificent beast, and through him to the spirits of the place they both currently inhabit.

Displacement was a way of life for Laotians and Cambodians during and after the U.S.-sponsored wars in those countries. Many Hmong and Kmhmu, whose families or villages had been caught up in conflicts between the Pathet Lao, on the one hand, and CIA forces and the Royal Lao Army, on the other, were driven from their villages by bomb raids, skirmishes, or military operations.[1] If they were not recruited directly into guerilla warfare, they lived precariously at its edges. With the destruction of farms and fields, many Hmong and Kmhmu subsisted on food supplied by the United States Agency for International Development (USAID) until the departure of U.S. forces in 1975, when a few thousand were airlifted to relative safety, while the vast majority were left behind to continue the fight or make their way through the forest and across the Mekong River to Thailand. When the Pathet Lao seized control of the government, Lao who belonged to the educated elite or military families also felt compelled to leave out of fear of being incarcerated in reeducation camps. As Douang explained,

> I saw many adults who were arrested. Many of my teachers escaped. And many of my friends also escaped. Everybody had some fear. My uncle who

was a military officer was afraid that they were going to arrest him and send him to a reeducation camp. After he escaped, he sent letters to me, urging my parents to leave or anybody to leave. . . . I talked to my parents. My father believed that the chaos would only be temporary, and things would get better, but I argued with my father. At first they tried to stop me, but they couldn't. My mother arranged the escape for me. She hired a saleswoman who had an import-export business between Laos and Thailand and went across the Mekong River a lot. I used a fake permit, as though I were a Thai citizen visiting Laos. It's tough when I think back to that. My heart—. That was really a hard time. Because she did not want me to go.

Even though Douang's parents urged him to stay, five years after he departed they also left, out of fear that his father might soon be arrested.[2]

Meanwhile in Cambodia (then Kampuchea) the Khmer Rouge relocated thousands of people from villages into communal farms, forcibly recruited young men sixteen or older into the armed forces, and evacuated Phnom Penh, the principal city, separating families into work teams organized by age group and often sent to remote locations.[3] Even after 1979 when the Khmer Rouge regime was overturned by the Vietnamese, Khmer were often unable to return to homes that were occupied by other families or the Vietnamese army. Dislocated in these ways, people subsisted in unfamiliar and shifting landscapes subject to unpredictable episodes of violence, but also vulnerable to wild animals, weather, and harsh terrain that might prevent or unexpectedly assist their survival. In these landscapes they were often forced to develop new bodily habits adapted to life in the forest.

The soldier at war, Elaine Scarry wrote, is

inextricably bound up with the qualities and conditions—berry laden or snow laden—of the ground over which he walks or runs or crawls and with which he craves and courts identification, as in the camouflage clothing he wears and the camouflage postures he adopts, now running bent over parallel with the ground it is his work to mime, now arching forward conforming the curve of his back to the curve of a companion boulder, now standing as upright and still and narrow as the slender tree behind which he hides; he is the elms and the mud, he is the one hundred and sixth, he is a small piece of German terrain broken off and floating dangerously through the woods of France. He is a fragment of American earth wedged into an open hillside in Korea and reworked by its unbearable sun and rain. He is dark blue like the sea. He is light grey like the air through which he flies. He is sodden in the green shadows of earth. He is a light brown vessel of red Australian blood that will soon be opened and emptied across the rocks and ridges of Gallipoli from which he can never again become distinguishable. (1985, 83)

What Scarry evokes in this unremitting rush of images is the way that a soldier (or anyone living in a combat zone) is shaped and transformed by physical landscapes. Starkly missing from this passage is any reference to the American, Vietnamese, Lao, and Cambodian bodies exploded and dispersed by grenades, or pressed into mud, to helmets tied with branches of Southeast Asian plants, or screaming bodies on fire running from thatched roof huts. These images, at least in some two-dimensional form, are not difficult to conjure, due to television footage, photographs, and feature-length movies proliferating the images of the American wars in Southeast Asia. One wonders if Scarry deliberately omitted images of the wars in Vietnam, Laos, and Cambodia, which by 1985, when the above passage was published, would have run the risk of being seen as if through the camera lenses of cinematographers for films such as *Apocalypse Now* (1979) and *First Blood* (1982).

Yet Scarry's prose makes vivid those sensory realities that elude a camera's lens, tracing a densely material interactivity of humans and landscape. The Lao soldier Lt. Somsy described to me the weeks he spent in the forest after escaping a prison camp.

> When it doesn't rain, I walked about sixty kilometers each day. I walked on the mud. The mud just gets collected on my shoes. So I would use a knife to cut the mud off, and then continue to walk. . . . Sometimes I would have to swim across the river. Sometimes there's very little food left, then gone, then you have to look for food again the next day. . . . Most of the time I would eat leaves. Some of them smell really bad. Sometimes it doesn't taste bad, but it does taste oily. But I didn't get poisoned by these leaves ever. I was hungry and just ate more. . . . I never got lost in the jungle because I learned in the military school, they said when you're in the jungle at night and you want to know the direction you look at the star. There's one star called diamond star. This diamond star is always in the north.

The diamond star and the oily leaves were not, I suggest, merely technical means of subsistence for Lt. Somsy, any more than the muddy earth and the river were merely obstacles. They were possible foes and allies in a densely tangled intimacy among human, earth, plant, and sky. They were forcefully interceding, not passive, but active, not simply the background scenery of history, but historical agents themselves, compelling him into new bodily practices.

Becoming Landscape

In 1975, Sodoeung's family was forcibly removed from their home near an army base where her father had served as an officer.[4]

The group of soldiers gunpointed us saying, "If you don't leave, we're going to shoot you." We said goodbye to our house and friends. And then we just walked with other people. I was scared. But then I was mad because they made us go and everything was destroyed. They wouldn't let us take anything. They said we were free to come back three days afterwards. It was not three days. It was almost three years. . . .

After three or four months, they tried to get all the different ages put into different areas. My older sister was put in with other old kids like eighteen, twenty, twenty-two. I was fourteen at that time. I was in a younger group of kids, teenagers. My other sister was ten. So she was in a group with ten-year-olds. The youngest one was seven. So she was with other kids her age. They split us up. . . . I don't know where they took us. But it was in the jungle. . . . A lot of trees. They just let us live there. No tent, no nothing. We just slept under the trees. No bedding, no mattress, nothing. . . .

I had to go to a place where they were building a dam, a powerful one. [The pit] was six meters deep. For the ladder they had cut a tree. And you know a tree, when it is fresh, there is a sticky substance that comes out. When it rained and you walked on the step, and there was no handle to hold onto, it was just like in a circus. A lot of kids fell and broke their arms and legs. Later on they could not carry anything. Some of them were not able to walk. We carried the dirt with a stick of bamboo across our shoulders. On this side and that side. They gave each one an area of ground to take out, one meter across and one meter down. Every day you had to do that. If you could not finish it you did not get food to eat. That was my job. I think I was there almost two years. . . .

So I was carrying dirt, digging the dam every day. And I was falling sometimes. Because we didn't have enough food to eat. And not enough salt. Sometimes they had just a small amount of rice for us. We worked hard, like eighteen or twenty hours a day, with only four hours of sleep. Even at night they had electric lights in the field and people would just carry dirt. At first they gave me just one meter, and later on two. Because I was fast, because I wanted to eat, right? Two and then three. They kept increasing it. If I finished early I could not leave, I had to help other people so that everybody could eat. I would not just go out there and eat by myself, no. Some kids couldn't make it and they suffered a lot of abuse. Hitting, spanking, kicking.

For the baskets that they used for the dirt, they used rope from cow skin. When it rained the skin got soggy and became just like meat, and it smelled. And flies would follow you everywhere, everywhere you walked. And you smelled like death. . . . Sometimes we didn't have food to eat, and we used those ropes. We just put them in the fire. Sometimes it was not cooked. A lot of us did that.

Sometimes in the evening, after we got off work, I couldn't sleep. There were a lot of trees. We could not see the sun. It was very dark. There were a lot of cobra and a lot of poisonous snakes, also scorpions, centipedes. Sometimes they got into our clothes and our backpacks. . . . When it rained I would go out to catch some frogs. . . . I knew one of the leaders who was guarding us. I told her I just needed to go to the bathroom. She said, "Yeah, okay." I liked to go just to look for something to eat. I knew one place where I could get mushrooms. They are very hard to find, they grow underground. When you open them on the top, the inside comes out all over, just like hair. You can eat it raw, or you can make soup, but too bad, we could not boil anything! We shared it.

I took a bath every one or two months. There was no shower and it was very hard to find water in that area. So most of us shaved our hair because we had a lot of lice. There was no soap and water. And every time they took us to take the shower we had to walk two or three miles. It was not a road. We just walked across the forest, through the trees and the bamboo. They are short but they are sharp. We walked barefoot and they stuck our feet. You could not just walk the way you walk here. You ran. One of them would ride on a horse wagon in front, and two of them would ride horses behind. It was just like, I don't know, maybe a dog. I don't know what word to use. Maybe they were just guarding a dog, taking the dog to have a bath. We ran to take a bath, and after that we came back and ran again. You got wet with sweat because it is hot there.

A lot of my friends got killed. Some of them were a little bit older than me, like sixteen, seventeen. They got raped before they died. They killed them. I know some of them were really worried that someday they would be taken away. And I told them, "I know. Because we cannot get away."

At that time we were thinking about god a lot. You believe in the spiritual? I believe in the spiritual. The trees, the big trees mean a lot to me. There we could not talk to our friends when they were around; we could only whisper when they were not around. At night when we were sleeping, they walked around to see who was asleep and who was not. If you were not asleep they would kick you and move you to a different place. So we had no freedom to talk to each other, to express our feelings. There was no regret, no grief when somebody died or somebody was taken away to be killed.

Then after that they sent me to two other places. One place they were digging another dam. When that one was finished, then I went to a different one. There the area that we had to dig was over the river. The river just fell there;

the water was very heavy. A lot of kids died there because they couldn't swim. We would walk and carry the dirt and rock, and how could we hold the river with our bare hands? It was crazy. If they wanted to kill people, why didn't they just kill them? They just used them and starved them. That was the technique. Some of the people just could not do it. You could see that when we sat, our knees were taller than our head. We were skin and bones. A lot of us were like that. I was the same way. I almost got drowned there. But I was lucky. Someone saw me and saved me. The water was flowing very hard, the current. A man saw me and my hat. I always wore a hat. They gave a hat to everybody, an old and broken one. I put a flower in it, any flower that I saw. I like flowers. To decorate the hat. Some of them knew that that was my hat that was floating there. I was drowning and my hat was there. The man tried to get me out. He asked the leader, "Who does she belong to? Which group?" And the leader said, "She belongs to me." That's what my girlfriend told me. I was unconscious. And then the [Khmer Rouge] woman said, "Just leave her there. Is she dead? Just throw her in the water." My friend cried and they told her, "If you cry, you're going to live here with her." The man tried to save me then. He knew how to do CPR. After that I became conscious, I was choking on water. I started to have a fever right away. Maybe the water got into my lungs. They warned the man, if he did that again he was going to be killed. And they watched him. But that man is still alive. After the Khmer Rouge left I met him again. Without him I probably would have drowned in the water and would be floating there. I said thank you to him and he said, "That's all right because I had a family, I had a sister, and they are all dead. This was a way that I could do a good thing."

After that the big head of the Khmer Rouge in the province came. He tried to sit there and encourage us and give us compliments. "You know you are good kids. You all decided to do this work for the Angkar" [Khmer Rouge leadership] or whatever. And then he said, "You are really good. You belong to Angkar. You do not belong to your parents. Don't listen to your parents." I was the smallest in the group. I was sitting with my knees up like this. [Hanging her head over her chest] I was skinny and very tired because I had just drowned. So I couldn't bear to sit straight. He came and tilted my head back and looked at me. I thought maybe I was dying. He talked really loud. Sometimes I got it and sometimes I didn't. He said, "Who are you?" I didn't say anything because my lips were all dry and broken. Even to open my mouth hurt. My tongue felt infected. My legs too. Every part of my body, my head, was infected, and my arm and my neck, all over, because I had blisters from carrying dirt. I had nothing to eat, and no water. When you put that all together, it's just, oh—. I didn't say anything. I tried to open my mouth. My friend cried for me. She said, "Oh, she is the girl who was drowning." And the guy said, "Why?" "Because we are working on that dam." And then he said, "Who let you come? You are little ones." We didn't say anything because we were scared. We could not just tell him. He said, "How long?" The girl told him. I didn't know how many days. I couldn't talk. I couldn't hold myself up. Anywhere I sat I wanted to sit by a tree, to prop myself up. She was holding me so I would not fall. After that the guy said, "Okay, I will let you girls go. I won't let you stay in this place." We were still working there for a while. Then they sent us back to work in a different place.

But after that, I heard the launching in the area where they were bombing, the launching and the shooting, and I saw the Khmer Rouge running for their lives with their horses. Some of them had bloody arms and legs and cuts. They came to the girls' camp, and our leader told us to prepare to go with them. And I knew that my dad had told me, "If anything happens and you see them hurt, then you'll know something has happened." So I knew that I would not go with them. I planned. My goal was just to escape from them. At that time they brought the boys from a different camp to go together with the girls. There were three to five hundred kids. I told my leader that I needed to go to the bathroom. That was my excuse all the time. [Laughing] "I need to go to the bathroom." She knew that I didn't talk, I did whatever they told me, I worked. She believed me. I said, "I will just go close to here. Don't worry. I will be back. You can keep my backpack."

Then I was sitting there. I just sat and thought about it. What should I do? There were a lot of people and they had horses. I was afraid that I could not run faster than a horse. Everyone had a scarf. Our scarves were old and broken apart. One of the other girls always covered her head with her scarf. I did the same. I hardly let people see my face. She went to the bathroom too, and then she went back. Those leaders were confused. They mixed us up. The leader said, "Sodoeung you came back?" That girl didn't respond to her. She just walked past. They were on a hill and I was below. I heard because of the wind. It blew so hard that anybody could talk and you could hear very well. So I thought, that's good. But that woman was still counting. And she counted and counted and everybody said, "Oh, we are missing three or four." I didn't know who else. Three or four! And then the leader tried to get two Khmer Rouge [soldiers]. But the one who had a horse was hurt. So he didn't come back. Two others came and looked. They said, "All you girls, if you don't come out, I am going to shoot you, blow your brains out." One of the girls jumped up from a bush and ran back. I didn't even know she was there. She was scared and she went out, and then they shot her. The soldiers came closer and closer, and the other two tried to escape, and they caught them too. The boys. I was the last one to run. I ran fast. Ten times faster than anyone. No one can run the way I did. I don't know how. I was sick, but I was determined.

I ran, and they shot at me, and I didn't get hurt. It only went through the side of my clothing. The sun was setting. There was a red sky. It was harvest time. The rice was ripe already, and people were harvesting. They said, "You can hide anywhere in the rice fields. It's okay." But I was afraid to hide. So I ran and ran and ran, and they shot at me until they used up all their bullets. And then one of them said, "We have to get the horse." They went back but it was too late. I left and hid myself in the water. I had to cross a creek, and at that time I didn't know how to swim very well. I remembered that my brother had said that you could use bamboo, you could use a long bamboo to flip. So I flipped. But my legs were still in the water. By the creek there was a lot of bushy grass. I hung onto that so the water would not take me. It was deep. So I flipped and I got there. All my sisters were with my parents. I was the last one. And they asked me, "Where were you? We are here, we were waiting for you." Everybody was mad at me because I was late. And I said, "What? I tried to get out with my life."

. . . In some villages they have a house for *neak ta* [the guardian of a place], just like a Buddha's house. That's a place that is set up under a tree somewhere far from the village. Sometimes people offer food, especially fruit and bananas, to *neak ta.* Sometimes when they walk past they go there and just pay their respects. *Neak ta* is a spirit who takes care of the villagers who live there. I saw them everywhere when we were in the jungle. I saw them near mountains, the little houses for *neak ta.*[5] Sometimes they build something like a stupa. When people offer food they always call *neak ta* to come to eat the food they offer them and to take care of everyone, so they will be healthy and nobody can hurt them. . . . I always heard my mom praying. When we had been separated, and then we met again, she prayed and offered the food at night and then prayed, "Oh, I am glad that all my kids have come. There are just two missing. Thanks for helping them to come home." That's how she would pray for those two. When we go to the temple we pray to the Buddha. But when we go to the jungle and see the big trees, we pray to these people, these spirits. I sometimes prayed to the trees too during the Khmer Rouge time. There was no one to talk to so I talked to the trees. They cannot talk back, but you can talk to them. You talk to the tree and then when the wind blows you feel like, "Oh, they answered. I got the answer!"

. . . Later on we went back to our hometown. This was in 1978. We walked for two days. When we got there we saw that everything was there except for the house. They destroyed our big house to build three small houses. The land, the trees. We had every kind of fruit tree surrounding the house. And big wells. We saw a woman with three children and no husband living in the house. There were other families living there too. They asked us, "Who are you?" I was sitting under the coconut tree and my father went to look in the well, and he said, "Oh, it is clean. We can come back." Then when he saw the woman with her kids, he said, "No." The woman said, "You can come back. I can go to my hometown. My husband got killed." The three children were swollen and malnourished. My dad's face changed. He was sad. He asked us before he decided. "What do you think? You see her, she has small kids and no husband. She cannot work, you know that. At least here she can take the coconuts that we have, and the milk fruit, and she can sell them and raise her kids. We can live too because you are all grown up." My youngest sister was mad. She said, "I miss home. I want to come here." He said, "No, we better go back to the place where they put us." The lady was so happy that we let her live there. Everybody was happy and said, "Thank you for your help." Then we went to our fruit farm. But the Vietnamese army was there. They told us not to come in. My dad spoke some Vietnamese. He chatted a little with them. Then he came back and told us that we had no place. "I thought we could go to our farm but now we have nothing."

We went back to the place where the Khmer Rouge had put us. Those people who lived there did not want us there. We were not welcome. We had never been welcome. One family who was nice to us let us live on their land in a small house that we built out of bamboo. Later on I grew vegetables. My dad just told me how. . . . My older sisters got married during this time and left. My two younger sisters and I were living with our parents. I worked, I grew fruit, and I went fishing. My dad went along with us to the ponds or to the creek. He would tell us, do this and do that. We tied a hook to get the fish. My younger sister would take it to the market and sell it.

Soon after this, Sodoeung made the journey into Thailand for rice recounted in the previous chapter, which led to her guiding her family out of Cambodia.

Her story is one of phantom impressions of possible deaths, imagining her body floating on the river's surface, hearing the soldiers yell their intention to blow her brains out, watching them shoot the other children hiding in the bushes, smelling like death, losing her ability to speak through cracked lips, hearing her own name (assigned to another girl) carried on the wind, feeling a bullet rip through her clothes. These possible deaths culminate in the moment recounted in the previous chapter, when her family mistakes her for a ghost. Yet, at the same time, her story is also one of tactile details of the landscape, where water is heavy, bamboo is sharp under bare feet, mushrooms spring open like coiled hair. Sodoeung's senses, like Lt. Somsy's, become differently attuned during her time in the forest. She develops new physical relationships with nonhuman beings: flipping herself across the river with a bamboo stalk, grasping onto tufts of grass, learning to hook a fish, catching frogs, digging up mushrooms, gripping rain-soaked rope, slipping on a log slick with rain and sap, shaving her head to discourage lice, choking on river water, sleeping on the ground among scorpions and cobras, running through rice paddies under a red sky. As she becomes alert to the pulling strength of river water and the stickiness of resinous logs, she also learns to speak to trees, and to listen for their windy answers. In this world she is treated like a dog, but also perhaps acquires the acute senses, hungers, and skills of one, running uncannily fast, chewing on rawhide rope for food.

This is not a landscape saturated with elegiac memories, but rather a militarized zone of random violence and a habitat of beasts, ghosts, and bandits. It is a place of shadow and camouflage, a place where one can hide, but also where one is at risk from whatever else may be hiding there. Surviving in this landscape is a matter not only of hard labor, foraging, or running fast, but also of hearing comfort in the play of breezes, praying to and offering food to the *neak ta*. The nonhuman agents in these stories are not only signs or omens, like Lt. Somsy's diamond star, but figures with jurisdiction over the jungle. The closeness of death and the omnipresence of terror threaten to drive Sodoeung into a nonhuman realm of existence, but this realm also offers unique and unexpected opportunities of survival. Displacement in this context is less cultural dislocation than entry into an animated landscape that is a site for metamorphosis, whether through violence or through miraculous intervention.

Place spirits such as the Khmer *neak ta* or the Lao *phi ban* or *phi muang* (village or town spirits) who watch over an area are said to be the spirits of those distant ancestors who founded that village or district (Thipmuntali 1999, 154; Chandler 1996, 28; LaFreniere 2000, 12).[6] Yet people may refer to such ancestral spirits as if they are not simply overseers of an area, but somehow one with it. Insofar as they are spirits of the dead, they are spirits of the remote dead, partially blended into the land, capable of being offended by those who cross their territory, or of offering them sanctuary. As Sodoeung suggests, when *wats* were destroyed and monks murdered or forced out of monkhood, and when people were forced out of the city into the countryside, even relatively educated Khmer found themselves seeking assistance from the spirits of the forests.

Mrs. Sann told the following story of an encounter with *neak ta*.

> During Khmer Rouge, you were not supposed to believe anything. They didn't have a belief system. So they trained the younger generation well not to believe in religion, in any kind of superstitious belief, or even in one's parents. You were not supposed to trust and believe them. When they put people to work, the younger adults who were not married yet but still single, they put in one group. My child was in a younger group.

They came upon a chest, and it was in the middle of nowhere in the forest. They opened up the wooden chest, and they saw pans, kettles, and spoons and all of that. They looked around and didn't see any owner. They said, "What do we do?" Since there was no owner they decided to destroy it. After they destroyed the chest everyone in that group got sick. The symptoms were dizziness, fever, and headache. They just got sick and died. . . . I was so worried when I heard about it. I believe that the *neak ta* who was taking care of the land and the forest gave them the chest of silverware to use because at that time they didn't give us anything to use. . . . Probably the *neak ta* who was taking care of the forest and the land was angry with them; that was why she took their lives away. I was so worried but I could not do anything.

One night I saw a person with long hair to her breasts, dressed in white. She came and was shaking my toe. She said, "What are you doing? Why are you still sleeping? Your child is very sick." After that I could not do anything. I worried but I didn't know if it was just a dream. Later in the day, my brother told me that I had to go and see my child because she was very sick. My child had fever and headaches. It was not a coincidence.

When my brother told me that, I was crying. I went to the two group leaders, and they were kind to me. They said, "Just go and take care of your child." I think that the *neak ta* brought those two leaders to be there at the same time. During Pol Pot, when you asked for rest time, you had to go through certain channels, and it was very hard. This time it was so easy. I believe that the *neak ta* was very kind to me.

When I got to my child, she was very sick. She had diarrhea, and she was exhausted. . . . I saw the hospital personnel swinging in the hammock and not doing anything because they were Khmer Rouge. They separated my daughter and me so far, like five kilometers. I had to walk with my brother there. . . . I don't know exactly how [she got well], but I believe that the old lady who takes care of the land and the forest helped my daughter, because all they gave to my daughter was the medicine [herbal medicine pills referred to as "rabbit turds" (North 1995, 306)] that I described earlier. They didn't give anything else. I kept praying to the old lady who takes care of that area and to Buddha and the higher powers. Everybody who went to that place, if they were sick they never got cured. They died from their sickness. I don't know why my daughter survived. . . .

I think the old lady who took care of the land and the forest helped me because my daughter was sick for two weeks and she lost almost all of her hair. When you are dehydrated and you don't have anything to eat, then the body swells up like a balloon. That was the condition of my daughter. She decided to ask permission from the Khmer Rouge to come back with me, and they allowed her to come. When I arrived, the leader asked, "Whose relative is that? Who belongs to something like that?" A woman told the leader that I was the sick girl's mother. He said, "She should ask permission to stay with her mom." She hadn't said anything because she was afraid that whatever she said they would kill her for it. When he said that, she decided to ask him. He allowed her to stay with me for thirty days. I was very fortunate that the old lady was taking care of me. . . . That's why the leader was kind to me. . . . *Neak ta* has very high power and if *neak ta* is mad at anybody her power is so bad it can make you sick and kill you. . . . It is considered a superstitious belief. But that is why I think the old lady came into my dream. . . . *Neak ta* was taking care of my daughter.

Although Mrs. Sann feels constrained to say that *neak ta* is considered superstition, Penny Edwards notes that oaths in Cambodian courts are still sworn not in the presence of either Buddha or the state, but in the presence of *neak ta* (2008, 150). Such practices gesture toward an older mapping of the landscape that is still visible behind the political divisions of the modern state. David Chandler suggests that the region now known as Cambodia was once conceptualized as "a sum of places, arranged in *mandala* form where *nak ta* were honored and sacrifices took place" (1996, 42).

It is among the trees that these *neak ta* are said to reside, in the *mluap*, the protective shadow of the forest (Edwards 2008, 149), which is paradoxically both dangerous and benign. Citing Ang Choulean (2004) and Miech Ponn (2001), Edwards observes that the Khmer soul-calling rite *hav praloeng* calls back the vital spirits of a person who may have been lured into the forest by ghosts, but may also have sought out the woodlands for rest and recuperation (2008, 148–49). Forests, she writes, are associated not only with asocial chaos, but also with "transition" and "transformation" (151). As Chandler (2008) convincingly argues, the categories so salient in Khmer folklore of *srok*, domesticity or civil order, and *prei*, wildness, may at times shift and merge in risky yet creative inversions that are sometimes catalyzed by social violence and chaos. He recounts a folktale of two girls, deliberately abandoned by their mother in the forest, who are defended from predatory animals by a sympathetic *arak devata* (local guardian spirit similar to *neak ta*) and manage to survive by embracing wildness, eating raw snails, fish, and grain, until finally they become birds, their clothing turning to feathers, their fingers curling into claws, their lips hardening to beaks, and their arms unfolding into wings. Having lost the ability to speak human language, they communicate with one another in bird song (Edwards 2008, 145), while knowing "in their hearts" that they are human (Chandler 2008, 34).

The manuscript in which this tale is found dates from the mid-nineteenth century, toward the end of a period when Cambodia was repeatedly invaded by Thai and Vietnamese armies, a time that, as Chandler (2008, 31) observes, resembled the 1970s in its extremes of violence. Comparing the tale with a poem chronicling the fate of a Khmer family during the first half of the nineteenth century, Chandler notes that the girls' experience in the forest resonates with the fate of many Khmer of that time. Exiled from their home and fleeing the Vietnamese, the family in the poem enters the forest where they eat lizards dug from the earth and soup made from roots. Eventually both the father and the son die alone in the forest, despite performing virtuous acts on behalf of their family. For Chandler, the poem and tale, taken together, suggest that in a time of social turmoil there was "no explanation for suffering that would allow any but the magically endowed to overcome it" (2008, 45). Although it remained resistant to assimilation by a moral order, the forest became a refuge from the violence that had overtaken the civil realm. Survival was possible only by trafficking with nonhuman beings, or becoming them, through a willingness to engage in parahuman magic that alone had a chance of prevailing against human aggression. In the folktale the *arak devata* even assists the girls in transforming the landscape they inhabit from wild forest stalked by predatory animals to a corn field, frequented only by gentle herbivores such as deer, pigs, monkeys, and squirrels (Edwards 2008, 146). Such potentially nurturing spirits embedded in the landscape offer the wildness of the forest as a powerful if unpredictable source of protection during a time when the civil order itself has undergone a terrifying metamorphosis. It is worth noting that such spirits are anarchic beings who, even in peacetime, defy the quotidian violence inherent in social hierarchies.[7] This history of iconoclasm may make them especially ready to interfere in more murderous forms of status quo. In the face of the transformation of villages and farms into war zones, such beings offer a countertransformation of violent social life into a wild survival that partly embraces animal existence.

Figures of Animality

The figures of animality most often evoked in narratives of war or state terror are "inhuman brutes"—such as bandits or soldiers—who kill indiscriminately like wild predators on a rampage, and "subhuman" creatures who are subjected like livestock to captivity, forced labor, and slaughter. "They treated us like animals," the Kmhmu soldier Lt. Phanha said of his time in a Thai refugee camp. "They did whatever they felt like." Tellingly, this figure of captive animality appears also in stories of U.S. medicine. A Lao friend of Douang's who worked in a hospital told him, "Man, if you don't have friends or relatives, you're going to be miserable if you're dead in this hospital, because they put you there like a pig, like an animal." As such medical sites serve to remind us, both these figures of animality, the vicious predator and the abject livestock, fit comfortably into a biopolitical narrative whereby animals, like the sovereign, exist outside the moral and political order (cf. Derrida 2009, 2:39, 60).

Yet there is a third figure of animality that appears in the stories of animistically inclined emigrants who survived the covert war in Laos or the Khmer Rouge regime in Cambodia: the wild animal as transmigrated ancestor or possibly sympathetic spirit. This last figure of animality, like the cobra in Oeur's poem, is a magical animal who might be motivated to intervene in human affairs, perhaps especially at times of social upheaval. Such wondrous beasts offer another vision of animality than that evoked by biopolitical theory, less subhumanity or hypersovereignty than a paradoxical mix of productive alterity and interspecies kinship or fusion. Their willful subjectivity defamiliarizes such creatures, intensifying their otherness, while also drawing them uncannily close to humans. These animals possess agency, the capacity for thought and communication, as well as an ambivalent morality that might benefit the humans who encounter them.

In Southeast Asian folklore, it is small animals who are most often helpful. In Cambodia, for instance, birds who enter a house are considered to carry messages from ancestors (Edwards 2008, 143), while in Kmhmu lore, humans are often assisted by animals such as anteaters or insects (Lindell, Swahn, and Tayanin 1977–95, 4:17). According to the Kmhmu storyteller and folklorist Kam Raw, small wild animals who enter a domestic environment are thought to embody the soul of a living friend or relative who is close to death.

> Birds, squirrels, and rats are shy animals. . . . When an animal of this kind enters our house, it is drowsy and we can catch it; it is not shy at all. The soul of a person has entered it; the soul of a friend or a relative comes to us as an omen. If an animal of this kind comes and behaves as I have mentioned, and we manage to catch it, we should tie a string around its legs and set it free. When one takes the string to tie it around its legs, one should say the following words:
>
> Oh soul of a friend, of a relative,
> soul of an elder or younger brother,
> soul of a father- or brother-in-law,
> stay with me, eat with me!
> Do not run away, don't escape!
> Stay with your father- or brother-in-law,
> Stay with your elder or younger brother!

After these words are spoken, the animal is released, so that it, in turn, will free the soul to return to its human body, allowing the dying person to become well. Kam Raw also speaks of ancestors who appeared as barking deer to alert their descendants to danger, cautioning them not to cut lumber or work in the field that day.

Similar human–animal interactions are woven into the memories of Southeast Asian survivors of war or state terror. In his memoir of escaping from the Khmer Rouge, Daran Kravanh describes the assistance he received from his maternal grandfather in the form of a reptile. When his grandfather died his family buried him near a rice field. At the hundredth-day mourning feast they offered food at the grave. As they were praying a lizard crawled out from a fruit tree and ate some of the food. Kravanh's mother cried, "Father you've come back to life." Thereafter when they visited the grave they called to grandfather and the lizard appeared. Kravanh recalls spending many hours alone at the gravesite, listening for his grandfather's advice. "The voice I heard from him," he said, "was not a human voice but one of nature—of that place where my grandfather had returned" (LaFreniere 2000, 10). Much later when Kravanh was living in the forest, hungry and wounded from a fight with Khmer Rouge soldiers, he saw a lizard and reassured his companions, "It is my grandfather come to help us" (68).

Among Hmong, the exchangeability of human and animal souls is ceremonially enacted in animal sacrifices when, for instance, the soul of a pig is offered to the spirits as replacement for the soul of an ill human. Such exchange of souls may happen in less scripted ways as well. Pheng, a Hmong counselor, recalled that as a child in Thailand, he once spontaneously pointed at a bird flying overhead and said "drop dead." When the bird fell to the ground, he took it home to his father who roasted it and gave it to Pheng to eat. Three months later when his father fell ill, a *txiv neeb* told them that his father's soul was being requested in "trade" for the bird. When you touch or injure a wild animal, Pheng told me, it can injure your spirit. Hmong hunters in Southeast Asia have been known to smear blood on their crossbows after a kill in order to placate the spirits of their prey (Livo and Cha 1991, 3). One Catholic Hmong man, Mr. Lo, distancing himself from such ideas, commented ruefully, "Non-Christians still believe that humans and animals can connect together as spirits."

Richard Davis describes *su khwan* (soul-calling ceremonies) performed for water buffalo in Northern Thailand, in which the animal's soul is asked to forgive the hard labor and beatings to which it has been subjected, praised for its patience, and asked not to wander and consort with wild animals but rather to stay in its body and enjoy the sweet grass. As in *su khwan* for humans, the animals are offered cigarettes, betel, rice, bananas, and cooked chicken (1984, 167). These interactions with beasts of labor call to mind the interactions with domestic buffalo in a South Indian village discussed by Anand Pandian (2008). Pandian traces what he identifies as a locally specific biopolitics whereby thieving or violent humans are compared to disobedient buffalo not only in their lack of self-conduct, but also in their determination to remain unyoked. In that setting, the bullish traits of social rebels who may be either animal or human are alternately governed, excused, and celebrated.

I suggest, however, that the animal–human interactions in the stories I retell here might be thought of less as an alternative biopolitics than as a zoopolitics, an ethics and politics grounded in animal existence. Zoopolitics might be understood as a branch of the cosmopolitics evoked by Marisol de la Cadena (2010) following Isabelle Stengers (2005), in which nonhumans are not simply the province of scientific investigation or management, but enter agentially into political struggles and questions. In zoopolitics, animality would figure not for cruelty or subservience, but for a subjectivity that exceeds bio-politics, chasing questions of power into cosmological terrains. In zoopolitics, power would no longer be singular, a homogeneous substance moving from one scale and one site to another: individual, family, village, city, nation, multi-national entity, or species. Rather power would become plural, pushing political power into communication with magical powers, the heterogeneous capacities of spirits and deities.

Zoopolitics might encompass cross-species interactions that are governed by their own peculiar rites, customs, and hierarchies. Southeast Asian folk-tales, for instance, emphasize that interspecies border crossing is risky and subject to shifting rules, which, if violated, can have devastating consequences. Cheuang, a Kmhmu healer, told me the story of two sisters who were brush-ing their hair. After they finished they decided to brush the dog's fur as well. That night it rained so hard that by midnight the village was flooded and everyone drowned. Only seven people, who were away hunting at the time, survived. "I could go now and still look at that hole," he said. "It's as big as this room." *Prayong róoy*, a dragon spirit who sometimes materializes as a snake, had punished them for addressing the dog as if it were human.

If prey animals are often benevolent, magical predators, as this caution-ary tale suggests, are dangerous. Kmhmu tales refer to humans who are pos-sessed by tiger spirits and become fierce and aggressive, killing and eating their neighbors' water buffalo. In one Hmong story, a tiger abducts a woman from her family's field and makes her his wife (Johnson 1992, 415). She gives birth to a tiger cub without a tail. When her visiting sister admires and cuddles the cub, the tiger father grows angry. He stalks the sister, killing and eating her. Her parents then curse their feline son-in-law, as much for his disrespect as for his savagery. Despite the tiger's attempts to conciliate them by offering gifts of money and paying a friendly visit, dressed in human clothes, he and the cub are eventually killed by his father-in-law, who then soaks his daughter in a bath of cow dung to restore her to more domestic human–animal transactions.

In Laos, Lt. Somsy told me, an animal spirit would sometimes fall in love with a Lao woman and marry her. At certain phases of the moon she would leave her husband's bed to sleep in a different room with the animal spirit. Lt. Somsy had heard of one woman in southern Laos who married a *phaya nak*, a sea serpent, and gave birth to five human children.

> There are some curious people also that wanted to know if she was really married to the *phaya nak* and followed her. And what they saw or described is that they saw her walking down to the river by herself. She would go under the water, just like walking downhill, and then disappear in the water for a few days and then return from the river safely. And then when she had children, she would put the children on her back and walk down to the river and then disappear into the river the same way.

"It is unbelievable to me also," he exclaimed. "The husband is *phaya nak*, an animal, and when they have children together, how come it is human? Why?" For Lt. Somsy, as for others, such stories are often told with a mix of wonder, fascination, and doubt. This skepticism, no less than the conspecific instability and ambivalent kinship of these interspecies intimacies, makes them especially marvelous.[8]

How different the tigers and sea serpents in these stories are from Agamben's werewolf, the mythic animal figure for one who is reduced to "bare life," exiled from the polis, neither entirely human nor entirely beast (1998, 105–8). The wolf, Jacques Derrida notes, is stealthy (2009, 1:21), too stealthy perhaps to play the emblematic role she is assigned in Agamben's text. To be a wolf (or a tiger or perhaps a sea serpent) is to take your prey by surprise, after all. What is missing in Agamben's werewolf is not only subjectivity, desire, and will, but also (and these are not unrelated) miraculousness and magic. More importantly, perhaps, Agamben seems to have overlooked how a werewolf (or weretiger) might smuggle alien powers not simply into the city but into the intimate space of kinship networks, sparking expectations of reciprocity and hospitality, invoking less biopolitics than *zoopolitesse*. The Hmong tiger husband, for instance, is not entirely reducible to an allegory for a banished savagery within the human. As a jealous family member who loses his temper, forgets his manners, seeks forgiveness, feigns humanity, and offers gifts, he exemplifies the difficulties of finding one's way in the ethical thicket of injurious love and comfortable captivity. Similarly, the Lao sea serpent is not only a figure of predation but also a lover and father, seductively attractive to his human wife, charismatically commanding her loyalty, and demanding to know his human children. These are moral and contradictory creatures who make choices and mistakes, never entirely caught in a maze with only one moral lesson.

Bang Fai, the rocket festival that occurs in Laos and Thailand at the beginning of the rainy season, is a signal for the *nak*, the phallic bringers of rain, to awaken. The festival is celebrated partly by boat races in which the vessels themselves are crafted to look like sea serpents. These boats are said to drive the *nak* out of the river so that they can fertilize the fields, returning to the river again at the end of the rains (R. Davis 1984, 217). *Nak* move stealthily, we might say, between domesticity and wildness, benevolence and aggression. A U.S. reporter visiting Thailand for a Bang Fai festival in 2002 was shown a postcard sporting a photo of a group of American soldiers, supposedly stationed in Laos during the 1970s, holding an eight-meter-long silvery eel-like fish. Locals told him that the *nak* later escaped the soldiers who were said to be carting it to the United States for "scientific study." The photograph, which also circulates in Laos, matches one taken in 1996 by the U.S. Navy to show off a giant oarfish found off a Pacific coastline. Yet that doesn't prevent the postcard from drawing on the power of the *nak* to trump both U.S. military prowess and laboratory science. At the time of the 2002 rocket festival Thai locals assured the U.S. journalist that "all of the men in the photo met with messy ends" (Gagliardi 2002).

Such animal–human interchanges and transmigrations have implications for the biopolitical story about humanity and animality that prevails in much contemporary social analysis, especially to convey the bestialization of war and state terror that afflicts both perpetrators and victims. In the stories told above this bestialization is answered by a counteranimalization, perhaps a "becoming-animal" (Deleuze and Guattari 1987), whereby escape, protection, or rescue is sought from fantastic creatures.[9] Those who are threatened with dehumanization, susceptible to being abused like livestock, or to killing others like savage predators, have the possibility of imagining and evoking alternative subjectivities through collaborations and fusions with nonhuman creatures. In so doing they abandon a seemingly futile insistence on rehumanization, turning instead toward a productive merging of human and other-than-human.

Rather than holding out for the restoration of a peacetime morality or becoming resigned to the end of morality altogether, they gamble on temporary
assistance involving morally ambivalent beasts. Faced with the "inhumane-
ness" of human society, they turn to a broader realm of sociality in which
humans and animals form risky alliances, speaking, sympathizing, and bargaining with one another, exchanging souls and substance. In these stories
the lawlessness of a society at war is displaced by the lawlessness of animals,
who do not so much defy the law as supersede it. It is as if the extraordinary
animals in these stories talk back to human violence with an ethos that spo-
radically rewards reciprocity, hospitality, compassion, and bravery though
with a capriciousness that mocks human moral logic. Yet such magical animals, along with other spirits of place, appear to be largely erased from diasporic social worlds.

Spirits out of Place

Bouakhay's first husband was a soldier with the Royal Lao Army. On the eve
of his expected arrest by the Pathet Lao in the wake of U.S. withdrawal from
Laos, the family fled the country by night.

> Talking about this, I still feel afraid; my hair stands up. We almost died to be
> able to get here. We almost died. . . . I asked protection from the guardian of the
> village *[phi ban]*. And when I got to Thailand, I sent a message to my mother
> back home, asking her to do the ceremony for me, to keep my promise. And
> my mother did the ceremony for me. The reason that my hair stands up is
> because when we crossed the Mekong River, there was a black log that came
> and hit our boat, and to us that was the guardian of the village who came with
> us, trying to protect us along the way. And that was incredible. . . . We were
> not really living by or believing totally in the *phi ban*. But everybody in the vil-
> lage believed in it or respected it, so we had to do like everybody else did.[10]

Any temptation to hear this narrative as an illustration of Bouakhay's belief
in spirits is given pause when she says that her family was not "believing
totally" in *phi ban*. This village spirit had not been, for her family, especially
important, or even, perhaps, especially real. It is in light of this skepticism that
it "was incredible" when the log hit the boat speaking to the presence of *phi
ban*. For Freud, remember, an encounter with a spirit becomes uncanny insofar as it disrupts a rationalist understanding of the world. In a similar vein,
Dipesh Chakrabarty has observed that it is "the disjunctures in the present"
that make it possible to encounter spirits in modern life (2000, 112). At the
disjuncture of escape from Laos, *phi ban* is tangible in Bouakhay's embodied

practice, her prayer for protection and the spirit's answer. This spirit connected to a particular landscape is a key figure in her memory of leaving Laos. The log gliding through the dark water dividing Laos (site of her abandoned home) from Thailand (where she would spend months in a refugee camp) tangibly marks her exile from her homeland and her new relationship with this homeland from exile. Indeed it might be said to mark the nascent coalescence of the very idea of "homeland," a sharpened orientation toward national-cultural belonging that emerges through emigration. The encounter with *phi ban* is not so much a continuance of everyday religious practice as a sudden and intense personification of place flaring up during a dangerous flight out of Laos. This liaison with a spirit who, among others, was officially condemned if not actually outlawed by the government of the Lao Peoples Democratic Republic (LPDR, established by the Pathet Lao in 1975) in its campaign against "superstition" (Evans 1998, 72; Van Esterik 1992, 44) makes Bouakhay's escape transgressive not only of national borders but of national policy. It is hardly surprising, then, that the absence or scarcity of topological spirits in diaspora might take on a particular resonance.

Many emigrants categorically deny any significance of landscape spirits in the United States. When I asked the Kmhmu woman Kampheang, for instance, if anyone in the United States still fed *róoy mìang* (guardian spirits of particular districts) she said, "No, we don't do that here. No more *róoy.*" Similarly a Hmong man told me, "In this country there are not many *dab* [spirits] around." Of course, some emigrants do wonder about the guardian spirits of North America itself. Christine Desan notes of Hmong in Philadelphia that "while many refugees reason that spirits may be as ubiquitous in the U.S. as they are in Laos, they conclude, 'They are not our spirits; we don't know them, nor do they know us. So how can they affect us, and us them?'" (1983). One Khmer man, Charles, told me of a monk he knew who attempted to consult the guardian spirit of Chicago for a winning lotto number. He told Charles, "He's too strong, too powerful. I tried to get the number from him, and he wouldn't give it to me." Mrs. Sann concluded her story of *neak ta* by saying, "Even now if I go to Canada and my children buy a lot of food, before we eat I reserve a little bit of everything and put it on a plate and put it under a tree somewhere and just pray for the spirits of the place to take care of us. It's my habit because of my Khmer Rouge experience." While Lt. Phanha no longer maintains relationships with Kmhmu *róoy* in the United States he wondered aloud about the spirits portrayed on U.S. television. "Do American people actually see spirits?" he asked, "In our country we don't actually see them." I had no idea what to say. Perhaps the deliberately uncanny effect of televised ghosts requires visibility to inspire sufficient horror. Having transferred their encounters with spirits almost exclusively to entertainment media (V. Nelson 2001), most North Americans have no way of comparing spirits on TV with spirits who cause illness or make noise in the night.

Despite their rarity, however, Southeast Asian topological spirits register violence and dislocation in complex ways, marking the wresting of emigrants from specific places, as well as the transformation of many of these same places to bombed-out wastelands or killing fields. Spirits evoke the breakup of extended families and the abandonment and/or destruction of rice fields and vegetable gardens. In some stories spirits themselves have been driven from the very places they have long overseen. Douang knew of one village guardian spirit who, when asked for help in escaping Laos, replied, "Sorry children, I cannot help you. I'm having a hard time too. I also have to flee this place." With such words the spirit acknowledged the impossibility of carrying out his protective work under a regime that was executing or denouncing not only monks, but also *nang tiam* (female spirit mediums, sometimes called *moh tiam*), *moh phi*, and other spiritual practitioners. Similarly Daran Kravanh commented that under the Khmer Rouge there was "so much terror even the protecting spirits of our ancestors ran in fear" (LaFreniere 2000, 30). Grant Evans reports that in 1977 in Luang Prabang, an LPDR leader, having first declared that all spirits attached to the temples in the old royal capital were "feudal," conducted a ceremony at a spirit shrine to inform all the spirits that the king had been deposed and sent to "seminar" (reeducation camp), and the spirits must choose whether to follow him, become monks, or flee the country (1998, 73). Yet even as many Lao, Kmhmu, Hmong, and Khmer were admitted to the United States, often through sponsorship of Christian churches, spirits seem to have largely been turned away at immigration. Their absence comments on a deep-cutting exclusion that underlies the emigrants' ostensible welcome.

Nonetheless spirits of place still make their absent presence felt at times of crisis. After recounting the story of her promise to *phi ban*, Bouakhay told us that pledges made to Lao spirits should ideally be fulfilled within Laos itself if only by proxy. She knew of others who broke promises to *phi ban* or to *thevada* (*devata*, deities) and became critically ill. When their relatives in Laos consulted *moh du* (diviners),[11] the emigrants were directed to make good on their promised offerings, and when they did so, their health was often restored.[12] The Kmhmu woman Kampheang told me that over the course of her life she has paid homage to *róoy*, Buddha, and Christ, depending on where and with whom she was living. Her father maintained (or when appropriate, avoided)

relations with *róoy,* while her mother's family converted to Catholicism, severing all connections with Kmhmu spirits. Her first husband also interacted
with *róoy,* while her present boyfriend in the United States is a Buddhist. She
said that whenever she tried to practice a relationship with both Buddha and
Christ simultaneously she was disturbed by nightmares.

> I don't go to church any more, since I met this boyfriend. I don't want to mix.
> When I mixed I got too confused. I had bad dreams. . . . *Sai bat* is the tradition
> for the Lao people.[13] Everybody puts the rice and whatever they want to offer,
> they put it there. Every time I did it, for the first two or three years after we met,
> I had bad dreams. Like somebody was going to come and get me, or some peo-
> ple were fighting each other about me. Or this person grabbed me on this side,
> and that person grabbed me on this side. And I knew, I said, "Okay, that's
> probably the Christians and Buddhists." They are fighting each other to get
> me to protect. I better keep up one.

Kampheang's dreams are reminiscent of a story (retold by LaCapra) in which
a forced Jewish convert to Christianity dreamed that God divided him in two
with an axe. This man, LaCapra notes, understood the dream not as the fragmentation of his self into Jewish and Christian, but rather as God's attempt to
kill him (2001, xiv). Similarly Kampheang's dream signifies for her less a religious conflict enacted within her being than an attack on her person from two
powerful and conflicting directions. Since that time she has kept a shrine to
Buddha in her house, making offerings of rice and water every morning. In
practicing as a Buddhist Kampheang has not decided that Buddha is more real
than Christ, or even than *róoy.* Rather she addresses her complex social location as a Kmhmu woman living with a Lao Buddhist boyfriend in a Christian-
dominated country.

Recently, however, Kampheang found it necessary to fulfill an old debt to
róoy mìang. In 1996 as she planned a trip back to Laos, her mother suffered a
stroke and lost her ability to speak. Her father then revealed to her that before
he left Laos, he had promised to offer a pig to *róoy mìang* in exchange for his
safe arrival in the United States. The promise had never been fulfilled. "It's
because you are going back home," he told Kampheang. "They hurt your
mother because of my promise." The family was being held accountable to this
spirit of place when Kampheang was traveling back to the place in question.
Kampheang made arrangements for the offering while she was in Laos, and
back in the United States her mother began to talk again. "The doctor didn't
treat her," Kampheang said, "but now she is almost like she was before the
stroke." Kampheang's brother, a psychologist, was angry with her for traveling

to Laos while her mother was ill in the United States. "He just ignores *rit* Kmhmu [Kmhmu customs]," she said. "He tries to forget how we worshipped before. Not me. If you ignore it, you will receive it." If, in conformity to new social worlds, you give up the care of specific spirit powers, those spirits who seem to have vanished may reappear, reminding you of your connections to villages on the other side of the world. If you ignore *rit* Kmhmu, you will "receive" its effects in your bodily existence. *Róoy* are not just objects of religious choice or symbols of cultural identity, but agentive forces asserting their authority across national borders.

Douang also recalled a time that a spirit of the land exerted its power when he traveled back to Laos.

> I visited my uncle in Laos four years ago. When I visited him he told the spirit of the guardian of the village, "This is my nephew who is visiting me. As the great spirit who protects the village, please look after him, take care of him." I stayed overnight with him for only one night. The next day I left for Vieng Chan. Then one week later I came to the U.S. I heard that he had become ill. He took medicine, and his illness did not go away as fast as he expected. He believed that if it was just a regular illness, it should be gone fast. Within a week after taking the medicine he should feel better. But this had been more than a week. I talked to his son in the U.S. here and he said that one reason that his father became ill was that, when I left his house, he did not tell the spirit of the village that I had gone. Like, "Thank you for taking care of him. Now he is gone." A way to show some respect. He did not do that. So he had a little ceremony to ask for forgiveness from the spirit, the protector of the village. He offered one chicken, one bottle of alcohol, flowers, candles to the spirit. And then he became better.

Similarly Mr. Chea, an elderly Khmer, told me of an illness and healing related to *neak ta* during one of his recent visits to Cambodia.

> My children don't know the name of the rice plant. It's different from the name for rice that is ready to cook. Some people from the airplane see a rice paddy, and they say, "Oh look, there's 'rice' [cooked rice]." So when we got to the relatives' house, I asked them to take us around and show us how to say [the names of] trees and other plants. When we came back home, I felt like somebody had put something in my ear. I couldn't talk, and my head was very heavy. I just lay there. For a long time they coined me, but I didn't get better. Then at around six o'clock the monk came. He had come to do a ceremony for the family members who had passed away. But when he noticed me, he asked why I was lying down. We told the monk what had happened and he

said that I had stepped on *preay* [a malicious spirit, usually female] and *neak ta*. He told us to do a special ceremony for that. We had to pray, light incense, and offer a plate of fruit. We prayed that if I got better then we would do another ceremony in which we'd make an offering out of a banana branch, with candles, incense, different colors of rice and food, betel leaf, and chewing betel. And I got better; I was able to hear and talk again.

Here the appearance of landscape spirits speaks obliquely to the further remove of emigrants' children, who might learn the names of rice plants not as daily necessity, but as cultural lore. The sickness acts as a physical insistence that the animated landscapes of the Cambodian countryside are more than passive focal points of cultural affiliation for those living elsewhere. By inscribing the claims of space spirits in Mr. Chea's body, the sickness suggests his tangible connection to places that have left their material traces in his bodily substance and practice. As Talal Asad writes,

> The body's memories, feelings and desires necessarily escape the rational/ instrumental ambitions of [national] politics. This is not properly understood by those well-wishing critics who urge Asian immigrants to abandon their traditions, to regard some of their collective memories and desires as not essentially their own, to embrace instead the more modern conception of self-determination underlying the European nation state in which they now live. (2000, 24)

Even if the country in which Mr. Chea currently lives encourages him to understand his practices of worship or healing as inessential cultural attributes appended to his U.S. existence, the sickness he suffers during his visit to Cambodia insists forcibly that these practices are matters of his life and breath.

Even Charles, educated in the United States, who laughed at most references to spirits, recalled an encounter with *neak ta:*

> *Neak ta* sometimes live in a big tree, big humongous tree. People who do something or say something insulting would get sick. Sometimes the big tree has a lot of fruit, and you go and pick the fruit without asking permission. You bring the fruit home and eat it, and you get sick. It happened to me! It's for real! It happened. I was shocked. I went way into the jungle in the countryside. This tree had lots of fruit. I picked a lot of it. I cut part of the branch and took the whole branch home because there was a lot of fruit in it. It's somewhat like a tangerine, but we don't have it over here. I brought it home and we ate it. My brother and everybody else ate it. I'm the one who got sick. My brother, my parents, they don't get sick. I was sick really bad. Couldn't figure out what's going on. I told my mom and my mom said, "Oh it must be some

preay or *neak ta* that lives in that tree." You disturbed them so they made you sick. She did some praying and I got better.

The storyteller's amazement ("It happened to me! It's for real!") marks his alienation from the spirits honored by his parents, his rational assessment of practices that his cosmopolitan education has named as superstition, and therefore the intensification of the incident's uncanny effect. His sickness, however, bypassed both his alienation and his rationality, asserting the force of place in his body.

Patricia Lawrence recounts the increasing turn to spirit oracles in Sri Lankan villages wracked by fifteen years of violent encounters between the Liberation Tigers of Tamil Eelam and government security forces. Against the many kinds of silence—self-protective, intimidated, shell-shocked—in which they live, survivors articulate their terror and grief through consultations with the oracles of local goddesses. Lawrence notes, "It has become the [oracles'] work to address agonizing doubts about lost connections, memory which cannot be erased, and wounds which cannot heal" (1997, 198). Similarly, emigrants from Laos and Cambodia may deliberately invoke spirits of place to ward off misfortune, or inadvertently offend them during visits to the homeland. In either situation, the spirits speak to lost connections and un-healed wounds related to violence and exile. They speak, however, less through words than through afflictions that require the body to actively engage with spirits of the land. John Pemberton (1994) writes of Javanese who do not deny spirits exist but say they have left a place that has grown too noisy and crowded. Similarly, emigrants do not deny that *róoy, phi, neak ta,* or *dab* exist but speak of their absence in U.S. social worlds. At the same time they suggest that spirits of the landscape resist their exclusion in deeply embodied ways. This absence of spirits of place, along with their uncanny reappearance, fore-shadows a similar absence and haunting by spirits of the dying and the dead at those U.S. medical and mortuary sites where death is alternately prevented or permitted.

The Wages of Mercy

The medics tell me he's been ten years
in the nursing home, dwindling
the past few weeks, refusing to eat,
asking only for his Winstons
and to be left alone.
Tonight when he spiked a fever,
and quickly became unresponsive,
with no family, no friends
to contact, the nurses asked
he be brought here, to the Emergency Room,
the open hands of strangers.

His color is awful. He's barely breathing.
I wonder for a moment what all
the commotion is about,
nurses frantically starting IVs
and drawing blood and
placing EKG electrodes;
it's only death—
as if we hadn't seen death before.

I shine a penlight into vacant
eyes, touch his heaving chest
and abdomen with the bell
of my stethoscope, listening
to the pneumonia crackle and pop.

The nurses ask what I want to do,
as if we must do something, anything.

I stroke a lock of matted hair
away from the old man's brow,
order a liter of saline and
some oxygen, biding time with comfort
as I sit at his bedside,
rifle through his voluminous chart.

Cardiac monitors beep and whir,
keeping guard with their syncopated melody.

The telephone rings three times, then stops.

—Peter Pereira

Chapter 3   Disciplines of Dying

FIVE YEARS AFTER MAJOR SAMSUTHI ARRIVED in the United States his first wife was diagnosed with liver cancer and died. He told the story in Lao to our interpreter, who in turn retold it to me. Then, as if this mediated account were insufficient, Major Samsuthi addressed me directly in English, saying "My wife. Liver cancer. No doctor in the world can treat liver cancer." He attributed her illness in part to the years they spent with their three children in a reeducation camp in Laos. It was there that her health problems began. "During those thirteen years . . . we did hard labor," he said. "When we fell ill we had no medicine. We didn't get enough to eat so our health was poor. . . . If there had been no change of government in Laos, maybe my wife would not have died. We would still live peacefully." In this account, her hospital death, the very one that elicited nightmares after our last conversation, borrows some of its troubling force from the permission to die (Foucault 1990) that prevailed in the thanatopolitical space of the reeducation camp.

In U.S. hospital wards permission to die is extended to patients who hover between life and death, often on mechanical ventilators, unable to breathe on their own. In wartime Laos and Cambodia, on the other hand, such permission was experienced in combat zones and camps, where the wonders (and horrors) of life-prolonging medical technologies were remote. Emigrants remember stepping over dead bodies, giving away children, and watching as Buddhist *wats* were turned into torture chambers. Death took the shapes of starvation, landmines, and guerilla warfare, more often than the shapes of cancer or car accidents. During those same years, other memories accumulated for U.S. publics: the media-ted memories of technologically prolonged lives (and deaths) that eventually prompted calls for "natural dying" and "death with dignity." These memories were organized more by the dread of a lingering mechanized death than of a violent death among enemies. Even as rumors circulated in Thai refugee camps and U.S. housing projects about premature deaths resulting from medical experimentation on refugee bodies, stories of mechanically prolonged lives were repeatedly featured in North American media. If the stories told in Southeast Asian communities reiterated the chronic risks of medical inadequacy, disregard, and neglect, stories told within the U.S. mainstream reiterated rather the dangers of medical excess.

When bioethicist Jennifer Beste raises the question, what if dying is not losing a war, she voices what sections of the U.S. public have been asking for decades. If death, Beste argues, is not an enemy to be fought to the bitter end, then surely there is no need to instill hope in the patient in order to raise her morale for a last rally (2005, 229). Beste's call for the pacification of dying follows a trend in U.S. popular discourse since the 1960s. At that time a demilitarization of death, in which doctors and patients were invited to lay down the technological weapons and psychological defenses that had been marshaled against mortality, resonated well with a nation grown tired of a seemingly endless war in Southeast Asia waged with seemingly useless though expensive technological hardware. While those who were living in the war zones faced a lack of medical technology, many in the United States were worried about an overuse of medical technology. And while for those in Laos and Cambodia, death was often the result of losing a battle in a literal sense, many in the United States worked to imagine death without struggle. This image of peaceful death, I will suggest, is not only locatable within a backlash to militarism, but is also embedded within a specific numinological vision, in which nature is the privileged site for the release of a Christian soul from the medical technology that would entrap it in matter.

Pacifying Death

Psychiatrist Elisabeth Kübler-Ross begins her influential book *On Death and Dying*, published in 1969, with an elegiac memory from her Swiss childhood in which a dying farmer spoke with family and friends, arranging his affairs with equanimity, saying goodbye, and sipping a favorite wine rather than a sedative (1969, 5). Following the death, she noted, the man lay in "his own beloved home which he had built." "In that country today," she continued, "there is still no make-believe slumber room, no embalming, no false makeup to pretend sleep." Without overtly referring to the farmer's death as more natural than the deaths she was attending in a New York hospital, she commented on the impossibility of going "back in time" to the "experience of a simple life on a farm with its closeness to nature, the experience of birth and death in the natural surrounding" (15). Five years later, addressing a question on the desire of some dying patients to hasten their own death she asked,

"Where does this tremendous need come from, to be in control even of the time and way of one's death? If a patient is not afraid of death and dying, he is then able to give up this control and wait for his natural death" (1974, 58).

Jenny Hockey (1996) has cautioned against a romanticism whereby pre-industrial death practices constitute a prototypical natural death that is imagined to offer redemptive possibilities for a modern death that is mechanized, emotionally stoic, and presumably repressed. Others (e.g., Gilbert 2006; Kaufman 2005; Webb 1997) have pointed out the elaborate logistical and technological arrangements necessary in order to, paradoxically, orchestrate a "natural" death.[1] While both these interventions are critical, I want to pursue here a different problem: the circumstances through which a figure of natural death became compelling. Writing her first book amid the 1960s peace and antinuclear movements, Kübler-Ross suggests that contemporary societies have bolstered their psychological defenses against death in direct relation to an intensified vulnerability to the technologically driven deaths of modern warfare.

> In the old days a man was able to face his enemy eye to eye. He had a fair chance in a personal encounter with a visible enemy. Now the soldier as well as the civilian has to anticipate weapons of mass destruction which offer no one a reasonable chance, often not even an awareness of their approach. Destruction can strike out of the blue skies and destroy thousands like the bomb at Hiroshima; it may come in the form of gases or other means of chemical warfare—invisible, crippling, killing. . . . This is how science and technology have contributed to an ever increasing fear of destruction and therefore fear of death. (1969, 11)

What interests me here is not the causal force of this connection between modern management of death and modern warfare—though it has been forcefully suggested by various scholars (e.g., Gilbert 2006, 135–63; Bourke 1996), and resonates with Benjamin's (1968) account of how modern warfare together with the removal of death from modern life have undermined storytelling. Rather I am intrigued by the relationship between military and medical hardware. The quest for death with dignity arose alongside the mass-televised spectacle of the meaningless or ignominious deaths of young American soldiers or napalmed villagers in Vietnam. At a time when advanced technology very often took the form of weapons, machines that prolonged life could become linked in the public imagination with machines that destroy life. The cry for natural death drew language from a broader resistance to the technocratic solutions of a military-industrial complex.[2]

Shortly after North American publics accumulated video memories of the Vietnam War they also assembled journalistic memories of legally contested and highly publicized artificially prolonged deaths of patients like Karen Ann Quinlan and, later, Nancy Cruzan. These memories compose a different set of nightmares of a different kind of terror from those of the emigrants consulted for this book. These media-informed nightmares are structured around a cyborgian death (or uncanny afterlife) hooked up to machines. The scenarios invoke a peculiarly Euroamerican type of restless ghost, a Christian soul locked inside a body that is kept alive by mechanical devices. In popular imagination these mechanistically prolonged lives carry a frightening ambiguity,[3] motivating the call for "natural death" that eventually culminated in the Patient Self-Determination Act of 1991, requiring that all medical facilities receiving federal funds inform patients that they have the right to an advance directive, a legal document in which they specify their preferences for the use or nonuse of life-prolonging technologies in the event that they can no longer communicate. This legislated right to refuse specific treatments is popularly understood as a way to refuse a cyborgian death, while simultaneously claiming a natural, dignified death as inscribed in public imagination and the media.[4]

The backlash against mechanized death persisted postmortem in public response to the descriptions of embalming and cosmetic alteration of corpses in Jessica Mitford's (1963) best-selling book on the U.S. funeral industry, a work that may have helped to prompt a turn in the United States toward cremation (already a preference in Europe).[5] Mitford's account of mortuary practice aroused not only pragmatic concern about the funeral industry's hard sell of expensively altered corpses, but also repugnance at the graphic accounts of corpses drained of blood and infused with preservative liquids. For North American reading publics of the 1960s, the dual technologies of prolonging life and preserving bodies evoked similar fantasies of zombie-like hybrids (cf. Haraway 1991). While corpses in themselves are often experienced as hybrid entities, existing uneasily on an edge between human and nonhuman (Bradbury 1999, 138), the simulated animation of corpses has the capacity to intensify their ghoulishness. This ghoulishness, while capable of sparking a pleasurable horror or fascination in entertainment contexts (ranging from horror films to the immensely popular Body Worlds exhibit, in which actual cadavers are reanimated as three-dimensional anatomical models engaged in activities of daily life), takes on a more repellent cast when attached to a deceased family member or friend. As Philippe Ariès commented, "the death of the patient in the hospital, covered with tubes" has become more horrifying to contemporary publics than the *transi*, the half-decomposed corpse of medieval European "macabre rhetoric" (1982, 614). The call for natural death suggests that the horror of decomposition—now made invisible by closed coffins, refrigeration, and embalming—has shifted to horror of a loved one who has become part mannequin. It is not surprising that Mitford's exposé of the mechanical processes through which such a mannequin is produced evoked in readers a revulsion at the prospect of their own loved ones as vivisected and revivified. If the mimetic body of repose produced in the funeral home constructs, as Mary Bradbury suggests, a false narrative of a peaceful death (1999, 2, 127), then it is also subject, through that very construction, to exposure as a technological effect manufactured by surgical means. When wheeled into view, the body of backstage embalming, like the intubated body in the ICU, is revealed as an uncanny body symbiotically merged with mechanical effects at once familiar and alien.

Natural death therefore remains, for many North Americans, a compelling moral and aesthetic image, even though the refusal of life-prolonging technologies can hardly guarantee the kinds of deaths imagined to be natural. As bioethicist Margaret Pabst Battin has observed, many imagine that "natural death" will allow time for "reviewing life and saying farewell, for last rites or final words." These ideas, she notes,

> are the product of literary and cultural traditions associated with conventional deathbed scenes, reinforced by movies, books, news stories, religious models, and just plain wishful thinking. Even the very term "natural" may have stereotyped connotations for the patient: something close to nature, uncontrived, and appropriate. As a result of these notions, the patient often takes "natural death" to be a painless, conscious, dignified, culminative slipping away. (1994, 33–34)

Battin goes on to offer graphic details of several possible deaths without medical or mechanical intervention: abrupt death by heart attack; slow delirious death by infection; death by kidney failure accompanied by nausea, vomiting, hemorrhage, and convulsions. "Many patients who are dying in these ways," Battin points out, "are comatose or heavily sedated. Such deaths do not allow for a period of conscious reflection at the end of life . . . or other features of the stereotypically 'dignified' death" (34). As Sharon Kaufman has shown, the phrase "let nature take its course" and the designation of particular mechanically managed deaths as "not natural" are rhetorics employed most often by physicians in the context of persuading families that it is time to discontinue life support (2005, 122, 124).[6] The negotiation of the "natural" may be, she concludes, "the most fundamental feature of hospital practice today" (325).

Hospice is that site where desires for peaceful, natural death—against the more ostensibly violent death of technical intervention—are most deliberately institutionalized. A radical notion in the 1960s, hospice is now an integral part of the medical system, offering coordinated end-of-life care involving medical treatment (as considered appropriate), pain management, grief support, companionship, and assistance with advance directives. To be hospice-eligible in the United States, it is typically necessary to receive a doctor's prognosis of no more than six months of remaining life. In the late 1990s the hospices I visited required a Do Not Resuscitate (DNR) order signed by the patient to indicate her agreement to not be revived in the event of death (cf. Gleeson and Wise 1990). Nearly a decade later many hospices have become more flexible, sometimes requiring only the physician prognosis rather than a signed DNR order. If patients are already attached to ventilators or other life-prolonging equipment when they are transferred to hospice care, they are rarely required to be unplugged. Nor are they necessarily forced off hospice if they fail to die in six months, although they may lose eligibility if their illness is considered to have gone into remission.

While the logic of hospice depends on a relatively recently conceived distinction between curative and palliative care, in practice the distinction is blurry. Some hospice personnel freely acknowledge that a particular treatment may be curative in one context and palliative in another, palliative in intent though partly curative in effect, or otherwise falling ambiguously between the cracks of these two categories. At the same time, however, the structure of health-care finance, whereby hospitals are reimbursed only for treatment of specific conditions but not for pain relief (Kaufman 2005, 29, 102), and hospices are permitted only pain relief but not treatment, assures that the distinction between palliative and curative care is discursively and institutionally reinforced. Meanwhile, hospice emphasis on patient comfort continues to raise questions about the slippery slope between pain alleviation and assisted suicide or euthanasia, requiring hospice workers to sustain a delicate and rigorous language and practice in which death is permitted but not facilitated and pain medication is administered to ease death but not to hasten it.[7] For caretakers, opiates may constitute one more factor in the nagging ambiguity of causes of death.[8] Trained by hospice staff to read my father's moans as signs of pain, I faithfully squirted the breakthrough medicine in the side of his mouth during his last night. But how could I be sure that these moans were cries of pain, and not efforts to speak through a narcotic haze that mangled his language? How did I know that they arose from physical distress rather than anguished memory? The next morning as his hospice personal care provider was turning him for his sponge bath, she called my siblings and me to his bedside, telling us that he was "slipping away." Her words seemed to offer a soothing reassurance that he was dying in peace, bringing to mind David Moller's remark that hospice constructs a controlled space in which the "horrible" is reduced to the "ordinary and 'natural,'" and "anguish" is "channeled" into "acceptance" (quoted in Gilbert 2006, 200). Peaceful dying, like the more obviously cyborgian death, requires orchestration, acquiescence, paperwork, precise doses of morphine, and medical expertise.

In the mid-1990s I accompanied a hospice nurse on several visits to a Filipino family. In the car on the way to our first visit the nurse told me that the family was "in denial." The previous day when their mother was gasping for breath, they had called an ambulance. The nurse had cautioned them that emergency resuscitation was not "hospice-appropriate" and that hospice is for keeping people "comfortable and symptom-free" while they die. When we arrived, the mother was sleeping, mouth open, tubes taped to her nostrils, face muscles twitching, feet moving restlessly under the blanket. The daughter said that she wanted her mother to be comfortable, animated, and "well." "I guess that's not very logical," she added. The nurse reminded her that the family had signed a DNR order. "Do you know where the copies are?" she asked. The son dug out a loose-leaf notebook, found the form, and handed it to the nurse who showed it to the daughter. The daughter conceded: her mother had agreed to this so she must have understood it. But when she had asked her mother point-blank recently whether she would want to be resuscitated, her mother had said yes. "Maybe your mother changed her mind," the nurse suggested. "When she's coherent you need to ask her again. You need to make a decision. The purpose of hospice is not to prolong life." The daughter confessed to her own "ambivalence." "I want my mother to be at home and comfortable, but also I don't want to let her go. I guess I want to have my cake and eat it too." "No," the nurse said gently, "you just don't want your mother to die." She asked the brother, a certified nurse, what he thought. Lowering his voice, he said that he would like his mother to be able to die "peacefully."

The daughter recalled that when they left the emergency room she told her mother, "Now you're going to be okay," and her mother answered, "Yes, yes, I'm going to be okay now." "She could have said, 'No, no, I know I'm dying,'" the daughter pointed out. "Maybe your mother is trying to protect you, to comfort you," the nurse suggested. "And I am trying to comfort *her*," the daughter replied, adding, "I understand you have your protocol." The brother piped up that he realized hospice couldn't provide a respirator. "No," the nurse corrected him, "it's not that we *can't* provide a respirator." The daughter tutored her brother: it's because it's not consistent with "their ideal" of comfortable death. "Tube-feeding and respirators are more invasive," he volunteered. "You mean for example if she goes into respiratory arrest then we wouldn't call hospice?" the daughter asked. "We'd just let her go, we wouldn't call 911 to revive her?" "That's right," the nurse said. "I would like to just play it by ear," the daughter said. "No, we can't do that," the nurse said. "We need to know which direction you're going to go, whether you're going to stay on hospice or move into more aggressive care."

Before our next visit, the nurse mentioned that the daughter and son had nearly come to blows because the sister had accused her brother of trying to keep their mother alive by feeding her. On the other hand, the nurse added, the daughter herself was "forcing shark cartilage [a home remedy] down her mother's throat." During that visit, the son told us that either he or his sister slept by his mother at night. He said that he had just bathed her and changed her clothes. The nurse asked him if he was getting out at all. No, he said. Sometimes he went over to his sister's house but then he just thought about his mother so it was better for him to be here. The only way he would go out was if he could go dancing. That is my "weakness," he said. But he couldn't find anyone to go with him. Everyone is too busy. The nurse listened to his mother's heart and took her blood pressure. She went through the calendar pillbox, replenishing the medicines. The son pulled out some papers. One was a bill for the emergency room visit. He was concerned that hospice might not pay the bill, because he had signed a "revocation" form. The nurse assured him that she had consulted with her supervisor and hospice would pay. She returned both copies of the revocation form to him. She told him that she'd noticed a "decline" over the previous week and that his mother might die soon. Hearing this, he touched his hand quickly to his cheek. He told us he had asked his mother to forgive him for being a "juvenile delinquent," and she told him that she'd forgiven him long before. He told her he loved her, and she also said she loved him. When he tried to feed her cereal she ate only a couple of spoonfuls. He told her, "You say you want to live but you're not eating. If you want to live, you have to eat." The nurse replied that his mother might be saying she wanted to live in words, but saying something else by refusing to eat. She asked him what he would do if his mother died. He answered that he'd cry, and then clean her up. "Do you know who to call?" she asked. "I'll call the funeral organization," he answered. His sister had mailed in the membership fee. "No," the nurse said, "you just call hospice and we take care of everything." "Oh, it's a test," he said, and he and I laughed.

The nurse added that if he calls 911 the police will try to resuscitate his mother because she's still "full code." "I would like to resuscitate her myself," he said, "not have the medics do it." "I know you know how to do it," the nurse said. "But even if you succeed she might be brain-dead. You might break her ribs or lacerate her liver, and when she was revived she would still have cancer." She added that a resuscitation attempt might be "traumatic" for him as well.

At our next visit, the mother was unusually alert. The nurse asked whether she still wanted cardiopulmonary resuscitation (CPR) if she stopped breathing. "We've discussed this before," the nurse said. "We've discussed it before?" the mother asked. "Yes, twice before," the nurse replied. "What did I say?" the mother asked. "You said different things at different times," the nurse said. "When your daughter asked you said no. But when I asked, you said yes. After you're revived you'll still be sick. Do you want the aid car to come or not?" "Your sternum might be broken," the son added, "your brain might already be dead." "What do you think?" the nurse asked. "Do you want CPR or not? Would you want them to resuscitate you?" After a short pause, the mother replied, "Yes." "We don't want it to be an issue," the daughter said reassuringly, "but if it were an issue—." "There is a paper that has to be signed," the son said. "You check one box if you want to be revived and another box if you don't." "My mother," he added, "is just asking for a French kiss. That's a bonus. Sometimes when I do CPR on people, they kiss me." "It will probably be a nonissue," the nurse said. "My mother is tough as a mule," the daughter said. "She's had miracles happen."

We moved back out into the living room. "I hope I'm not offending you by being a funny man," the son said. He and the nurse discussed the pain medications. Meanwhile, the daughter, sitting near me, told me quietly that resuscitation is "not an issue because we are trying to keep her alive. I heard the prognosis. I understand the academic of it, but there are other things too. Some of the stuff the doctor says is b.s. I'm not giving up."

Some weeks later I learned from the nurse that the mother had died. Toward the end her daughter had agreed to have her transferred to a nursing home. She died during her first day in the home, after her daughter left. The nurse thought that she probably needed her daughter to leave before she could die.

In this story of conflict and capitulation, misunderstanding and translation, both nurse and family tease out the ironies of hospice discipline, testing its limits even while reiterating its legitimacy. If the nurse's task is partly didactic, instructing the family, asking questions, and correcting the answers, the family is partly willing to play the foil, competing for the right answer, instructing one another, demonstrating their knowledge for the nurse. Yet in joking about this didacticism ("it's a test"), the son also suggests the absurdity of academic expertise on death. Even as he appears to bow to hospice discipline, his mimicry of its discourse has the effect of exaggerating its tropes. His graphic admonishment to his mother about broken bones and brain death enacts his mastery of the anatomy of resuscitation while also drawing attention to its impersonal tone. Similarly, in reminding her brother that hospice rules are based on "their ideal" of death, the daughter in one gesture disassociates herself from this ideal while demonstrating her command of it. Her responses to the nurse are a delicate dance of polite disagreement alternating with gently mocking accession. As phrases are traded back and forth they undergo quiet metamorphoses: "Maybe your mother is trying to comfort you," the nurse says, as if to say she knows she's dying, there's no need to hide it. "And I am trying to comfort her," the daughter replies, as if to say we comfort one another by not talking about death. Later, in her asides to me, she holds out for miracles and identifies medical "b.s." That b.s. might include not just the technical language of full code, lacerate, and brain-dead, but also the alternating techno-affective vocabulary of denial, letting go, and comfort, both linguistic registers scrambling to contain the enigma of death in a space of informed and autonomous decision-making. Meanwhile discipline leaves a paper trail, death's loose-leaf notebook, forms signed in duplicate or triplicate, other copies stashed in remote hospice and Medicaid files.

The mother appears agitated, even as she patiently works out once again the answers to the social work interview, the intake to death, the sales pitch for nonresuscitation, perhaps wondering how she can satisfy the nurse without hurting her children, or whether she is receiving quality or substandard care. Alongside the banality of information exchange is the strangeness of addressing, across a chasm of time and biological transformation, a corpse in the patient's future who is no longer her: when you are dead do you want the aid car? Such questions, which are at the very heart of advance directives, operate according to a peculiar logic whereby one is pressed to imagine oneself as dead, but with a choice in the matter. Even the end of this story confounds the disciplinary moral. Was this a peaceful death at last, as the nurse implies? Did the woman die when her daughter left her in the nursing home because she felt free, or because she felt abandoned, or by an utter non sequitur? The nurse's lesson that the dying need to be "let go" with its subtextual message of self-actuation and independence is simultaneously undercut by her recognition that holding on to the dying is a helpless gesture of love, which calls forth in her an equally helpless gesture of compassion. The story suggests less where the disciplinary mechanism of peaceful dying creakingly succeeds, but rather where it breaks down, as if jammed in its tracks by the ghost in the machine that is death's unmanageable remainder.

Permission to Die

Scenarios such as the above play out between hospice workers with conscientious aspirations to be culturally competent and patients and families acutely aware of their social marginality. For these families medical disciplines of dying dramatize the convergence of two versions of thanatopolitical subjection: social exclusion and terminal diagnosis.[9] In North America, even white elderly patients slide toward the margins from both these directions, their lives threatening to become what others might be tempted to classify as no longer meaningful. One British physician admitted, "life is more sacred, I suppose, when you are younger. Obviously. Much cheaper when you are old" (Bradbury 1999, 53). Several emigrants commented on this cheapness of aging life in the United States. As one Hmong woman, Mrs. Vangay, put it, "I think that the young and the youthful and children, the doctors have hope for them, and so they treat them well. But with elders they know that death is overdue so they don't really care. If they have good medication they don't use it for them." Many Hmong share this perception, Pheng told me. "For the old, people think the doctors probably say, 'Oh, she won't be able to live anyway. If we save her life, she won't be able to do anything. Or her Medicaid doesn't cover this or that. That's the way it goes.'"

Even Sodoeung, herself a health-care professional, had this to say about the hospital that cared for her father at the end of his life.

> They didn't really take good care of him. I know that he was an old man, and maybe they thought they didn't have to do that much. He could just die. They only came in to check him when we were there. . . . Sometimes he would pull all the tubes out and nobody had even come and fixed it. . . . He was supposed to come home on Monday afternoon. But the nurse called and said we couldn't pick him up because in the morning he had choked, and the food got into his lungs. They didn't even tell us until we were ready to pick him up. Later on I talked to him and my sister talked to him and said, "Dad, it's okay to come home." My mother was cooking all the food he likes and preparing his bath. My sister had headed to the hospital, right? And then at nine o'clock they called my mother and said, "Oh, he died." My sister called me and said he passed away and I said, "That's impossible. I talked to him and he was okay." They said he had pneumonia. I don't know if they helped him. My sister said that when she got there, he was having a hard time breathing and no one was

there. And they didn't give him any oxygen or anything. She called the nurse and they came and they tried to help him but they couldn't. It was too late. . . . After he passed away we tried to find the doctor, and his doctor didn't call us or let us know anything. Later he said, "Oh he was old," and this and that. And I said, "Yes, I know my father was old. He was ninety-four, I know that. But he was doing okay. We expected him home. And my mother was taking good care of him." I wasn't happy.

When I asked a Kmhmu woman, Julie Prachitham, which of the old ways elderly Kmhmu were most concerned that their children follow, she replied without hesitation: "The most important thing is to not put your parents in a nursing home. We have lived [in this city] almost twenty years, and we have had only one Kmhmu family who let their parent go to a nursing home. It was because she was really heavy and they couldn't take care of her at home." Similarly one Lao man, recalling life in Laos, told Rob Proudfoot, "They take care of the mother and father when old . . . this way we are not alone . . . not like America where the old are put away. . . . I hope my children remember the Lao way" (quoted in Proudfoot 1990, 97–98).

The routinized permission to die that is structurally directed at the elderly is compounded for elderly people of color, immigrants, and recipients of public assistance. For emigrants it repeats the politics of dispensability they remember from war zones and refugee camps. In wartime Laos and Cambodia, medicine was understood as a possible staging area for death, whether by murder or by deliberate neglect. Under the Khmer Rouge, qualified medics were scarce, and the only readily available remedy in the rural areas was herbal medicine concocted by nonspecialists (Guillou 2004, 7). Infirmaries became places for the sick to die quietly, with little access to food and less to medical intervention. As Pin Yathay noted, "Only someone who was really sick, who didn't think they would survive anyway, would risk going to the hospital" (1987, 180). In wartime Laos, hospitals were expected to be politically partisan. "Because I was an important person," the Kmhmu Lt. Phanha recalled, "[my superiors] didn't want me to go to the hospital in Laos. They told me to go to Thailand, where nobody would know me. We didn't trust our own doctors; they might have killed me on purpose." Medicine had a similar reputation in Thai refugee camps. Rumors circulated of women who were given tubal ligations against their will, and children, hospitalized for stomachaches, who died on the operating table and then disappeared, exploited for medical experiments or body parts. The dread of scientific excess that prompted the call for natural death in the United States gave rise here to a different scenario, not the body bionically connected to machinery, but the body dismantled for its mechanical parts and secrets. In such rumors the invasive potential of biomedicine fuses with the institutionalized disregard for refugees' bodies. Such stories of modern medicine intuitively apprehend biopolitics as that thanato-politics wherein "letting die" grades into "making die."

Rumors of medical violence also thrive in the enigmatic bureaucracies of North America. The Hmong woman Mrs. Vangay recounted this story about an uncle living in another state:

> At the hospital the doctor asked the family, "Should we give him a shot so he can just die? Then you can take him home for the funeral." The patient wanted to come home. He was crying. He didn't want to stay in the hospital. But they decided to keep him there. And while he was in the hospital, the doctor grabbed him and did surgery on him with no anesthetic. It knocked him unconscious. They cut him open and he was moving a lot. He had bloody eyes and nose and was bleeding at the mouth. After the surgery was done, instead of sewing him up, they just put tape over the incision. The relatives went to visit him and called his name. He woke up and talked with them. But the nurse and the doctor were angry and told them not to do that. They gave him some sleep-ing pills and killed him again and that time he just died.

It might seem to defy plausibility that a late twentieth-century U.S physician proposed euthanasia, operated without anesthesia, and deliberately hastened a patient's death, in violation of several laws. The import of this story, how-ever, lies not in its accurate relation to a particular event but in its grasp of a thanatological ethos. The physician in question might have recommended high doses of pain medication, spared a "dying" patient the discomfort of stitches, and asked the family not to wake the patient from a sleep that meant a brief respite from pain, according to logics of medical futility and compassion. These acts would be consistent with a standard of palliative care for patients con-sidered to be dying and yet could look like negligence to a family still seeking a cure. Since some elderly Hmong say that the *plig* is liable to escape from a body that is opened for surgery, the failure to sew up the wound might have seemed an especially egregious offense. (Hmong shamans sometimes refuse to treat a person who has undergone surgery on the grounds that it will be difficult if not impossible to lure the *plig* back into the body once it has escaped.) Such rumors interrogate the different standard of care signaled by a shift to palliation. Of his father's decline Mr. Vangay said,

> At the hospital they weren't treating him or anything. They were just giving him painkillers and sleeping pills, so he was unconscious most of the time. We thought that was not a good idea, so we brought him home. We thought he

would be better off there. We thought he would probably live more days than in the hospital. And no matter how many days he was going to live, we were able to see him there.

Mrs. Vangay told a story of two local men, brothers, who had died in the hospital a few months before. "At the time I had a newborn baby so I didn't really know about it but my husband did," she said. "As far as I know they had difficulty breathing, like asthma. And all they were receiving was a numbing painkiller that made them fall asleep, and sleep and sleep and then go from so much sleep." On the other hand the Hmong elder Pao Chang laughed off the idea that U.S. doctors kill patients. "If a person is sick, and the doctor treats him and he dies, it's not that the doctor wanted to do it. It's because the person is already sick. . . . It's the same thing in Hmong culture. When a person is ill, they look for a *txiv neeb* to help. Somehow the body dies, and they complain that the *txiv neeb* didn't want to heal him."

Although the suspicion of negligence or malice is not unique to encounters with biomedicine, rumors of death-dealing medicine continue to spread, perhaps because they effectively condense a confluence of concerns not easily discounted: the devaluation of emigrants' lives, the hiddenness of medical decision-making, and the economic inequities of contemporary health care. Like those forms of mass media that rely on mechanical reproduction rather than oral transmission (newspapers, radio, tabloids, television), rumor acts as a forum for collective anxieties, spinning those speculative versions of events that best resonate with popular apprehensions and aspirations.[10]

As a powerful substance with a particular social history in Hmong communities, it is perhaps not surprising that morphine is a key player in Hmong rumors of medicalized death. When Hmong were fleeing from the Pathet Lao, they often gave opium to babies to keep them quiet, guessing at the dosage. These infants sometimes died. Opium use is further associated with rifts in families and masculinities set adrift. Since such substances do not simply shed their historical weight in U.S. hospitals, the opiated death of palliative care can become a site of distrust for some Hmong families. Like opium, blood is hardly a neutral substance. During wartime, blood for transfusions was scarce, and loss of blood was a frequent source of weakness and death. If morphine allows sick people to slip into a sleep from which they may never awaken, blood flows too copiously from opened bodies. Pheng recalled one clinical interaction for which he served as interpreter. "The doctor took some blood from the guy, and he said, 'Are you going to take my blood to eat, to drink, or what? You are taking so much, I'm going to die now, you know?' . . . Nobody likes that. They think that the blood is for someone else. It is going to be added to someone else." As in the refugee camps, medical encounters in the United States are shadowed by a fear of commerce in bodily substance. Mr. Vangay was mostly content with the care his father received at the end of his life. "The only thing I was concerned about is that when my father was dying, the doctors took about 50 cc of his blood to check on something. He was really weak; he was hardly eating anything. Why were they still taking his blood like that?" Elderly Khmer are also wary of blood draws. One Khmer health-care provider commented, "They think that if you draw blood, you lose the blood, and you are already sick, you are already weak, you're already low in blood count." Such fears are partly locatable within histories of interaction with specific substances, which carry traces from other regimes of permission to die.

Within biomedicine divergent historical positions are framed as cultural difference, which health-care professionals are disciplined to acknowledge and, to some extent, accommodate. In this process, medical professionals seek out anthropologists, cross-cultural researchers, and representatives of cultural communities, inciting a body of literature outlining diverse approaches to death among culturally defined groups (e.g., Bliatout 1993; Kalish 1980; Parkes, Laungani, and Young 1997). Such literature reinforces the view that cultural communities are relatively static entities with codified systems of belief—which, in Povinelli's (2002) terms, bow to genealogical imperatives— rather than fluid affiliations of people improvising lifestyles according to shifting political conditions. Research investigating cultural preferences at the end of life separates subjects into discreet cultural groups such that the results necessarily reinforce the assumption of culturally linked preferences. By contrast, studies without any prior commitment to the salience or nonsalience of cultural difference have concluded that cultural affiliation is a poor predictor of patient responses to critical illness (Drought and Koenig 2002; Koenig and Gates-Williams 1995; Hern et al. 1998). Even though cultural crib sheets are a grossly inadequate substitute for becoming acquainted with patients (Guneratnam 1997; cf. Surbone 2004; Hern et al. 1998), the structure of U.S. health care assures that few physicians take time to seek out their patients' bodily knowledge or life stories. By the same token, few patients have the chance to become acquainted with the physicians who order their surgeries, monitor their pain, or determine that they are dying. In this respect hospice care offers more sustained opportunity for dialogue between practitioners and families over ethics of care. Nonetheless during a conversation at one hospice serving several immigrant communities, staff voiced anxieties about their cultural knowledge. They noted that some patients and families were not comfortable signing DNR orders. They suspected there were ways to broach the subject of death of which they were ignorant. One family, they said, refused to speak of death, and yet purchased a "dying gown" for the ill person. Some immigrant families seemed to be wary of their loved one dying at home lest the spirit keep hanging around, while others emphatically preferred her to die at home so they could care for her body in specific ways. The staff recognized that they needed to spend more time with the families if both parties were to understand one another's ethos. But where would this time be found?

Ultimately, one wonders if the anxiety over gaps in cultural knowledge might be displacing a deeper paradox of this hospice's work: the irony of easing death for those who seem to have been more exposed to it in the first place. At weekly meetings, hospice nurses and social workers discussed new admissions and ongoing patients with the team director and medical director. My fieldnotes on the running commentary at one such meeting indicate the institutional and emotional complexity of negotiating permission to die with those who already face social abandonment on other fronts. It also suggests how the wild contingencies and idiosyncrasies of dying elude and confound bureaucratic management.

A forty-two-year-old man with a rare brain disease. He won't last long. Are there signs of pain, such as wrinkling of the forehead or moaning? He should probably have morphine. The man's sisters would like more aggressive treatment, but the wife feels differently. The situation is a "real heartbreak" because the man just finished an alcohol treatment program.

A man with severe aphasia, alert, not in a coma. He's appropriate for hospice because he doesn't want to be revived. He refused antibiotics. He needs a chaplain, social worker, and home health aid. He can understand but he can't speak. He needs companionship. Whoever spends time with him should read the newspaper.

A patient with esophageal cancer, very afraid of dying. When they talked it became clear that he is mostly afraid of leaving his family alone. Once they discussed how his family would be okay, he decided to stop tube feeding. His wife was relieved. She would still like a more aggressive painkiller. She stays awake at night worrying about whether the pain control is effective. His doctor can be cavalier and ungenerous. Could the man be persuaded to change physicians? The medical director comments that if the person who has coverage for his regular physician after hours is "human," then maybe he doesn't need to change doctors.

The patient is eighty-one and not declining very fast. He is worried about Medicaid issues. The daughter worries to the hospice staff about "when you drop us." How can the daughter get supplies and equipment she needs for the patient's care after he's taken off hospice?

A sixty-six-year-old man with lung cancer. There seems to be substance abuse in the home. The woman is emotionally flat. There doesn't seem to be any income. When they heard the hospice nurse was coming they quickly rushed to set up the hospital bed that had been delivered. The woman doesn't want him to have no-CPR status. Meanwhile he's declining quickly. When the nurse told the woman it wouldn't be long she started crying.

A woman suffering from heart disease. She has no pain with her edema, but she can't get out of bed because of it. Should they treat the edema? There is no need to treat it, the medical director says, since the patient is not in pain.

This patient is into natural therapies. Does anyone know of a natural therapy for nausea? Ginger snaps, someone suggests. Candied ginger, ginger beer, ginger ale. There is also an acupressure strap.

A thirteen-year-old with leukemia. He just received a bone marrow transplant. The father doesn't want to tell him he's dying. The mother feels they must tell him. They did tell him that his cancer has returned. Some of his friends are finding out from their parents that he's dying, but the son himself has not been told. He goes to get platelets twice a week. Staff are advising the parents to tell him. People need to know sooner rather than later. The kid wants to remain active. He takes painkillers. He is an independent "neat" kid. The hospice staff will work with the father to get him to agree to tell the kid. How long does he have? He could die at any time, the director said, or he could last two months. His DNR status is ambiguous.

A sixty-one-year-old man with AIDS, lives with his partner, well connected to services. He's also connected with Compassion in Dying (a group that offers information on hastened death). He doesn't want to commit suicide but he also doesn't want to be bedridden. Everyone should be aware of his connection to Compassion in Dying.

A seventy-four-year-old man, always short of breath. He sometimes forgets to take the oxygen off when he's smoking. There are eight very involved kids. The kids think his decline is due to not fully grieving the loss of a nineteen-year-old son in a car accident a few years back.

This man has lung cancer. He is fairly independent but has poor short-term memory. Can he cook for himself? Someone needs to be sent to "make an assessment." His wife is planning to quit her job. She doesn't seem to realize that she can't get Medicare for two years.

An eighty-six-year-old man with lung cancer. When he was offered a nurse, he said, "Hell no, what do I want a nurse for?" He is probably drinking. He goes up and down stairs by himself, has lots of visitors, smokes a pack of cigarettes a day. His house is clean. He's "in denial" and very frail. He doesn't want anyone living in the house. What would it take to rearrange the house so he could live entirely on the first floor?

This patient is seventy-five and "actively dying." The hospice worker told the son-in-law what to do at the time of death. They are using morphine and Ativan for the pain. The patient is unresponsive. When he grimaces they give him morphine. He has a lot of support. He's a private man, though. He wouldn't want people to see him like this.

This person needs "social work," is living on Insure. The cat is the significant other. The primary caregiver is the patient himself. He's weak and anxious and says he wants to die. He abandoned his son when he was eight years old. They contacted each other recently and his son sent him a TV. But he can't forgive himself. He doesn't have any spiritual practice. His medicines are a mess.

This patient is a child. There's no change. The hospice workers are doing mostly "social work." The mother is drinking. There's no phone; the electricity may be turned off. How far can we go to keep him on hospice? He was expected to die more quickly. The family signed a DNR order. The main concern is to make sure there's eight hours of nursing care. There's a need to "touch base" with the doctor to find out what is happening medically.

Forty-six-year-old patient, with tube feeding, still "full code," wants aggressive treatment. How should the pain be managed? He can't use his mouth because his tongue is huge from edema. His mother doesn't want to take care of him at home any more. He has to write to communicate and in his writing he "screams" that he doesn't want to leave home. There is an in-home mental health counselor visiting now. How about a conference of the family and the caregivers? Even if the mother had power of attorney, she can't force him to go to the hospital.

The patient is still "full code." The person with power of attorney wants him to be revived if "something can be done." "What does that mean?" someone asks. (No one bothers to answer. The question is rhetorical.)

The patient and hospice staff have talked about how no one knows what they want till they get there. Right now he thinks he wants to stay home and have "comfort only" treatment.

This patient has prostate cancer. If it's reasonably stable, the medical director says, it could be years before he dies. If he's not terminal within six months he'll have to be discharged. Otherwise it could be considered fraud. The decision is made to discharge him now. A week will be taken to prepare the family and make sure he has everything he needs.

At times during the meeting staff openly wept. At the end, in a rite of mourning, they read aloud the names of those who died the previous week. The idiosyncrasies of this group of patients went beyond extant cultural categories, which seldom entered the conversation except for oblique references to social and economic class. Yet in the conflict between palliation and treatment (where a treatment may be justified to remove pain, but not to enhance mobility); in the competing desires to domesticate care with home remedies and rely on medical authority; in the need to simultaneously monitor hospice eligibility and creatively patch together care options; in the wisecracks questioning mental health, family functionality, and physician humanity; in the awareness that hospice, whether appropriate or not, is sometimes the only care available; and in the sense of responsibility to offer patients a foreknowledge of their death alongside a reluctant respect for the refusal of this knowledge on the part of some patients or families, it seems clear that a sense of being socially expendable cannot be answered with any simple calculus of end-of-life protocol.

In one reading of this meeting, hospice personnel display a deft practicality as they labor to obtain permission for death from impoverished, lonely, sometimes neglectful or demented families. In another reading, personnel strive to unflinchingly face the absurdity, heartbreak, and (sometimes) relief of death, bypassing the rules when necessary and possible. Like the staff at the emergency psychiatric unit described by Lorna Rhodes (1991), the hospice staff reflect on the impossibilities of their own positions and that of their patients through a dark humor edged with sadness. They also reinforce in one another a conviction that an inescapable and primary aspect of their work is to witness and participate in grief, despair, and exasperation. Even as they attempt to encourage peacefully permitted deaths, they readily entangle themselves in much less disciplined scenes of dying. Within this hospice, then, the lack of security in rational decision-making, self-conscious recognition of inherent ironies, and seat-of-the pants improvisation open a space for dialogue over permission to die. The more smoothly a negotiated death is managed, through selective use of machinery, documentation, and pathways of care, the more it resembles a decision of life or death by a sovereign bioethical power. Insofar as hospice care stumbles over the unmanageability of dying, it relinquishes such an illusion of sovereignty.

Negotiations

In the 1990s the American Hospital Association estimated that 70 percent of deaths in the United States were "timed or negotiated, with all concerned parties privately concurring on withdrawal of some death-delaying technology or not even starting it in the first place" (quoted in Webb 1997, 189). In the twenty-first century medicalized dying remains a negotiated practice in which decisions to use or not use life-prolonging technologies are hashed out among physicians, nurses, patients, and families. Kaufman's account of negotiated death examines patterns of rhetoric and protocol through which hospital, insurance, and state bureaucracies shape the temporal arc of dying. She traces a jagged historical convergence of life-prolonging technologies, healthcare economics, divisions of medical labor, and shifting public and professional discourse. When first invented, mechanical ventilation and CPR were used only for specific medical conditions. By the mid-1960s CPR became standard procedure for patients whose hearts had stopped beating, and by the early 1970s ventilators became standard equipment for patients unable to breathe on their own (Kaufman 2005, 90, 117). Despite public outcry against mechanically prolonged dying, and the legal inauguration of DNR orders in 1974, both ventilators and CPR were in wide use in the first decade of the twenty-first century, even with severely ill patients. Not only do patients understandably change their mind about equipment like ventilators, when faced, for instance, with shortness of breath, but the wide scope of scenarios in which patients might be revived or kept alive is not adequately addressed by a prior generic refusal of mechanical life support (162).

The very existence of life-support technologies, then, necessitates difficult decisions about their use, such that physicians, families, and patients are inevitably burdened with the responsibility for either prolonging or facilitating death (Kaufman 2005, 57). Physician ignorance or overriding of individual DNR orders make it clear that the principle of patient autonomy competes, in practice, not just with the confusion and fear of patients and families, but also with hospitals' de facto charters for appropriately timed trajectories of dying. As Kaufman demonstrates, medical staff acknowledge that families and patients need time to accept impending death, while harboring implicit expectations about how much time is reasonable (115). Moreover, physicians often subtly or not so subtly communicate to patients and families which of the apparent choices is actually viable. Many decisions involving hospitalized patients who are not responding to treatment probably unfold like this one: "I mean, we discussed it, but honestly they weren't really decisions. They were 'treatment's not working, this is what we have to do now.' It wasn't a matter of 'we can do this, or we can do that'" (quoted in Drought and Koenig 2002, 121). Kaufman partly attributes the discrepancy she observed between medical personnel's and families' or patients' ideas on when to shift from sustaining life to permitting death to the "doublespeak" of physicians who hedge on terminal prognoses (2005, 123, 176). Physicians attribute their obliqueness to uncertainty, as well as to their own experiences of miraculous (if temporary) recoveries (123). It would seem, then, that the "doublespeak" reflects not only habitual euphemisms or unconscious evasion, but also the insistent twists and mysteries of dying itself.

Even in the wake of studies suggesting that advance directives have little effect on end-of-life decision-making,[11] there have been efforts to render them relevant across chasms of language and historical experience. In the late 1990s I was introduced to an informative pamphlet on advance directives that had been translated into several languages. One day I spent an hour or more with Lt. Somsy and an interpreter poring over the Lao version of the booklet. Lt. Somsy's first comments were tactful. "It helps the reader understand what to do when you are ill or need health care. But the book uses vocabulary that would be hard to understand except for those who've gone to school for many years." As we closely examined specific passages, certain key confusions emerged. The Lao words used for "benefits" and "risks" of treatment, for instance, implied to Lt. Somsy the possibility of monetary loss or gain. As we continued to plow through the book, the interpreter, literate in both English and Lao, struggled to make sense of the Lao sentences. Lt. Somsy commented that the text had been translated word for word. "It should be translated from the full sentence," he said. Meanwhile the interpreter was stalled for a long baffled moment at the Lao phrase used for "artificially sustained." In the end, he was able to understand the booklet only by referring to the English. A Khmer graduate student voiced a similar response to the Khmer version of the booklet. Even if it were not an awkwardly literal translation, it would be useless to most elderly Khmer, who are not literate even in Khmer. The only Khmer, he mused, who would be able to understand the booklet were those who were literate in English, and they would find it easier to read the booklet in the original.[12] Meanwhile, the difficulty in finding an equivalent for the medical sense of "artificial" invites speculation about the historical specificity of a contemporary Euroamerican distinction between natural and artificial dying.

Like those interviewed by Kaufman, when Lao families are asked to weigh in on the use of technological life support, they often postpone the decision of acceding to death. Lt. Somsy's wife was undergoing surgery for cancer in her knee when her heart stopped for about twenty minutes.

> The doctors, they come to help her. And she is beating again. . . . They use oxygen to help her breathe. She could not talk then. So they cannot solve the problem. So they asked me if they should take off the oxygen, but if you take off the oxygen, she would die suddenly. So I told them not to take off the oxygen yet. They sent her to a nursing home. Then she died in the nursing home.

The possibility, however unlikely, of unexpected recovery inevitably influences families' thoughts about life support. Douang recalled the story of a Hmong friend's six-year-old daughter who failed to wake from anesthesia after a tonsillectomy. The physician in charge recommended removing her from the ventilator, but the family refused. Many people, Douang explained, consider a coma to be a long sleep during which the soul is visiting heaven or hell. A year later, the friend's daughter awoke from her coma and began the process of relearning how to walk and talk.

Nonetheless when people understand how violent biomedical resuscitation can be and how different dependence on life support is from a return to daily life, they often choose to allow death. Of the decision to sign a DNR order for her father, Sodoeung said,

> He was admitted to the hospital six or seven times in the last year before he died. In January or February he was in the hospital and the staff asked, "In case he is 'out,' do you want us to code him or something?" I didn't know what the doctor was talking about at first and I asked him, "What are you going to do? Shock him?" And I said, "No, I don't like that." . . . No one wants that. CPR is fine, but not shock. That's what we told the doctor when he asked me about my father. We said, "He is too old. We don't want to hurt him." We signed the paper. When we told my mom, at first she said, "I want them to help him." We said, "No, it won't help him. They do electric shock and stuff." Seeing how skinny he was, we decided to just let him go whenever he wanted to. What is the point of hurting a person?

For Mr. Chea and his elderly Khmer friends the question of resuscitation provoked a complex ethical discussion:

> If a person has been sick for a long time and then goes, just let him go. But if a person just got sick, and goes, then the doctors should try to help as much as they can.

Everybody has his own karma. But if the person has been sick for a long time with a chronic illness, getting better and worse, and then one day he decides to go, but someone decides to help him, that is *also* his karma. If you help him to come back and there is nothing he can do but lie there and breathe, that's all, he can't talk or anything, then *that* becomes his karma.

There are two kinds of people. One wants to live and the other doesn't. A person who has a chronic illness and has been on a ventilator or in a coma for a long time, and then suddenly goes, is someone who doesn't want to live. If the family says, "Oh, can you help him to come back?" and he is still breathing but cannot talk or do anything, it's not worth it. Just let him go. Don't keep him. But if a person is still walking or using a crutch, and suddenly passes away, then the doctor should try to help him as much as he can, because that person wants to live.

Sometimes the family wants a patient to be resuscitated so that someone can come from Cambodia to see them before they go. We all want to be with someone as they go.

Few would choose to consign a loved one to a bedridden, unconscious state for months, or even weeks, at a time. Nonetheless, it can be difficult to make a decision that may evoke memories of life-and-death choices in wartime or trouble relations with the dead. Sodoeung told me that some Khmer who authorized DNR orders were later tormented by their choices. "They still talk about it with regret. They keep thinking, 'Oh, if I let them help him with the "full code," he would probably still be around.'" Sodoeung suggested that the decision to resuscitate or not should be lifted from families.

If the doctors say, "We know that you love him, and you cannot throw him away; we feel sorry for him, but this is the reality," people will understand that. They know about life and death. They know. Then they don't have to make the decision. They can take time to take care of that person and talk more to them. When they have to make a decision, it's such a big decision, life and death. They feel like they helped that person to die.

Julie Prachitham knew several Kmhmu families who agreed to have loved ones disconnected from life support after a few days, and several individuals who had signed DNR orders. "More and more of our people now have kidney problems and they suffer for a long, long time. And those people sign right away, because they see their friends suffering and they don't want to be like that." Her husband, John, told me,

It's hard for me. I think it's hard for others too, to decide something like that. It depends on the situation. My uncle's mother was breathing with a respirator for one week in the hospital. When we went there, she didn't know anybody. It's hard to say just stop it, and take everything out, let her die. But . . . if they live, then day by day, year by year, it's going to be like that. So my uncle said, "We can't make her suffer like this. Let her go."

Similarly, the Catholic Hmong man Mr. Lo recalled. "I know of a few cases when Hmong people were told by a doctor that the problem could not be cured. 'Even if we put in the tubes or connect him to the machines or whatever, he can only last for a few weeks.' Then most of the time the family members agree not to use anything. They feel, 'Just let him go.'" Pheng thought that many Hmong, facing a doctor's recommendation that someone not be revived "would want him to keep trying." Nevertheless, if the patient still doesn't come back to life, "no one can force it."

A few spoke vehemently about the importance of attending death in a way that resuscitation procedures disallow. When a Kmhmu person is dying in the hospital, Julie said, ten or twenty people, including young children, will crowd into a room, crying loudly. When they leave, another fifteen cram into the room. After the person has died, everyone touches the patient to make her aware of their love. Doctors and nurses, Julie observed, find this practice "weird." Julie vividly recalled being shut out of the room during efforts to revive her father-in-law:

> They pushed me away from the door. "Just wait in the waiting room." Then two or three minutes later they said, "Oh, we tried our best, but he died." In Laos, when someone is going to die, and they know it for sure, they let the family members in. Everybody is there. But here, they have everybody go out. And people don't know what they're doing. That's why some old people say, "Oh maybe it wasn't time for that person to die. Maybe the doctor did something wrong, maybe even on purpose."

Resuscitation efforts from which the family and friends are excluded easily become focal points of suspicion. Cheuang, the Kmhmu healer, said,

> The thing I don't like, which happens many times, is when a patient is really sick, and then the doctor says, "Okay, everybody, get out of this room." That's the thing other people don't like also. We wonder, "What happened? Did they kill him or what?" That's what we worry. It would be good if the family members and friends could see when the patient actually dies.

Since most attempts at CPR are unsuccessful, more patients undergo it as their final moment of life rather than as the first treatment in their recovery

(Kaufman 2005, 118–19; Timmermans 1999). The exclusion of family members from resuscitative efforts therefore often means their exclusion from the dying process itself. Moreover, resuscitation, as Stefan Timmermans notes, is "often a depersonalized event in which, for the sake of saving a human life, the person being resuscitated is reduced to clinical parameters" (1997, 153). Doctors exclude family members in order to maximize efficiency and minimize the need for bedside manner. One emergency technician told Timmermans, "When I am involved in a resuscitation, I want that time to become a machine, not to be human at that point" (160). "But on the other hand," he added, "as a parent I defy you to keep me out of that room where my child is being resuscitated. I'll be in there whether you like it or not. I can see both sides of this."[13]

Emigrants also sometimes question the sudden detachment of medical staff after death. Continuing the story of her father's death, Sodoeung said,

> The doctor never came when he died. He never saw even saw him. . . . And then we never heard anything from them. Nothing. Just from our family. . . . I think the provider should at least ask someone to call, a social worker or some support person, to ask the family how they are doing. Most of them would talk, they wouldn't refuse, if you just came over or called them. Sometimes they don't want to talk on the phone. Just come over and stop by. You don't need to stay. Just stop by for five or ten minutes and then they know that you care about them. That's all. My mother kept saying, "He's been going to see the doctor for a long time, and now he has died, and nobody—." And I said, "Mom, they are doctors. They are not supposed to come." She said, "I know, but at least somebody could call and ask about us, say something." I said, "Mom, you don't need that, you have your kids. For those people who don't have a family, they should. But for us, we have family." But she still was mad at the hospital.

In Sodoeung's perception, the medical neglect of an aging man persisted in the quick dismissal of his grieving family. While hospice care, geared toward easing death, includes up to six months of bereavement support for the family, hospital care, geared toward cure, ends abruptly when the patient dies, with the exception of postmortems and temporary storage of the body. Yet it's not clear whether even a hospice offer of bereavement support would have answered Sodoeung's mother's sense of abandonment. The division of labor in hospice care assures that those who administer medicines (nurses) are different from those who give baths (personal care providers), those who explain about funeral homes and DNR forms (social workers), and those who offer bereavement support (counselors). As a British physician told Bradbury: after a death "you say goodbye to the relatives, who invariably ask you 'So what do we do now?' and I go 'I don't know, it's not really my job to deal with that, it's the relative liaison officer's'" (Bradbury 1999, 59). Sodoeung's mother is missing not so much an offer of expert assistance from a bereavement specialist as the ongoing concern of those who cared for her husband at the end of his life. Another Khmer health-care professional, Sheila, told me that many Khmer mourners say, "This doctor is so mean. He was so nice when my husband was still alive. But when he died he didn't even come and bring a candle and incense. It doesn't cost a lot of money to do that."

The hospice nurses I knew through caring for my father and for a friend with ALS were invited to the respective memorial services, and came, though each one mentioned that she didn't usually attend such events. "People are afraid to ask," Sodoeung said. "They think, 'Americans don't know and don't care.'" "That phrase—'they don't know and they don't care,'" Sheila clarified, "is used very frequently to refer to Americans, mainly hospital staff." In that phrase, she explained, the Khmer word for "they" is a derogatory word for outsiders who cannot be bothered to learn Khmer ways. One Khmer man was evidently not afraid to ask his physician, poet Peter Pereira, to grieve with him:

> Voice coarse from weeks of chanting,
> he tells me one hundred nights have passed
> since his son was killed, time now for his soul
> to emerge from the bardo,
> enter a new life. But he fears his grief
> like an upturned root
> will cause his wandering son to stumble,
> make him a shadow forever. . . .
> He asks me to go with him to the pagoda,
> help chant his son toward a happy life.
> Amid dizzying incense and ringing bells
> I join him singing the *phowa*,
> and dwell for a moment in that radiant doorway
> where birth becomes death
> and death becomes birth:
> one hand washing the other.[14]

The poem reflects the response to death that Sodoeung and others dare to imagine: a physician contemplating death, its grief, its secrets, alongside his patients and their families.

Medical Eschatologies

Contemporary disciplines of death have been shaped not only by a backlash to life-prolonging technology but also by eschatological narratives. Derrida coined the term "globalatinisation" to refer to "the effect of roman Christianity which today overdetermines all language of law, of politics." "No alleged disenchantment, no secularisation comes to interrupt it," he writes. "On the contrary" (Derrida 2001, 32). Nor does secularization interrupt the traces of Christianity in the language and ethos of medicalized death. Battin has suggested that an ideal of acquiescence toward unavoidable death deriving from Christian creation stories of death as punishment for original sin are built into contemporary bioethics (1994, 94). Gilbert, sifting through English poetry, finds as much indignation as quiet dignity in the face of death (2006, 200). Yet raging at death may also bear traces of a relationship with a Judeo-Christian personal God, whose demands for Jobian suffering prompt not only surrender but also sometimes the shaking of fists. While anger is considered one legitimate stage in a psychology of dying, dignified acceptance has been institutionalized as the most desirable response, from which the dying person hopefully will not backslide before they quietly "slip away." Moller suggests that the admonition to die with dignity works to suppress the anguish of dying in a way that "minimally disturbs and threatens the world of the living" (1990, 51), and, we might add, the world of medicine.

Theological undertones sound not only in the emphasis on dignity, but also in the deeply ingrained assumption that death represents a radical rupturing of body and soul. One physician noted to Kaufman that a man had stayed with his mother for an hour and a half after she stopped breathing. He was also "amazed" that it took the son so long to "let her die" (Kaufman 2005, 109). In his comments, the excessive time the son took to agree to the removal of the ventilator grades into the excessive time he spent with his mother after her death. Patients are implicitly disciplined to withdraw their affective attachment to the bodies of their loved ones soon after they are declared to be dead or brain-dead. Hospital discipline operates according to a hidden eschatological assumption that a dead body is, almost instantaneously, an empty shell (cf. Lock 2001). In this way a Protestant numinology organizes the modern management of death from the sidelines.

Significantly, moreover, the yearning for preindustrial dying noted at the start of this chapter is not accompanied by a parallel longing for preindustrial disposition. If the natural birth movement has prompted a revival of midwifery, the natural death movement has not provoked a return to the "deathwives" who once cleaned and laid out bodies (Bradbury 1999, 13). There has been no dismantlement of the association between odor and hygiene that developed in nineteenth-century Europe. In late nineteenth-century Britain debates over cremation still weighed a new sensory revulsion and a perceived "barbarism" of visible bodily decay against the lingering possibility of a literal resurrection of the body (15). Over the course of the twentieth century, however, the doctrine of resurrection took on a symbolic cast more compatible with a lack of cemetery space and the increased repulsiveness of the corpse. Resurrection worries bowed to clerical reassurance that "the immortal soul should, in theory, not be affected by the mode of disposal" (15). Those who find the idea of embalming and cosmetic alteration macabre can bypass viewing altogether and opt for cremation followed by the scattering of the ashes, often in a mnemonically meaningful locale.[15] Transforming the body discreetly to cremains might accommodate, even better than embalming, an implicit Christian theology that is pervaded by an anxiety about the relationship between spirit and flesh (Keane 2006).

As body and soul are increasingly disconnected in the eschatological imaginary, Euroamerican mourning has become dominated by an emphasis on memory of the living person, as previously suggested. Speaking of the Jivaro, Nigel Barley comments that "it is above all the dead who feel desperate grief and loneliness" (1995, 31). The loneliness of the dead recognized in the global south becomes noteworthy insofar as it fails to be referenced in Euroamerican rites. Despite statistics on avowed belief in afterlives (Bradbury 1999; Gilbert 2006), ethnographic accounts of Christian cemetery visits during which relatives converse with the dead (Francis, Kellaher, and Neophytou 2005), and letters to the dead posted in cyberspace (Gilbert 2006, 247), there is a self-consciously therapeutic or symbolic cast to Euroamerican interactions with the dead. The point is not that these encounters are empty of genuine belief. After all, relations with the dead among Lao, Khmer, Hmong, and Kmhmu emigrants are equally complicated by skepticism.[16] The point, rather, is that messages to the dead in Euroamerican mourning are largely detached from an imagination of the desires of the dead in an ongoing existence.[17] Memorialization epitomizes the globalatinization of attention to the dead.

The following story was told to me in several installments by a hospital staff member, Bruce, as the event unfolded at his workplace.[18] Like the story of hospice told earlier in this chapter, the story plunges us into a crisis of discipline, this time postmortem discipline with its unacknowledged but anxious attachment to cosmological stories about the relationship between matter and spirit.

A well-educated Hindu man called 911 when his mother, visiting from India, died in his arms at his U.S. home. His mother was taken by ambulance to the emergency room where she was resuscitated before undergoing another cardiac arrest. This time the EMTs were unable to revive her. Her body was transferred to the morgue, and then to a funeral home, where the son had arranged to prepare the body for cremation. He was extremely disturbed, however, to find that his mother's body had been transported naked to the funeral home, since, as he told the hospital, a married woman's body should be clothed at all times. He asked the hospital to return the garment in which she had died, so he could cremate it with her according to family custom. The garment, however, had been cut off during resuscitation efforts and could not be retrieved. One staff member suggested that the man was displacing his anger at his mother's death onto the hospital. Ultimately, there were several meetings between the son and hospital personnel. The hospital consulted an expert in cross-cultural care, who reportedly offered two suggestions: to advise the man that it was his mother's karma to have a second death; and to suggest to the man that since the gown was removed when his mother was first resuscitated, she didn't actually die in it. Meanwhile, the woman's body lay two weeks in the funeral home awaiting a resolution before the son finally had her cremated. He intended to take her ashes to the Ganges River at Benares, but a Brahmin priest advised him that his mother's soul was not yet at rest.[19]

The hospital eventually offered to make a change in their standard policy of transferring bodies unclothed to the funeral home. The son was invited to understand this procedural change as part of his mother's legacy. The man countered with three requests: a sum of money to compensate him for mental anguish; an unqualified apology; and a special service in the hospital chapel. The hospital staff were shocked. During all the negotiations, the son had always said that he wouldn't consult attorneys and wasn't interested in money. At the time, one of the hospital personnel had even told the son that this was refreshing to hear, since most Americans are only thinking of money. (In an aside, Bruce said: I have talked to so many people at the end of life, and no one ever says, I wish I'd made more money. If they have any regrets at all, they wish they had been kinder or got in touch with who they really were.) One of the administrators suggested that if a Catholic died in an Indian hospital, there might be no priest to provide the sacrament at the time of death. The man purportedly replied that his culture was "ancient," a remark that the staff interpreted as an assertion of cultural superiority. Bruce speculated that the son was projecting onto the hospital his own guilt at calling 911. If he had simply let his mother die in his arms, she would have had "the perfect death."[20]

Eventually the hospital agreed to the apology and the special service and completed a twofold policy change. First, a question was inserted into the "death list" (a list of questions to ask the patient's family immediately following death) regarding religious preferences in postmortem care. Second, each dead body would now be clothed in a paper gown for its departure from the hospital. Soon after the policy change was announced, the son said that he intended to make a donation to a charity within the hospital in honor of his mother. One staff member commented that the man must have realized that fighting with the hospital was not an appropriate way to "remember" his mother. The son had come to believe that his mother's spirit was responsible for the policy change. Bruce agreed.

This story serves as an allegory for the way that spirit and matter figure in contemporary postmortem disciplines of death. Culture plays an ambivalent role here as well, as the cross-cultural expert mines cultural knowledge for creative mediations to conflict, even to the point, when necessary, of tripping up cultural practice in its own contradictions; and as the hospital administration experiences a backlash to cultural competence, retracting from their initial accession to stereotype—when they admired the son's antimaterialist values—to resentment at his assertion of cultural antiquity. Yet cultural conflict and multiculturalist disillusionment seem mere side plots to a more central antithesis, at the heart of this tale, between religious conviction and money. As hospital personnel take offense that the son has translated his concern for his mother's spirit into a request for compensation, the story's driving undercurrent becomes indignation at the violation of the taboo against mixing material and spiritual agendas. From the hospital's perspective, the sincerity of the man's grief and his concern for his mother's spirit is undermined by the act of requesting money and validated by the act of relinquishing it. (Presumably, there is no need for the hospital to demonstrate its sincerity of grief or concern for the spirit.) How quickly the man's mourning becomes legible when he resorts to the convention of making a donation to a hospital charity in his mother's memory. The charitable gift can be read symbolically as an act of memorial homage to the dead, whereas a demand for compensation is read as a confusion of monetary gain with spiritual solace. "Talk about materialism," Webb Keane notes, "seems to incite people to a certain dematerialization in their understandings of the world. This is evident, for instance, in the effort to treat material goods as merely symbolic" (2006, 315). The way this dematerialization works, he goes on to show, is by treating material objects (such as the son's charitable donation) as signs of an immaterial value (the remembrance of his mother). Ultimately, the lesson about money and spirit is authorized by the words of the dying themselves as Bruce invokes that most pervasive of contemporary end-of-life parables, that the dying never speak wistfully about material possessions but only about kindness and self-actualization. The change in hospital policy reconfirms religious/cultural identity as the primary disciplinary category through which alternative post-mortems might be negotiated, while the paper gown enters the paper trail left by death, except that this slip of paper will be recycled rather than filed. It was the hospital's version of perfect death that the man ruined by calling 911— a peaceful death preserved from any regret by a (retrospective) foreknowl-edge of the futile and excessive technological interventions that it foregoes. Finally, there are hints of slippage in the remarkable convergence wherein Bruce agrees with the son that the credit for the new policy goes to his mother's spirit. For if the son imagines that his mother actively influenced the course of events, Bruce likely conceives of her as an absent figure in whose memory new policy was made.

What's Written on the Body

He will not light long enough
for the interpreter to gather
the tatters of his speech.
But the longer we listen
the calmer he becomes.
He shows me the place where his daughter
has rubbed with a coin, violaceous streaks
raising a skeletal pattern on his chest.
He thinks he's been hit by the wind.
He's worried it will become pneumonia.
In Cambodia, he'd be given
a special tea, a prescriptive sacrifice,
the right chants to say. But I
know nothing of Chi, of Karma,
and ask him to lift the back of his shirt,
so I may listen to his breathing. Holding the stethoscope's
    bell I'm stunned
by the whirl of icons and script
tattooed across his back, their teal green color
the outline of a map which looks
like Cambodia, perhaps his village, a lake,
then a scroll of letters in a watery signature.
I ask the interpreter what it means.
It's a spell, asking his ancestors
to protect him from evil spirits—
she is tracing the lines with her fingers—
and those who meet him for kindness.
The old man waves his arms and a staccato of
diphthongs and nasals fills the room.
He believes these words will lead his spirit
back to Cambodia after he dies.
I see, I say, and rest my hand on his shoulder.
He takes full deep breaths and I listen,
touching down with the stethoscope
from his back to his front. He watches me
with anticipation—as if awaiting a verdict.
His lungs are clear. You'll be fine,
I tell him. It's not your time to die.
His shoulders relax and he folds his hands
above his head as if in blessing.
Ar-kon, he says. All better now.

—Peter Pereira

Chapter 4   Dangerous Language

THE POEM "WHAT'S WRITTEN ON THE BODY" by the physician Peter Pereira transports us to a scene of medical practice, which over the past couple of centuries has increasingly become a primary site for communication with the dying. The verse alerts us to the way a prognosis can be a verdict of life or death. It also offers an opening for thinking through the different genres of language used to address the dying on the part of medicine and on the part of Southeast Asian laypersons and healing practitioners. Both linguistic registers are powerful in their effects, but a medical prognosis and a message to the spirits printed on the skin exercise power in different ways. While it might seem that one is a technical language of matter, and the other a magical language of spirit, each of these languages is informed by a distinctive understanding of the relationship between matter and spirit. These alternate understandings offer different possibilities for confronting death.

Lt. Somsy spoke once about the *chom mon,* or mantras, which had kept him alive during his time as a soldier in the Royal Lao Army from the 1950s to the early 1970s. He had walked for a month to reach the *achan,* or teacher, who taught him to repeat a stream of sacred words. "Instead of saying in order the Pali language you say it in reverse to make it magic, to protect the bullet from going through your skin." Before imparting the words, the *achan* tested his bravery, having him jump in a pit of sharpened bamboo and grab a thorny vine that pierced his skin to the bone. The *achan* healed the wounds by speaking magic syllables, blowing into his hand, and then touching the wounds.

Minutes later Lt. Somsy began to speak unprompted of another memory, a memory of near death from which these same *chom mon* had protected him, a memory of another pit, other barbs, a hole in the ground, covered with barbed wire, where he was held captive in a Pathet Lao prison camp. Some nights he was taken blindfolded into the jungle.

> They told me that they was going to kill me. They have spade and shovel for me so that I would dig my own grave. They told me to dig the grave, and I didn't. They hit me. Then they took me back and put me in the same underground cell. . . . They used the butt of the gun, and hit on the knee. It was swollen. . . . The man wouldn't give me any medicine. Maybe because I have the magic power that I have learned, or maybe because I have done good deeds, the power has protected me. The swelling has gone by itself.

Later he segued into an account of his escape from yet another pit in another prison camp, this time Vietnamese. He sketched a diagram of the camp on a scrap of notepaper, the guard tower, the path of the patrols, the route he had crawled on a rainy night after he and his cellmates had managed to unravel a little of the barbed wire over the pit. "I was the first who got out and after me I saw two more people, there's three of us that got out. I didn't know if they were safe or not because then they saw and they fired on us. . . . I don't know if those two were alive or if they escaped." Later on that afternoon Lt. Somsy talked about the dreams of combat that our meetings often provoked. Our conversation had the power to call back old events, and invite new ones, to leave nightmares in its wake. Words, whether the *chom mon* he recited or the war stories he recounted, were neither neutral nor inert: they could be protective, or they could be risky, even injurious. If this is true for the words of ethnographic encounters, it is no less true for the words of medical interactions.

Confessing Death

In June 1999, while I was writing a report on the initial fieldwork that inspired this book, I spent the last two weeks of my father's life at his house in Massachusetts. At ninety-two he was suffering from cancer and congestive heart failure, and since I'd last seen him he had grown progressively weaker. He no longer left the house to tend his garden and bees, and he had given away his companion of many years, a horse named Moses. My sister and I arrived the same day, relieving one of my brothers and my sister-in-law who had stayed with him around the clock for some weeks. My father was receiving out-patient hospice care from a nurse, who monitored his medications, and a personal care provider, who came each morning to give him a sponge bath, change his pajamas, and brush his teeth. He had a DNR order taped to his refrigerator, but he was not interested in talking about his death. When the local minister, whom he otherwise liked, promised him that she would return to pray with him when it was time, he was visibly annoyed. One day he asked me what treatment the doctors were currently recommending. I replied that they recommended he continue with the same medications. "Okay," he said. By then swallowing was so difficult that the only medicine he was receiving was a skin patch for the pain and morphine squirted into the side of his mouth. My father was a reserved man who grew up on a New England farm and was given to understatement. He was also heavily sedated, often disoriented, and very tired. On his last Saturday he asked for poached eggs, toast, and coffee for breakfast, after his usual few spoonfuls of oatmeal, and then for dinner a hot turkey sandwich followed by chocolate ice cream. My sister and I rushed excitedly around, fulfilling his culinary requests. We had read the hospice pamphlet: we knew his interest in food was supposed to wane and that there was no reason any more to nourish his body. But there was little enough we could offer to a taciturn, self-reliant man who resisted anything resembling a heart-to-heart talk. We fashioned our love into small acts of physical nurturance and courteously averted the topic of death. A day or two before he died my father uttered his last coherent sentence: "The hay is ready," he said. "It's time to mow."

The difference between my father's death in 1999 and my mother's death in 1973 instructively highlights a quarter-century shift in North American ideas of communicating with the dying. In 1973 hospice was still a radical concept.[1] Nonetheless my mother, often ahead of her time, had read Kübler-Ross and Mitford and had signed a living will—stating that she didn't want her life to be prolonged through artificial means—before these were legal documents.[2] She had also arranged to donate her body to a local medical school, in order to preempt expensive cosmetic alterations of her body. After several months of treatment for uterine cancer, she was hospitalized with an intestinal blockage. The surgeon opened up her abdomen, closed it again, and then called the family. Even as the doctor told us that she would die within a couple of days, he told her that they would soon start another round of chemotherapy. I resented the deception but remained silent. Within a few days my mother understood what had not been said. She lived two more weeks, refusing morphine in favor of staying lucid. We sang songs at her bedside, while she told *us* to "let go." She wondered aloud why it was so difficult to die, and then, after falling into a coma, at last she did. That night two weeks of humidity finally broke loose in a lightning storm accompanied by torrents of rain.

Ironically, dying at a time when patients were protected from their terminal prognoses, my mother took the initiative to speak of her impending death, while my father, dying in an era when self-conscious death is valorized, avoided speaking of his death. Many emigrants from Laos and Cambodia seem to find themselves similarly seized by a historical moment not of their choosing.

One day I accompanied a hospice nurse on a visit to a Lao home. The patient, Mrs. Tha, had been diagnosed with pancreatic cancer. As we drove to the house, the nurse told me that the family doubted the diagnosis, suspecting the doctors were being less than conscientious because the family was on public assistance. The nurse was concerned because at her last visit she discovered that the family had removed the patient's "pain patch." The family worried that the pain medication was not good for her. Meanwhile they were treating her with herbal medicines imported from Laos by friends and relatives. When we entered the house, the patient was lying on a hospital bed just inside the front door. Her daughter was bathing her with a warm washcloth. The nurse took the patient's temperature, listened to her lungs with a stethoscope, and offered to wash her back. The daughter handed her the washcloth. An IV tube ran from a suspended bag to a needle in Mrs. Tha's arm. When I asked the nurse about the IV, which is not usually considered comfort care, she replied, "When it's already installed, we don't mess with it." Mrs. Tha's granddaughter arrived. As the only English speaker in the family, she was the one who negotiated the terms of her grandmother's life on hospice. She was smartly dressed, having come directly from work. The patient was moaning or cooing softly, and the nurse asked the granddaughter if she was in pain. The granddaughter said that the sounds were her grandmother's way of soothing herself. When the nurse asked if she had told her grandmother her diagnosis, the granddaughter answered tactfully but firmly, "This is not a good time to tell her. Both traditionally and emotionally, it would kill her." She went on to explain to the nurse that younger Lao people want to know about their illnesses, but that her grandmother lived in the "old way." With these comments she politely rejected the practice of disclosure as well as the idea of dignified death as one that is self-conscious and free of denial. In invoking tradition she engaged the presumed multiculturalist sympathies of the white nurse, making use of an ambivalence within a medical ethics that is simultaneously committed to cultural competence and patient autonomy. On this occasion the nurse did not press the point, though a half hour later a social worker arrived to explain DNR orders.

In refusing to start a conversation with her grandmother about death, the granddaughter resisted what Foucault called confessionalism, the institutionalized incitement to speak of hidden thoughts and feelings, which is the basis of practices of psychotherapy, social work, police interrogations, and autobiographies, not to mention ethnographic conversations (Foucault 1982b, 1990), and which has been introduced in recent decades to the deathbed (Armstrong 1987b). For Foucault, confessionalism has a specifically Christian provenance, originating with the "pastoral power" exercised originally by ministers who focused attention on the interior states of their parishioners out of interest in their salvation. "This form of power," he wrote, "cannot be exercised without knowing the inside of people's minds, without exploring their souls, without making them reveal their innermost secrets" (1982b, 214). Eventually pastoral power became "an individualizing 'tactic'" productive of "truth—the truth of the individual himself" (215). In contemporary medicine, the truth of the individual who's been diagnosed with terminal illness is the truth that she is dying. Indeed, one of the most common terms for conveying a terminal prognosis to a patient is "truth-telling." The medical gaze long dedicated to "opening up corpses" (Foucault 1973, 124) turned to opening up subjectivities (Arney and Bergen 1984). The hospice nurse had been trained to honor what she understood to be a universal human need to acknowledge and speak of one's death. It was not unusual for her to comment that this or that family who wanted more aggressive treatment for their loved one was "in denial." Denial is one of five institutionally recognized psychological stages of dying (or grief) usually credited to Kübler-Ross.[3] While many scholars point out that these stages can have the effect of pathologizing those who fail to move gracefully through the sequence (Littlewood 1992; Bradbury 1999; Kleinman 1989), the notion of denial has nonetheless lodged tenaciously in popular and medical discussions of dying.

It's noteworthy that Kübler-Ross herself identified denial as more of a problem for physicians than for patients. She repeatedly insisted that medical staff should neither inform the patient that they are dying nor predict the timing of their death, since either of these might undermine their hope. Instead Kübler-Ross advocated informing patients of their diagnosis and inviting (or in Foucault's terms, perhaps inciting) them to discuss their feelings about it (1969, 1974).[4] She observed that in her experience many patients predict the timing of their own death with more accuracy than any statistical average provided by a physician. At the same time, however, she implied that in the ideal process of dying a patient would eventually arrive at the stage of acceptance through a process of anticipatory grief (1974, 36). The concept of "anticipatory grief," David Armstrong notes, is the keystone of the practice of "truth-telling," in which, as he puts it, "the chief mourners became the dying themselves" (1987b, 654).

The tenacity of a psychological narrative of denial might be due in part to its redoubling in historical accounts. Denial is framed not only as a crucial phase in a programmatic approach to dying, but also as a pivotal shift in the history of European attitudes toward death. Philippe Ariès argues that from the mid-nineteenth to mid-twentieth centuries death was removed from the heart of community life into funeral homes and hospitals (1982, 109; 1974). His account traces an arc in which death is openly acknowledged during the Middle Ages and beyond, then undergoes a hundred years of repression, and then in the late twentieth century is exposed again in a flurry of discursive unveiling of what we might call, following Michael Taussig (1999), a public secret.[5] In this narrative, the practice of disclosure becomes a liberating moment in which the patient is encouraged to confront the truth of her death. Ariès's history can be retrospectively situated as a part of the "death with dignity" movement of the 1970s in which Kübler-Ross was also a major voice. Yet Armstrong (1987b) points out that a historical account of an insti-tutionalization of denial that is resolved by a turn to dignity obscures another history, the proliferation of modern discourses of death that range from ter-minal diagnoses to biological definitions of death, from death certificates to autopsy reports, from the public files registering the time and causes of each death inaugurated in the nineteenth century to the "bereavement packet" tucked under the arm of the hospital personnel with the job of speaking to a family about the death of their loved one (Gilbert 2006, 94). These forms of speech and documentation about death were developed over the same period in which Ariès noted an intensification of denial. Within these discourses, talk of death became not taboo, but rather public, official, and scientific. Con-temporary emphasis on truth-telling then appears less as a liberating moment than as an expansion of discourse from mapping the dead corpse and its causes of death to mapping the dying patient's subjectivity and her anticipa-tion of death.

The questions Foucault asked of the often told story of sexual repression (1990, 10) have not yet been asked intently enough of the equally prevalent story of the repression of death. Is the repression of death historically accu-rate? Is the working of power in relation to death primarily repressive? Geof-frey Gorer argued in 1955 that "death and mourning are treated with much the same prudery as sexual impulses were a century ago" (quoted in Gilbert 2006, 249). Yet, as Foucault notes, the prudery about sex that prohibited "a certain way of speaking about sex, a mode that was disallowed as being too direct, crude, or coarse . . . was only the counterpart of other discourses, and perhaps the condition necessary for them to function" (1990, 30). Trans-posing death for sex in Foucault's text, we might ask:

Is it with the aim of inciting people to speak of [death] that it is made to mir-ror, at the very outer limit of every actual discourse, something akin to a secret whose discovery is imperative, a thing abusively reduced to silence, and at the same time difficult and necessary, dangerous and precious to divulge? . . . What is peculiar to modern societies, in fact, is not that they consigned [death] to a shadow existence, but that they dedicated themselves to speaking of it *ad infinitum,* while exploiting it as the secret. (35)

If death, like sex, seemed to become a dirty carnal secret over the last century and a half, it also simultaneously inspired a fascinated attention. The often noted modern embarrassment at death (Gilbert 2006, 247–64) has been the counterpart (and perhaps the necessary condition) of bureaucratic discourses of death, insofar as that very embarrassment has enabled a scientific language to masquerade as plain talk and the singularity of dying to be subsumed in psychological prescription. In the sheaves of paperwork faced by contemporary mourners, documents such as hospice pamphlets about the physical changes to be expected in the hours before death slip easily into place alongside older documents of death like death certificates, tracing a chain of bureaucratic injunctions to hold death under scrutiny. Writing of deaths in the UK, Bradbury notes that "survivors find themselves embroiled in the very complex business of unraveling the dead person's citizenship," which involves "a series of queues in private waiting-rooms and a series of interviews with professionals and pseudo-professionals in pseudo-office spaces together with endless cups of tea or coffee" (1999, 71). She goes on to observe that bereavement therapies "invariably involve even more talk" (187). The pathologization of grief has brought bereavement too under medicine's purview, generating diagnostic codes, pharmaceutical prescriptions, counseling sessions, and charted courses of recovery. Rather than a repression of death that is finally being lifted, the proliferation of inscriptive and interrogative discourse of death suggests rather an attention to death that has expanded its temporal span from the final days of the deceased to months of anticipation in one direction and weeks of therapy in the other.

Armstrong suggests that the focus on a subjective truth of death intensified as the scientific truth of death—its exact causes and precise timing—became more ambiguous. "As the secret of death . . . no longer resided with such assuredness in the depths of the body, the court of judgment demanded less the body as evidence and more the person as witness" (1987b, 656). The use of a judicial metaphor is apt since confessionalism is linked to a discourse of the modern political subject that informs the legislated ethic of patient self-determination. Over the last few decades the biomedical model of care has shifted from paternalism to legal covenant, emphasizing not so much patient trust and physician reliability, but rather patient autonomy and physician liability. While patient trust is still considered essential to medical interactions, it is now more likely to be understood as fostered by the "forthrightness" of the doctor (E. Gordon and Daugherty 2003, 143).

Truth-telling is intended to influence the self-knowledge of the patient through the medium of medical fact or, in Joseph Dumit's (1998) term, factoid. Patients are implicitly invited to own their medical prognosis, to integrate it into their understanding of themselves and their lives. Psychiatrist Holly Prigerson has referred to the patient's willingness or unwillingness to assume a "dying role" that would involve acknowledging imminent death and agreeing to receive only "comfort care" (1992, 379). Yet in the prognosis of impending death, the assimilation of the medical factoid may misfire, resulting less in "objective self-fashioning" (Dumit 1998) than fear. As one physician mused,

> Actually this is a much more complex issue than just life and death issues. If you have a possible bad diagnosis [physicians] often feel compelled to tell you all this stuff right up front before they even know what the diagnosis is. . . . They'll tell you, "Well you know you could end up with a bone marrow transplant." And that's before they even know. . . . I think that ends up terrorizing people and causing a huge amount of distress. . . . People tell folks all kinds of stuff that in earlier, more paternalistic settings they wouldn't have done. Now there's an oncologist in town who doesn't do that. . . . He's seen by many people as one of the best oncologists in town. But he doesn't lay all kinds of stuff on you. In fact, he says he avoids doing that because he doesn't want to cause more pain and agony for people. They've already got enough.

Understanding that hearing a prognosis can result in anxiety as often as acceptance, bioethicists often assess the consequences of truth-telling in a language of risks and benefits, weighing the benefits of enabling informed decisions about treatment against the risks of doing harm by intensifying a patient's fear. Some argue that beneficence takes precedence over autonomy, given that autonomy, understood as freedom of choice and the capacity for rational decisions, is already limited for the severely ill (Cassell and Duffy cited in Beste 2005, 217). Others argue that respect for autonomy is a "necessary component" of beneficence (Beste 2005, 230), or conclude that truth-telling is necessarily beneficial because statistically it leads to "appropriate treatment choices" (Gordon and Daugherty 2003, 143). Still other bioethicists suggest respect for autonomy must embrace the right to nondisclosure for those patients who choose that option (Berger 2005; Cain et al. 1990; Seale 1991;

Fan and Tao 2004; Da Silva et al. 2003). Several scholars also suggest that for family-identified patients (who, in the medical literature, are often ethnically marked) autonomy is less primary than family harmony and interdependence (Blackhall et al. 1995; Mystakidou et al. 2004; Tuckett 2004). In China, families have taken physicians to court on the charge of harming a patient through truth-telling (Fan and Li 2004, 182).[6] To complicate truth-telling in this way with a commitment to cultural competence is to acknowledge that there are circumstances in which truth-telling may be impractical or offensive. Yet this exercise barely scratches the patina of the philosophical principles that inform truth-telling, even as it smuggles into the dialogue what may be the most deceptively benign evasion of ethical contemplation, the principle of cultural appropriateness. While bioethicists ask how far we can universalize principles of autonomy and privacy (Hartman 1996, 320; McCarthy 2003, 66; Zussman 1997, 174) that are contingent on a specifically European historical trajectory, I am seized instead by the question of why we should be more accountable, in end-of-life care, to philosophical abstractions rather than, say, to spirits.

Then again, perhaps bioethical principles are rooted in their own theory of ghosts. Jeffrey Berger argues that disclosure of a terminal diagnosis affords a crucial opportunity to "existentially, e.g. spiritually and emotionally, experience the illness." He writes that while hearing a terminal prognosis may be painful, it helps to "form one's life narrative," leading to "insights, understandings, and other transforming events" (2005, 95–96). Berger's remarks make it clear that the communication of a terminal prognosis is not just a medical pronouncement on the condition of a person's body, but an active intervention in their life story. But his comments also presume that the experience of disclosure will lead to a deepening of self-awareness in a process of personal transformation that is consistent with the individuating thrust of Protestant Christianity. Patient self-determination, in this view, is not just a matter of decision making, but also a matter of a purposeful interior gaze.

During a hospital ethics meeting I attended in 1999, staff were discussing a conflict with an Ibo family over telling their father his terminal diagnosis. After evoking the principle of patient autonomy, one doctor remarked that if he went along with the family he could tell himself "I'm great; I'm going with the cultural flow," resting in a multiculturalist self-satisfaction. On the other hand, he worried that "hiding the truth" from the patient would foreclose an opportunity for spiritual growth. The patient should have the chance to reflect on his life, sound his depths, and confront his death. Here the pastoral past of confessionalism comes full circle in a modern medico-spiritual agenda. Truth-telling institutionalizes an ideal of an expressivist, introspective, and autono-mous self (cf. Taylor 1989), confronting itself in its final moments.

One Khmer family on hospice refused to tell their twelve-year-old son that he was dying of a brain tumor, continuing to seek out all treatment options from acupuncture and Chinese herbs to emergency resuscitations. As the boy's white stepfather commented to me, "A five thousand-year-old medicine must have something going for it." One morning, after the boy had been on hospice only a few weeks, he was coughing blood and could not be awakened. His mother called the nurse to ask if they could call 911. Although the nurse often warned families that a call to 911 could revoke their hospice status, in this case she agreed. The hospice for which she worked had what they called an "alternative pathway" for children in which they bypassed the DNR order and allowed more aggressive treatments, permitting the children to be "pla-teaued," remaining on hospice even if they were not "progressing in illness." The boy was taken to the hospital and put on a ventilator. When the family later agreed to have him removed from the machine, he breathed for a short while on his own and then took three deep breaths and died. The hospice nurse voiced to me her regret that the boy had never had a chance to "articulate his fears." Not only had his family been unwilling to talk with him about dying, but also, on advice of the boy's grandmother, they had not made any funeral arrangements in advance. After his death, they declined hospice's offer of bereavement counseling and dedicated themselves instead to preparations for a seven-day funeral. During that ceremony, as I elaborate in the next chap-ter, death would have been openly discussed for the benefit of not only the family, but also the boy himself.

Here, the commitment to nonresuscitation is deliberately abandoned, the ideal of conscious and counseled death is refused, and the advice on prepar-ing funeral arrangements in advance is ignored. In the language of bioethics, a principlism that weighs the values of autonomy, beneficence, nonmalefi-cence, and justice has given way to a narrative ethics in which moral choices are shaped to fit the life stories of the people involved (McCarthy 2003). While principlist bioethics is a morality of strangers that privileges systematicity and neutrality, narrative ethics is a morality of relationship that prioritizes situa-tion and intimacy, exploring the tensions among different life trajectories. In narrative ethics, nursing scholar Joan McCarthy observes, "vulnerability and suffering haunt each ordinary encounter and cannot be acknowledged or addressed simply by obedience to rules" (2003, 69). Interestingly, McCarthy's choice of words here opens bioethics, perhaps unconsciously though not by chance, to the uncanny. In haunted encounters, we sense the presence of spirits that might otherwise be reasoned away.

Risky Words

Whether or not the Khmer boy with the brain tumor would have chosen to openly discuss his death, his grandmother, who lived with the family and was continually consulted by the boy's mother and stepfather, worried that such discussion might weaken him further. The communication of impending death that in the view of the doctor at the ethics meeting was an important spiritual intervention seemed, for this family, a risky spiritual interference. A Khmer Buddhist monk confirmed that most Khmer would prefer that the physician convey a terminal prognosis not to the patient herself, but rather to the family. Telling the patient directly might have the effect of making her even more ill, he said. A Khmer medical interpreter told me that when she's asked to interpret a terminal prognosis to a patient she tries to avoid using the word for death. If it's not possible, she may tell the patient, "This is how this country works. But I hate to say this word to you. I'm sorry to say this word." "Instead of going straight across the bridge," she said, moving her hand in a straight line from one point to another over the surface of the table between us, "I go the other way." And she glided her hand in a semicircle between the same two points. She cited a Khmer adage that to directly name an event is to invite it closer. Sodoeung offered, "I know the doctor has an ethic that they have to tell the patient. . . . Sometimes it makes it worse. If they are supposed to live two years, and you tell them, they will probably just live one year or six months. . . . It makes the patient afraid. . . . They don't want to talk to anyone. They become depressed and isolated."

One Lao man Lt. Somsy knew was asked if he had made arrangements for his burial. "'Have you bought a place for your grave yet? Did you save your money for your funeral?' It made the person think a lot, couldn't sleep for many days, and later fell ill and died." Lt. Somsy went on, "The doctor should not tell the patient that he or she is going to die. . . . Let the family members know in secret without letting the patient know. . . . If the patient knows, he would be very discouraged, be heartbroken. He would be very depressed and would think too much." "It's not a good idea to tell someone," Bouakhay agreed. "If I received that kind of news I would be very upset and frustrated and sad." Like physicians in the United States for much of the twentieth century, health practitioners in Laos rarely discuss the possibility of death with their patients. "Usually they just tell the relatives secretly," Major Samsuthi said, "because they don't want to disappoint the ill person." As Douang put it: "People say that it's bad luck. Sometimes the patient says, 'If I die, I want you to do this and that.' Even then the children tell the person, 'Be quiet. Shut up, you are not going to die. Let's not talk about that.'" "It shocks people," Douang added, "the way the doctor [in the United States] says it. . . . The danger of telling the person directly is that it could exacerbate the symptoms or shorten the person's life." As Mrs. Tha's granddaughter said during the hospice visit, "If I tell grandmother now, she will give up hope." A Lao monk spelled out the spiritual danger of disclosure from his perspective: "Telling the truth to the patient will discourage him and weaken his *khwan* [usually translated as souls].[7] A hospital patient has already lost some *khwan*. And when the doctor tells him, 'You have this kind of illness,' that scares him into losing more *khwan*." To talk about a person's death in advance is precisely the wrong sequence of powerful words, a dangerous linguistic performance with the power to weaken the patient's souls or jolt them out of the body. If certain words, like Lt. Somsy's *chom mon*, have the power to protect, other words have the power to harm.

Raising the question of truth-telling with Mr. Chea and his friends provoked a lively debate. Most thought that whether or not a physician should convey a terminal prognosis to a patient depended on the patient's temperament. Some said they themselves would prefer to be told, so that they could arrange to travel or see friends before they died, but that others are too afraid of death. Everyone agreed that the doctor should consult the family first about whether or not a patient should be told, and follow the family's guidance. As Mr. Chea put it, "For people who are afraid to die, precaution is best. If the doctor has told someone that he will die tomorrow or the next day, and then he is still around, he might get angry at the doctor, just like at a fortune-teller, for telling a lie about his life." Here Mr. Chea puts a new spin on physician liability, where the doctor might be held accountable not for the mistake of allowing the patient to believe he can live, but for the mistake of wrongly predicting that he will die. In identifying the physician's prognosis as a form of fortune-telling, he reminds us of the uncontrollability of death, which does not conform well to predictions, whether statistical or mystical. He also politely suggests that in any given situation truth-telling might turn out to be a lie. Listening to such conversations it is clear that wariness of the powerful language wielded in U.S. hospitals is less a symptom of denial than a perspective emerging out of spirited ethical inquiry, in every sense of the first adjective.

Khmer and Lao suggest that communication about death should be initiated by the dying themselves or, in its more specialized vocabularies, by monks. Douang explained,

Monks talk about death; they talk about heaven; they talk about hell. People don't find it unlucky for monks to talk about death, because the monk usually talks in a kind of general way, not answering specific questions. If you say, "Your holiness, I'm going to die soon, the doctor told me," the monk would say, "Everybody who is born, dies. Have you done good deeds? If you haven't, then you should do something about that."

In the same conversation cited above, Mr. Chea and his friends also spoke eloquently about the Buddhist ideal of conscious dying. Many of them recalled the death of monks or practiced meditators whose ability to accurately predict their time of death was rooted in Buddhist austerity. "In Cambodia I've seen this happen many times," Mr. Chea said. "One person suddenly knew that he was going to die at two o'clock. He told his children to let everybody know and to invite the monk to do *saut kavada* and *saut pitam* [Pali verses chanted for the seriously ill or dying]."

> The family did as the man said. But they also wondered if it was really true that he would die because he seemed fine. When the monk started chanting everyone listened. They forgot to watch the ill person. Around two-thirty the monk realized, "Oh, he said he would die at two o'clock." They tried to listen to his breathing. They put cotton in front of his nose, but the cotton didn't move. And when they put a hand on his shoulder, his body fell back.

Another woman chimed in, "It happened to my brother too. He was a monk. He knew he was going to die at a certain time, at eleven thirty. He told his family members to provide him with four special dishes of food. They put it on a tray, and after he had a spoon from each of the dishes, he told them to put him to bed. He went to sleep and he died." "People like that," Mr. Chea said, "are people who don't have any sin in this world. No karma." The ability to inwardly sense one's imminent death is an attainment arrived at through mental discipline and merit. This knowledge, honed through Buddhist practice, differs from a prognosis fashioned from measurements of physical condition and statistical percentages. In these stories the dying person foretells his time of death not from a medical assessment, but from an intuitive or kinesthetic sense. The spiritual practice here is not to gracefully internalize the death announced by the doctor (as imagined by the physician at the ethics meeting referenced earlier), but to sense one's death and announce it to others. At first glance, this foreknowledge of death seems to resemble the self-knowledge that confessionalism seeks to instill in an autonomous, interiorized subject. The knowledge of the Buddhist adept, however, arises not out of a reflexive exploration of individuated selfhood, but rather out of a distancing from personal history through a recognition of the self as an ephemeral construction (cf. Klima 2002).

Cheuang, the Kmhmu healer, also thought that soul loss was a probable consequence of truth-telling. "If you hear that, your soul will leave right away. The *hrmàal* will go out of your body." Other Kmhmu spoke of a more ambiguous dispiritedness. One woman Kampheang knew was diagnosed with breast cancer. "From that day she was down. Down and down and down and down. In only six months she was gone. She got too disappointed. . . . Why let the patient know? Just let it go. And they will not be counting the days until they are going to die." Hmong told similar stories. Pheng recalled a man who died within one week of being diagnosed with AIDS. "I've had AIDS training," Pheng said. "Usually people don't die of AIDS right away. . . . He had no more hope."[8] Mr. Lo concurred, "Most people don't want the sick person to know his or her condition. They feel that could make the person even worse."

Speaking of death can be risky, not only because it weakens the patient, but also because words or acts that refer to certain scenarios might call those scenarios into existence. Lt. Phanha told this instructive Kmhmu tale:

> There was one guy who went hunting with his friend. His friend fell asleep under a tree. When he saw his friend asleep, he started crying and telling his friend to leave and telling him where to go, as he had heard people do when someone had died. While he was crying like that he suddenly realized his friend had died. He said, "Oh no, what should I do? What should I do?" So he cried in a different way to tell the guy to come back. And the guy came back. And then he knew that he shouldn't have cried the way people cry when someone has died.

The Kmhmu woman Julie Prachitham recalled an incident from her childhood in Laos when she was playing with a group of friends.

> We dug a hole and we put a friend in it, and then we cried, we pretended that she was dead. A month later she actually died, and her family "sued" four or five of us, saying that she died because we did that. We didn't have a court, but they said, "Okay you have to pay our *róoy kàan* [paternal ancestor] because you did this." They took the matter to the elders of the village. Each family had to pay a pig and a special French coin that is silver. We were Catholic, but that family was not. We didn't do it on purpose. We just thought it was a joke.

Although Julie's family might have regarded the children's play as mere mimicry of death, they were held accountable for the apparent sympathetic magic of their performance. One does not play lightly with the idioms of death.

From her birth, Julie's parents had considered her to be too vulnerable to have contact with the dead or the offerings to the dead. When she was born, a *móo du* declared her to be *luk tai,* that is, a "foreign [Lao] baby."[9] The *móo du* strongly advised her parents to limit her interactions with the dead. Even though her family was Christian, she visited a cemetery only once as a child. Afterward she was so seized with fear that she cried until a *móo du* performed a healing ceremony for her. After that she did not visit burial sites or view dead bodies except for once when her sister died, and then much later when her father-in-law passed away in the mid-1990s.

> My mom would say, "No, you can't go." Every time. "No, you can't go." So I never went. Even when my father's younger brother's wife's mother died, I couldn't go because my mother said no. But when my father-in-law died she said, "How do you feel?" I said, "I don't know." And she said, "Okay, you can go." So I went that once, and I felt like "Oh my God." I felt shaky afterward. I think it did disturb my *hrmàal.* Now I feel like I don't ever want to go back there. My brother-in-law, my sister-in-law, and my kids go after church on Sunday. They bring some offering to the grave. They always want me to go with them, and I don't want to go.

Several Hmong recalled people who chose to die in full consciousness of their death, even when this consciousness was mediated by medicine. Telling the story of her father-in-law's death, Mrs. Vangay said, "He had a chance to ask the doctor about his condition, and the doctor told him that he would never be cured. So if there was something he wanted to eat he should go ahead. Or if there was somewhere he wanted to go or visit or travel, he should go ahead. He should enjoy his life." Mr. Vangay recalled,

> When the doctor talked to the family it was not a private meeting. . . . I didn't have the guts to stand up and tell my father. But after the doctor told us we were crying. I said to my father, "Although the doctor said this, we will have hope for you, we will see how long you live." That's all. . . . I think the doctor did right. . . . My father's younger brother, he also said that it was the right way to talk. . . . Usually the *txiv neeb* are very weak. They don't have the guts to stand up and say, "You're going to die." They always say, "Oh, you're going to get well. You're going to get well." Just to cover it up.

Faced with the North American practice of truth-telling, some Hmong evaluate its ethic and find it consistent with their own. Pao Chang based his support of truth-telling in part on his respect for the doctor's knowledge.

I don't know about other people, but to me, I think that the way doctors open up honestly to the ill person is the best idea. To tell straight that the person is dying or they are not able to cure, so that a person can prepare him or herself. Maybe for someone else, no, but for me that is the best, the important thing.

Mrs. Vangay, on the other hand, was ambivalent about truth-telling. "As for me," she said, "I don't want to tell the patient, make him feel so sorry for himself. In my father-in-law's case, though, he actually asked the doctor, 'Whatever I have, let me know, tell me ahead. Don't hide anything.' So the doctor did that." She paused, then added, "He was still able to live life. He was eating and talking. When that happened I felt sad for him. I loved him. . . . That made me feel like, 'He's right here. How can the doctor say he's going to die?'" Working to contextualize Mrs. Vangay's feelings, the interpreter added:

> She didn't see the inside condition; she only saw the picture outside, his regular, daily routine. In her mind dying is associated with somebody who is bed-bound, who cannot see or hear any more. But her father-in-law was still able to talk. He was eating and walking around as usual, like any day in the past. . . . Also she loved him. That's why she would say, "You are not a sick person who's going to die." She loved him. The words came from the doctor's mouth and went into her mind. She felt a lot of worry. He was so worried too. He cried a lot. At the time that I talked with him he told me one of his worries was that he was scared of dying.

Here the interpreter, as ad hoc anthropologist, identified the specialized interior gaze of medicine on which contemporary terminal prognosis often hinges, contrasting it with Mrs. Vangay's focus on the rhythms of her father-in-law's daily life. Mrs. Vangay's comment alongside the interpreter's exegesis hint at conflicting intentions of language as conveyor of information or purveyor of emotion.

Pharmakopoetics

A bioethical turn from principles to personal narratives seems to clear a path from a restrictive language of futility, palliation, and pain scales toward more open-ended, heterogeneous languages. Yet attention to life stories, like Kübler-Ross's attention to affective experiences of dying, can easily devolve, in medical settings, into technical vocabulary. Recall the Filipino family in the previous chapter who took their mother to the emergency room when she began gasping for breath. The following day they were advised by the hospice nurse to consider their mother's "quality of life." "Would you like to be fed through a

tube down your nose?" Ironically, references to quality of life in medical interactions typically signal that medical staff have decided it's time to permit death
(Kaufman 2005, 151). In the late 1990s there was a move in hospice to
administer quality-of-life questionnaires to assess patients' priorities for their
experience of dying. Patients were asked, for instance, whether they were more
concerned about remaining lucid or averting pain. Some hospice workers I
spoke with thought that although the questionnaire was an admittedly Euro-
centric instrument it might nonetheless overcome the subjectivism of simply
having a conversation. Yet a narrative ethics that shies away from the subjectivism of conversation in favor of the apparent objectivity of a questionnaire
seems to reenter principlism by the back door. Can we imagine a medical ethics
that would have the grit to stay in the story without measuring the quality of
life? The quality of life of someone with a tube threaded into their nasal passage often works as the discursive inverse of the quality time that caregivers
are advised to spend with their loved one. When the Filipino patient's son
tried to talk to the hospice nurse about his mother's blood pressure and oxygen levels, the nurse suggested that he forget about the "mechanics" of his
mother's treatment and "concentrate on spending quality time" with her.
"Sing to her," she suggested, at which point, the woman's daughter interjected,
laughing, "Yes, I've been singing to her." The phrase "quality time" works to
assign commodity value to the helpless poignancy of offering spoonfuls of food
to someone who may not live to digest them. The phrase attaches a connotation of expertise and control to a dying that wildly exceeds either one.

Submersed in such languages of care, some resist truth-telling out of a
choice to confront death silently. As Pheng noted of some Hmong families,

> Deep inside their minds, they have a preparation for where they are going
> to bury him or her, what kind of [ceremony]. . . . But they don't say it out
> loud. . . . They say, "Try to save her, I don't believe she is going to die." Inside
> they have clear thinking. . . . But they don't want to mention it. It would hurt
> the person. For the person, "I'm not even dead yet and you are already prepar-
> ing." Like that.

When I asked Mrs. Vangay whether family members of a seriously ill person
would speak of their fears that the person might die, she responded, "They
wouldn't talk about it much. They would express it only with the burial clothes,
by embroidering them and setting them aside."

Of her first husband's death in the United States the Lao woman Bouakhay said, "He could sense that he would not make it. . . . He did not say much
to me. . . . He tried to prepare things and keep things in order. . . . I also knew

from the papers, the reports from the doctors, so I didn't ask him. He didn't say anything to me either about that he was not going to make it. It was just like we understood each other." For families who communicate without words when death is close, truth-telling can be overkill, even literally. As Sodoeung said, "People know. They are sick day and night, in and out of the hospital all the time. . . . They don't want to hear someone say, 'You are going to die. . . .' It shocks them. We know it and we keep it inside."

To read this silence as repression would be to assimilate it to the scandalous secrecy that truth-telling purports to expose. Stories of silence in which "we just understood each other" are not subsumable to either Ariès's history or Kübler-Ross's psychology of the denial of death. The ones who tell such stories also tell stories of frustration at being unable to smell and see the smoke of the cremation fire, and stories of grateful relief at being asked to clean the bones of a parent who has been dead and buried for a year. This silence suggests that we might most intimately touch the everydayness and enigma of death in the resonant spaces beyond and between what is said. This silence refuses the interpellation of a terminal prognosis (Althusser 1971), without pretending to refuse death itself.

If interpellation is a performative speech act through which a subject is constituted by an address (Butler 1997a, 24–25), truth-telling as interpellation is a performative utterance that constitutes a patient as terminally ill. The pronouncement of a terminal prognosis might seem to be a perlocutionary rather than illocutionary performative (Austin 1965) in that it does not so much instate its effects as provoke them, inaugurating a shift from curative to palliative care. The Lao monk and others, however, identify a performativity in truth-telling that borders on illocution, however inadvertent, by materially facilitating death. Judith Butler points out that no performative statement "works" without an accumulated, yet concealed "historicity of force" (1997a, 51). What she does not explicitly address are the ways that any given performative may be sedimented with different, even conflicting histories. For contemporary medicine, the communication of a terminal prognosis is an avowal of a once suppressed secret, an honoring of the patient's recently won right to foreknowledge of her death. For the family of an emigrant patient, on the other hand, the same communication may constitute an institutionalized abandonment of the elderly, the impoverished, or the racially marked that might set their souls adrift.

The linguistic status of truth-telling is more complicated still, however. From the perspective of medicine, truth-telling does not constitute a dying subject, but simply *unveils* her. Truth-telling is thought to name death through a reading of signs, not to summon it. Death, although in the future, is identified as foreknown, and therefore prior to and productive of the prognosis, rather than the other way around. Despite perlocutionary consequences, then, truth-telling, like other medical language, is treated as constative, in John Austin's (1965) sense, as conveying information, rather than as performative like Lt. Somsy's *chom mon,* effecting changes in the physical world.[10] Nonetheless fact-laden medical language is also obliquely perlocutionary, insofar as it maintains professional distance, manages patients', families', and physicians' emotions, and shapes compliance. As Shigehisa Kuriyama (1999) illuminates, biomedical language reflects a longing for clarity resting on a continually reinstated distinction between objective fact and subjective perception. Physicians have labored for centuries to minimize affective or poetic inferences in medical language. Yet neither the careful policing of relations between words and their referents nor a calculated flatness of tone can entirely filter out performative subtexts. It is hardly surprising, then, if some patients, attuned to the material power of utterance and the eloquence of silence, hear truth-telling not as an offer of information, but as a gesture of dismissal, a consignment to the community of the dying.

The social abandonment that may be communicated in truth-telling is accentuated by its enclosure in a field of medical performance that seems to emigrants to contribute to their marginalization or early deaths. On one visit to the Tha family, the granddaughter mentioned that she suspected that her family had been hurried out of the hospital because of being on Medicaid. The oncologist only spoke to them for five minutes, she said. The hospice nurse assured her that doctors have no time for any of their patients, no matter the payment plan. The granddaughter went on to say that one of the doctors had frightened her by implying that her grandmother was dying, while another failed to explain why her grandmother was taking a certain drug. Within such an ambience of suspicion, truth-telling becomes simply one of many life-threatening practices pressed on her family.

After faulting a physician for telling her Kmhmu friend she would die within a month, Julie's mother-in-law, Mrs. Prachitham, recalled, "Back in Laos, when you visit someone who's really sick, you always say, 'Oh you'll get better soon, don't worry.' . . . We feel compassion for the person's spirit." To understand such reassurances as dishonest or secretive is to mistake their primary force as the conveyance or withholding of information. These phrases are intended not as information, but as comfort. In their acknowledged performativity, they are capable only of being felicitous (or infelicitous), but not inaccurate (Austin 1965). Such statements communicate less through referentiality than through gentleness. They are more akin to washing someone's face, lifting her head onto a fresh pillowcase, or slipping spoonfuls of soup between her lips than they are to foretelling the future. As Kathy Culhane-Pera noted for Hmong, a refusal to tell someone she is dying is neither "lying" or "denying" but "expressing care" in a specific "idiom of support" (Culhane-Pera et al. 2003, 289).

If emigrants are wary of speaking directly to an ill person about death, they are no less intent on hearing what she might say to them from death's threshold. A Lao monk told me the story of a woman who was bitter because the hospital staff had not allowed her to stay with the patient. "It's very important for people to be with the patient just before the last breath," he said.

> Usually they know that it is the last day or the last hour. That's also why the patient likes to have their wife or husband or children nearby. There might be something they haven't told their loved ones yet, and they want to tell them at that moment before they pass away. When it comes to the last breath, all they can do is tell something to the living ones, so they want to do that.

Sodoeung noted that some hospitals do not have large enough rooms to accommodate the numbers of Khmer who want to visit the patient. "When they stay home they feel regret if something happens to their person and they are not there to see him, talk to him." Because of a longing to gather around the dying, many emigrants consulted prefer to take the patient home. Mrs. Vangay spoke of her family's decision to take her father-in-law out of the hospital.

> At home, at his last breath, we were able to raise him up and let the whole family see him. Everyone loved him and wanted to help him in his last breath. . . . I don't know why it's important for everyone to see his last breath. It's what the elders keep telling us, that at the last breath, we need to raise him up. The Hmong words literally mean "raise the mountain." It means to raise his head to see the ones he's leaving behind. At that moment he wishes good luck to the children and grandchildren. Whoever is left behind receives a blessing from him.

Lifting the head is also thought to allow everyone present to receive the dying person's wisdom (Anderson and Walker 2003, 274). In these accounts, rather than eliciting a patient's confession to her impending death, family and friends seek out her last words of advice and benediction for the living.

Within a bioethical framework, truth-telling works as a *pharmakon* in the sense considered by Plato and investigated more recently by Derrida, a statement poised between its dangerous power to frighten the patient and its beneficial power to deepen her spiritual engagement with her death. In Plato's metaphorical discussion of writing as *pharmakon,* Derrida (1981) finds intimations of an ultimately European ambivalence about writing, and about language itself. While in some passages of *Phaedrus* Socrates speaks of the *pharmakon* of writing as a useful remedial aid to speech and memory, in others he portrays it as a potentially harmful supplemental rhetoric that clouds the presumed transparency of memory's access to truth. Yet Socrates himself uses letters. He is therefore motivated to imagine a writing that would be mysteriously immediate to knowledge, inscribed "in the soul of the learner." "Would it be fair," Phaedrus asks, "to call the written discourse only a kind of ghost *(eidolon)* of [that other unmediated discourse]?" "Precisely," Socrates replies (cited in Derrida 1981, 148).

In the logic of bioethics as sketched above, a terminal prognosis sustains a certain pharmakological tension, provoking arguments that echo the ruminations of *Phaedrus,* over whether truth-telling is more (psychologically) harmful or (spiritually) beneficial. While, on the one hand, truth-telling grants the dying patient only a mediated, medical assessment of her death, on the other hand it might awaken a confrontation with death that, in a certain bioethical imaginary, is written in her soul. The *pharmakon* has the bite of a venomous snake, Derrida observes (1981, 118). Certain bioethicists accordingly imagine truth-telling as a bitter medicine for the spirit, for those who have the strength to swallow it. Any harm it might generate is understood as the emotional side effect of that potent drug that is the truth of death itself.

From the emigrants' perspectives, on the other hand, the words of a terminal prognosis sometimes seem to be dipped in poison, in the way that Lt. Somsy's *chom mon* or the words tattooed on the Khmer patient's back in Pereira's poem are infused with protection. Such words elude a European metaphysics that wrestles with writing's remove from meaning, or the separation of speech from the inner thoughts of the speaker. The words of Lt. Somsy's *chom mon* are powerful not as reference but as substance, spoken into his skin. This language does not so much represent safety as confer it, as the incantatory powers of the syllables themselves turn death aside. Understood from that angle, truth-telling can be dangerous in the same way that *chom mon* is protective, not as a pharmakological supplement to the patient's interior soul searching, but as sympathetic magic. Can we imagine a bioethics that would acknowledge both informative and performative, factual and magical, denotative and evocative dimensions of language?

Over the last decade a few hospitals have been inspired to develop a policy to permit consent not to be informed. Under such a policy, patients may choose the option of having their families informed, instead of themselves, about potential outcomes such as death. Inuit communities, on the other hand, have removed both informed consent and advance directives from their health-care services altogether (Robert Putsch, personal communication). A social worker at a nursing home serving Asian communities told me that interpretation of advance directive requirements has become more lenient in his state. Now, he said, it is possible for a family to sign a "values statement," an affidavit attesting, for instance, "I am a member of the patient's immediate family and I testify that his values are such that he would prefer not to be told he is dying." All such bureaucratic reforms, however, are still rooted in the concept of the subcultural exception whereby liberal tolerance is extended by virtue of philosophical arrogance. Joseph Carrese and Lorna Rhodes (1995) observe that many Navajo feel that the communication of a terminal prognosis violates *hózhó*—a word connoting beauty, goodness, and harmony. What might it mean to read such knowledge, not as a set of beliefs to be accommodated in limited ways, but as a theoretical response to the philosophical tradition that informs truth-telling? What might a bioethics be that was committed in the first instance to language that is beautiful, gentle, or melodious?

. . . return here, O soul, O spirit,
return to stay in our village,
return to stay in our house!
Return to live with your children and wife,
return to live with your father and mother,
return to live with your brothers and sisters!
Return to stay under the long crossbeams,
return to stay under the high ridge,
return to stay by the lighted fire at the cosy fireplace.
Return and eat the abundant rice,
return and eat the salt from the drying-rack.
During the season of rain continuous rain,
don't run away, don't roam
fearing spirits and tigers.

—from a Kmhmu soul-calling ceremony

Chapter 5 Syllables of Power

WHEN LANGUAGE IS WIELDED as sympathetic magic, certain words have the power to call death, and others, like Lt. Somsy's *chom mon,* to avert it. If trust in medicine was eroded in wartime Laos and Cambodia, reliance on magical healing may have intensified. As deaths and disappearances oscillated with miraculous survivals and rescues, war accentuated dependence on mysterious agents, including ceremonial syllables that might powerfully influence well-being. Such syllables work through a healing substance that inheres in the sounds or script, or through a direct address that lures a soul back into the world of the living or, after death, guides a soul to the ancestors. Either way, they are avowedly performative, influencing courses of life and death.

Sodoeung told this story of a monk she met during the Khmer Rouge years:

There was one temple where they put a lot of ill kids. At that time I was very sick, so they put me in that place. That was a hospital where they also tortured and killed people. My girlfriend was related to a monk who was 103 years old. He had an eyesight problem and couldn't see. He was very fat, and he was still wearing the red garments.[1] The Khmer Rouge tried to kill him a lot of times. Each time they went down on their knees and said good things to him. They had planned to murder him, but they could not do anything. I think he had some kind of power. He was still living in the temple, first in the big monastery. Then later on they transferred him to a small place under a tamarind tree. It was just like a birdhouse; it was very small. My friend went to visit him all the time. When she came back from seeing him she always brought something for me to eat. I didn't have enough food, because when you were sick and you couldn't work, they wouldn't give you food. One day I decided I would go to see him without my friend. I didn't knock on the door, I opened it, and he said, "Oh, I know you. You came with my granddaughter before. What do you want?" I didn't say anything. He just knew. He said my name. I talked to him in the way monks speak. And he said, "Who are your parents and where are they now?" And I said, "I don't know." He said, "How did you learn how to speak the way monks talk?" I said my grandmother was in the temple for thirty years and so I learned. And he said, "That's good." And then later on he said, "Don't worry. I know that they torture you a lot, but you won't die. You will have a long life, my child." I thought, "Am I dreaming or what?" That was the man who helped me. And he was funny too. I was skinny because of starvation. Every time I walked, I fell and passed out. Somebody had to drag me to that place and I had to lie down, because I didn't have anything to eat. He just said, "Oh, you're lazy."

Sodoeung laughed. "Then later on he said, 'Just eat a lot, okay?' and I said, 'I don't have anything to eat.'"

My friend began to bring me food. She said her grandfather gave it to her to share with me. I stayed there almost three months. I think at that time I also had some cholera or something. Diarrhea, vomiting. They didn't have any medicine for us to take. There was just an herbal medicine. The *krou khmer* [khmer healer/herbalist] made it from rabbit's poop. That was something they gave because they didn't have other supplies.

Later, after the Vietnamese had overthrown the Khmer Rouge, and Sodoeung was reunited with her family, she went to visit the monk again.

I was sick and I thought, "I need to see this person. Why can't they kill him?" That's why I went back to see him again. I had some kind of infection in my eye; on the right side I couldn't see. It was bloody. At that time there were no doctors. So I went back to him. I walked there, and he knew me from far away. He said, "Oh, that's you again. Come here. I know who you are. Why don't you go home?" I said, "I don't have a home, because they went through our house and took everything." He told me to come close to him. "I know you are sick. You have some kind of problem." I didn't talk that much. I said, "Oh, I just wanted to know if you can help me to see again out of my right eye. My left is okay." So he said, "Okay. I don't know. I'll try." So he just said something and he blew on my eye, and then I got home and I got better. I didn't take any medicine, nothing. Then before I left Cambodia, I went back to say goodbye to him. And he said to me that he would never see me again. And I said, "Why?" He said because he was old and he probably wouldn't live that long. He died in 1989. Some of the villagers sent a letter to me and a picture of his ceremony.

A number of tales of healing wind their strands through this story. Note, once again, the absence of reliable medicine. Note the temple that has been turned into a torture chamber-cum-hospital and the refusal of food to the sick. Into this absence of medicine and excess of violence, pour the monk's miraculous powers, his ability to see Sodoeung from afar with sightless eyes, his mantras and sacred breath, his talent for forcing the Khmer Rouge into a devotional bow each time they come to kill him. Picture his funeral when people of nearby villages would have offered a cornucopia of food and gifts wrapped with white string, and monks would have chanted for his spirit around the clock. Those who have long since fled the country, and so cannot dig through his ashes for lucky tokens, receive instead a snapshot of his death rite in the mail. Such photos offer a consoling contact with his death, an object touched by its light. Through it all, notice the healing words—like those the monk spoke as he blew on Sodoeung's eye—and their power to deflect death. Ignoring his interpellation by the Khmer Rouge as a person marked for death, the monk persists in speaking in another vein, and dying in his own sweet time.

Healing Syllables

The repertoire of healings and extensions of life available to emigrants in the United States are reminiscent of the powerful words and practices that offered protection during war and its aftermaths. Khmer still seek healing not only from monks but from *krou khmer* and other lay practitioners. One woman I met specialized in massaging broken bones and sprains.

> I use ointments, and I also know words to chant. While I'm doing the massage or releasing the bone I chant the words and blow air onto the person. If a person has dislocated her wrist or ankle, I feel the skin and then use tiger balm or some kind of ointment and blow on the spot and chant. The words are Pali or Sanskrit. Sometimes we translate them into Khmer. They are secret words. They cannot be told.

Some *krou* set broken bones with a flexible cast; others heal fevers with herb teas. Almost all these practices are accompanied by syllables that help to mend flesh and bone. When Mrs. Sann was a child, her mother consulted *krou* almost exclusively. "We didn't have money to go to the hospital. Once I had a fever. The *krou khmer* had some kind of oil. He mumbled some words and blew on the oil and put it on my face." Sometimes *krou* use not just spoken syllables, but script, like the one tattooed on the man's skin in the poem that begins the previous chapter. While living in Cambodia during Pol Pot time, Mrs. Sann sought help for her nightmares. "I bought a sheet of gold and took it to a *krou khmer*. He wrote some *thoa* [Buddhist teaching] on it. I wore it on a chain around my neck." A Khmer monk described his own healing services.

People who are ill or afraid that something bad has befallen them ask me to *srauch terk* [sprinkle water]. This includes reciting a *thoa* as well as giving an herbal medicine. I use a bucket of water along with candles and incense. I say the *thoa* over the water, and then sprinkle the water over the person to help dispel bad spirits. The power of the words goes into the water.

The words of these healings are not arbitrary signs, but signs that merge with matter and alter it. Their power inheres less in meaningful sound than in a material element that, when imprinted in water, gold, or oil, transmutes them to healing substance.

Sometimes a soul wanders toward death before her time as in this story Sodoeung told of a neighbor in Cambodia.

He was not that old. He had a very high fever and then he got better. Then the next morning his wife tried to wake him up and he just lay there. He was in a coma for two or three months, lying there just like he was dead. Every day we just walked across the street and went to see her and asked her how she was doing. She had five kids. My mom would bring them a lot of food and money. My mom said, "Why don't you go see the *krou teay* [astrologer, fortune-teller] to see if they know what's going on? Why is he like that?" His body was still warm, not cold. So they went to a *krou teay* and he told them that he was out having fun. When I heard that I laughed. "He's out having fun." How come? How can he be out when he's there? The *krou teay* told them to invite the monks to do a ceremony to call the spirit back. I don't know exactly how it goes. There is a ceremony to call people to come back who are not assigned to be dead yet. They did that ceremony every day until he came back.

The ceremony may have been *hav praloeng,* which involves chanting a specific text, making offerings to lost *praloeng* (souls), and tying a white string on the wrist to tether them to the body as in the Lao *su khwan.*[2] Khmer say there are as many as nineteen different *praloeng*. When one of the lesser souls *(praloeng tauch)* is lost, a person may become disoriented or sad, but when the primary soul *(praloeng tum)* is missing, then the person will die if the soul is not recovered. As one person put it:

If the *praloeng tauch* goes, then just a little of your soul is gone. You still remember. You can lose this soul temporarily from shock or panic, like from an accident. But if the *praloeng tum* leaves you temporarily, then you go into a coma or lose consciousness. And if you wake up you may not remember anything at all. (quoted in Smith-Hefner 1999, 41)

Soul loss may be due to a premature visit to the land of the dead. Mrs. Sann recalled a time that her sister-in-law's soul left her body.

She was shaking with fever and unconscious. Her parents decided to call a *krou khmer* who was very powerful and famous. He put all the things he needed around him and sat near her for three days and nights. Then she came back. He told them that he had gone to a certain mountain. That is, to us it is a mountain, but in the other world it is a house for people who are very truthful and honest. For those three days, he went to this mountain close to the village where they lived. He had to ask permission to go because that was the other world. He saw the girl's soul swinging a younger sibling in a hammock. He asked the spirit parent "What is she doing here? Her parents are sick and grieving. They are looking for her."[3] He asked, "Why are you keeping her here? Why don't you let her go?" The spirits said, "Well, we don't have anyone to take care of her siblings. So we need her to be here." He said, "Well, I am here to take her back because her parents want her back." Finally, the spirits decided to give her back to him. He was very well known and very powerful. He made potions that worked on ghosts, so that they did whatever he requested. She was alive for another year.

The *krou khmer* in this story operates within an undifferentiated continuum of virtual and actual, embarking on a trance journey to a geographic mountain (which, seen from the viewpoint of spirits, is a house for the honest), brewing potions that work on ghosts. The words he addresses to lost souls or to the spirits or ancestors who have lured them away compose their own interpellation, a counter to the Althusserian "hey you" of paramilitary death squads or medical prognosis, hailing the sick person as someone who belongs among the living.

Like Khmer, Lao speak of cures in which powerful words are infused into herbs or other healing substances. Douang recalled the following cure for cracked lips used during his childhood:

You get sticky rice that is still warm, and you put it here [pointing to the corners of his lips], and you say these magic words that mean: "Bring me back my lips, and take away your genitals." You're speaking to a chicken. You touch your lips with the rice, say that three times, and then throw the rice to the chickens, and the chickens eat it. So you have an exchange. I learned it from my grandmother. A few days later, it would be cured.

Herbalists often incorporated powerful words into their healings. Douang described the practices of one monk he had known in Laos:

Let's say that he had roots. He would grind them against a piece of rock with some water. He might mix many kinds of roots together in the bowl of water. Then he would say magic words into the water. And then he would give the water to me to drink. I would drink that five or six times a day. As I understand it, the words are to ward off evil spirits, and also to bring your spirit that is lost back to you.

Like Khmer souls, Lao souls may leave the body not only at death, but also at times of accident, shock, or illness. Under such circumstances, people say, *khwan* drift away, leaving the person alive, sometimes even conscious, but distressed, enfeebled, or confused. As Major Samsuthi explained:

If you drive and then have a car accident, and you lose your *khwan*, you lose your spirit. You were startled, you were surprised too much. Because of the accident, you almost died. . . . If you have a lot of money, you bring your money with you to gamble in the casino, you lost all of your money. Then not only did you lose the money that you had in your pocket, you also lost your car, and lost your house. So you are very, very sad. And when you are very, very sad like that you have lost your spirit.

While *khwan* are typically translated as spirits or souls, and understood as subtle aspects of a person or other entity, one monk defined them as thoughts that flit and scatter here and there in flickering instants of focus or distractedness.

When I talk about spirits or *khwan*, I am talking about spirit in the sense of awareness. Right now when we're talking to each other, this is one spirit. But then there is a spirit in me that might be thinking of something else. Like, for example, [to the interpreter] you just made a phone call because you have other things to do at work besides the things we are doing together here. That spirit is doing something else over there at the same time. So in our thoughts—we have many thoughts—we think of something else, we do something else, and we also have something else in mind. We have lots of spirits.

During *bai si su khwan*, enacted on Lao New Year, and during weddings, as well as during serious illness, offerings of rice and other food are arranged in a precisely folded banana leaf to attract wandering khwan,[4] and strings are tied to the wrist to fasten *khwan* more closely to the body (R. Davis 1984, 145; cf. Klima 2004). Describing *su khwan*, the monk said:

Everybody calls to the spirit, "Come on, spirits of the person, wherever you are. Spirits, whether you are in the rice field, or in the river, or wherever you are, spirits, please come here. We have these good things for you." When the ill person hears, she is happy that people are trying to help her, and trying to get the spirits back into her heart. We try to gather all of the spirits in the same place, in the heart. That is the center of a person's strength. The person gets more energy, and when the person gets more energy, then it is also a process of healing.

Richard Davis suggests that *khwan* is better translated as energy elements than soul (1984, 143). Morris defines them even more precisely as "distinct essences that together constitute the being of a person" or other entity (2000, 111). Humans are considered to have thirty-two *khwan*. "Water buffalo" and "kitchen implements," Morris observes, have less (112). The inadequacy of the translation of soul or spirit derives in part from the Christian connotation of disembodied subjectivity that adheres to those terms. By contrast, the understanding of *khwan* as energies, elements, or essences inherent in every being blurs the qualitative distinction between persons and things which Christian-inflected ontologies labor to sustain (Keane 2006), making the effect of banana-leaf offerings on mental states intuitively plausible.

Aside from *hav praloeng*, Khmer also spoke to me of the healing power of *saut kavada* and *saut pitam*.[5] Both texts are chanted in Pali, a language known only to the most educated of Khmer Buddhists, for those who are severely ill or in despair or fear about dying, though *saut pitam*, I was told, is more apt to be used when the person is unconscious or clearly dying. *Saut kavada* is usually recited by Buddhist monks, while *saut pitam*, Mr. Chea said, can be recited by any knowledgeable layperson. A Khmer monk explained that *saut kavada* delineates the four elements that compose a person—earth, air, fire, and water—as well as the four aspects of awareness: feelings, perceptions, attention, and consciousness.[6] The text therefore breaks down human existence into analytic, almost anatomical, detail, minutely decomposing bodily and mental attributes through language. In addition, the monk said, *saut kavada* outlines the three essential conditions of existence: *dukkha*, suffering, *anitya*, impermanence, and *anatma*, the lack of a discrete, underlying self or soul, which the monk explained by saying that no quality or feature of a person truly belongs to her. He went on to say that when people learn that nothing of their body actually belongs to them, they are less distressed about the loss or impending loss of their physical faculties or form. Although monks view these chants primarily as instruments of detachment from one's corporeal and perceptual existence, laypeople often understand them as techniques of healing. Mr. Chea commented that both *saut kavada* and *saut pitam* can add years onto a person's life span. Even the monk recalled that when he was invited to a hospital to recite *saut kavada* for an eighty-four-year-old man who wasn't expected to live, the man subsequently improved and returned home.

When *saut kavada* or *saut pitam* are performed, the words of the chant are again directed into a basin of water, drops of which are scattered over the person. These chants, like the spells of *krou khmer*, achieve their effect partly through the tangible power of the syllables themselves, as it is infused in water, and then absorbed by the patient. In Cambodia before the war, hospitals allowed patients to return home for *saut kavada*, and sometimes even contributed money for the ceremony. "Even if only a few people chanted *pitam* and *kavada*," Mr. Chea said, "the rest sat nearby to lend their support." U.S. hospitals are less conducive to these practices, however. Khmer people, Sodoeung said, are often afraid to ask hospital staff to allow the monk to do a chant for them. As Sheila said: "Providers don't understand. The person who's dying always says, 'I want to go home.' But the reason is that at home his family can do ceremonies for him." Recalling the monk who was allowed to perform a ceremony in the hospital chapel but not in the ICU, Sodoeung mused, "In the ICU everyone has to wear gowns and gloves and face masks." "The monk in a gown," Sheila joked. "The monk is already in a gown," Sodoeung said, laughing. Then she added that when her own mother was hospitalized she wanted the monks to chant for her but was afraid it would annoy her roommate. Ideally, Sodoeung said, there should be five or ten monks chanting these texts. It would have been hard to squeeze so many into the hospital room. In U.S. hospitals, where ministering to the spirit and caring for the body are spatially separated, Buddhist monks may be invited to chant in a chapel without the patient present to receive the material effects, or rarely in the ICU, saffron robe exchanged for sanitary gown, but without candlelight, incense smoke, or water to transfer the power of the words. The partitioning of spiritual and physical care reflects how far U.S. hospitals institutionalize a prevalent Protestant division between matter and spirit, enforcing a presumption that rituals work through symbolic representation rather than material contiguity.

In Hmong healings, a *txiv neeb* divines the cause of a spirit illness with two buffalo horns or pieces of bamboo, the *kuam*, which he throws in the air and allows to fall before reading their positions.[7] He then negotiates or battles with *dab* for the *plig* of the ill person.[8] Noting the scarcity of *dab* in the United States, Mr. Vangay said, "In this country illness is more a matter of the *plig*. For example, if a person turns yellow and has weak energy, it is because the spirit is not with the body. The spirit is trying to be reborn in some other place. It leaves the body to go be reincarnated elsewhere." Pao Chang told me that soul loss is suspected when a person has heard a noise or had a scary experience, and subsequently feels sick and loses his appetite. There are a variety of techniques to call back an absent soul, including *hu plig*, performed a few days after a child is born, and then thereafter in times of personal crisis. In *hu plig*, animals are sacrificed and eaten, prayers are said for health and long life, and white strings are tied on the person's wrist, again to attach the souls more closely to the body.

Mrs. Vangay remembered two kinds of shamans in Laos: those trained by an experienced *txiv neeb*, and those called to healing work through their own illness.

> My father was sick many times. He was even dead a couple of times. That's how they found out he wanted to be a *txiv neeb*. They called another *txiv neeb* over to help him. It turned out a dead *txiv neeb* wanted to be transplanted into his body, to use his body to do healing. He wasn't taught any lessons. When they put him in a chair and the *txiv neeb* blew colored water over him, he began to shake. Then he could feel what the spirit wanted to communicate through him, and he just said it. When he was just starting out, somebody had to blow water on him to get him to shake. Later on he pounded the drum and started to shake and was possessed by the spirit. The shaman who has studied learns the words by listening to others. But my father was not that kind of *txiv neeb*. Whatever came up in his mind, whatever the spirit told him in his mind, he said it out loud. After he made the diagnosis there was another ceremony. People killed a pig or other animal. They tied a rope to it and encircled the ill person with the other end, saying, "We are offering a pig." Then they killed the pig and cleaned it and put it nearby. Sometimes my father used a knife at the door. He would chop at the air and say he was fighting off the *dab*.

Mr. Vangay added, "If the *plig* is not with the body, then it has gone either to hell or somewhere else. That's when the shaman will ride a horse to catch up with the soul and bring it back." One of the tasks on the journey may be to renew the sick person's life visa, granted to her before birth by Ntxwj Nyug, the figure responsible for the existence of illness and death in the world (Chindarsi 1976).[9] Although the visa has a specific expiration date, *txiv neeb* can sometimes appeal for an extension. Here the performative languages of healing and politics interpenetrate as Hmong shamanism integrates the regulatory procedures of nation-states that permit or deny border crossing. Having crossed several borders over the last few centuries (from China to Laos, Laos to Thailand, Thailand to the United States), Hmong are well acquainted with the ways that migration is subject to the deployment of certain documents that are illocutionary in their effects.

Pheng told this story of a shamanic healing, filtered through his skepticism and affiliation with biomedicine.

One of my close friends, her daughter had a temperature and was going to have chicken pox. You should prevent it by avoiding strong scent, strong food. . . . The neighbor next door gave the daughter pizza, and it affected her illness inside. The chicken pox has got to come out on the skin, but instead it turned inside and it showed up on the lung. And the doctor believed it was bronchitis. But we believe that it is the outside turning inside. Back home the daughter would be dead. Here they used a machine to help her breathe. She was in the hospital for a month. My friend's husband went to get the medicine man to come in and make a magic blow, with a candle and a bowl of water. . . . He blew the magic into the water and tried to let the patient drink. . . . It was supposed to be the equipment and the technology of the doctor that got the credit. But the husband gave all the credit to the medicine man. Nothing at all to the machine.

When he works as a medical interpreter, Pheng encourages Hmong patients to distinguish physical illness from spiritual illness. "If you're physically, actually cut, then you need help from a doctor. . . . That's actually related to your body meat, not your spiritual side. . . . But if you feel like you hear a voice or you're scared, or you see a vision, you see something that is not actually real, then a medicine man or spiritual man can prevent that." Yet others do not necessarily separate material cures from spirit cures as tidily as he recommends. From a shamanic perspective, the power of words spoken into a bowl concretely passes into the water, and from there into the body of the patient as surely as a drug. Mai Chang, Pao Chang's wife, described a cure for fright in young children:

When a Hmong baby is frightened by yelling or a loud noise, she can get diarrhea. If the stool is loose and smells sour, we know the child was frightened by something, and we know a way to cure it. When my children are scared, my sister takes off the clothes they are wearing at that moment. Later on that night she shakes the clothes at the stove and speaks special words. The next day the children stop being afraid.

Once again, words and gestures work together to accomplish physical change.

Even though most of the Kmhmu emigrants I met had converted to Christianity in Laos, with all of the simultaneous conversion to biomedicine that usually entailed,[10] they still knew a variety of verbal and herbal remedies for healing sickness. For one of our visits Lt. Phanha (himself not yet a convert) invited a group of his friends who each possessed specific *kru*, or healing knowledge. Cheuang, an especially powerful *po kru* (healer), emphasized, "Just as doctors in this country learn all their procedures, so those of us in this room have studied as hard as any doctor." To learn *kru* an aspirant first offered a gift to a *po kru* who possessed that knowledge. When one had memorized the *kru* and was in the process of absorbing it, it was critical to remain celibate and avoid certain foods for a period of three weeks. Tellingly, given their history, everyone in the room, both men and women, knew a *kru* to stop the flow of blood from a wound. "The other day," Cheuang said, "boiling water spilled on me, but my skin didn't burn. This tells me that my *kaung* is still working." *Kaung* is very strong *kru*, he went on. "If one has *kaung* he has strong protection from his *kru*. A friend of mine who has *kaung* tried to stab himself, but he didn't succeed because his *kaung* wouldn't allow it. *Kaung* is the most powerful *kru*." Mrs. Prachitham, recalling the power of *kru* in Laos, said of *kru kaung*, "That means, if I have a gun and I try to shoot you, you wouldn't get killed, it wouldn't hurt you it all. That kind of *kru* is really important." She recalled that in Laos *po kru* (also called *móo kru*)[11] would speak Lao words into a bowl of water, then sip the water and blow it onto the ill person. Her daughter-in-law Julie, who knows Lao well, remembered that the words addressed the spirits who could heal the affected part of the body, saying, "Come and help me before other bad spirits destroy me." *Po kru*, she said, learn these powerful words, but do not necessarily understand them. Once again, the healing and protective force of the words depends not on the transmission of meaning, but rather on the transfer of a material essence inhering in the syllables, which in this case may draw some of their magic from their Lao and Buddhist alterity.

The Kmhmu ceremony *súu hrmàal* for strengthening the soul (Tayanin 1994, 124) is performed for good luck at birth, weddings, and the New Year, as well as during death rites. Similar to Lao, Khmer, and Hmong soul-calling rites, participants assemble a large platter of bananas, rice wine, flowers, sugar cane, chicken, and pig, "bless" the food (a verb that is both securely Christian and sufficiently ambiguous to not offend any ancestral *róoy* who may be hanging around), and then tie white strings onto people's wrists. In addition, if a *hrmàal* seems to have strayed, both non-Christian and Christian Kmhmu ask the *éem*, the ailing person's mother's brother, or, failing that, another male elder in the mother's family to call the soul. The *éem* breaks an egg, Lt. Phanha told me, and after pronouncing specific words inviting the spirit to return, he dips a string into the egg and ties it onto the ill person's wrist. He also fashions a bracelet for the person out of metal or other materials at hand. When Julie's sister's infant daughter was crying uncontrollably, her *éem* made her a bracelet of string, rice, and salt. "She cried like she was in pain," Julie said. "We tied on the bracelet and she was okay." Lt. Phanha related:

Just now someone called me from Laos to say that they want a bracelet from me for my sister's daughter. I am her *éem*. So I'm going to send it along with someone who is going to Laos. I'll buy a tiny ring or something, and over there they will figure out how to put it on. The bracelet doesn't have to be a big thing. It can be a little thing. If we lived close to each other I would give them eggs and cooked rice. But because I live far away, if I only sent that, it wouldn't be enough. So I'm going to send the ring. This is for her *hrmàal*. She isn't eating or drinking well, so they know that it must be one of the souls that has left the body.

When I asked Kampheang what signs indicated that a person's *hrmàal* was lost, she responded,

The person may get scared all the time. She may be skinny. She may not want to eat, or when she eats, she may feel like throwing up. There are many things that can happen. If you experience something very scary, that can make the *hrmàal* go too. Like myself right now I'm almost 100 percent believing that I lost my *hrmàal*. I got in an accident. I think my back is still not completely healed. Maybe my *hrmàal* is not here. Because I got so scared when I had the accident. I was so shocked. My boyfriend doesn't think I have a problem. But I know that every time I drive, if the car is changing lanes it scares me to death. This never happened before I had the accident. He told me, "Oh, it's because you were scared when you had the accident." But of course, if my *hrmàal* were here, I wouldn't be scared. That's how I feel.

Sometimes powerful words of healing are recited as if to counter the powerful words of terminal prognosis. When a physician told Mr. Prachitham, Julie's father-in-law, that he would die within two or three months, his family brought him home and arranged for a ceremony to extend his life. Cheuang told me: "We wrapped a long cloth around his head to make a cap and then had all the little children, two or three years old, stick flowers in the cap, and say, 'Have a long life like me. Have a long life.' After that he lived four more years." The same ceremony was conducted for his wife a few months after his death. After a funeral, Julie said, there should be two *súu hrmàal*, one in gratitude (and cleansing, in a non-Christian understanding) for those who attended the burial, the other for the family of the deceased.

You know what happened to our family? When my father-in-law died last year we just did one, we didn't do the other. A week or a month after the funeral we were supposed to do the one for good luck saying, "People who have passed away have passed away. Now we need to have better luck for ourselves." And now my mother-in-law is really sick. All the elders in the community are saying, "It is because you didn't do that." Everyone in the community has been saying, "You know, you need to do that one." So we did it last week. She feels much better this week. I don't know if it's because of that or what. We invited everyone. And after the string-tying we put a cap around her head and we had the little kids pick flowers and stick them in her cap. That is to make her have a longer life. We always want the kids to place the flowers. To connect the little children to her.

Julie is dubious, like many Christian Kmhmu, about the efficacy of healing words and their accompanying gestures. Yet her doubts do not keep her from following her elders' advice or from connecting her mother-in-law's recovery to *súu hrmàal*.

Temporalities of Dying

In some ceremonies performed for the seriously ill, preparation for death inter-mingles ambiguously with final attempts at cure. One Lao monk frequently visits hospitalized patients at the request of their families.

> What I do is comfort the patient and the family, and teach the patient about illness, that everyone becomes ill sometimes, and also that everyone will die sometime. The important thing is to always keep your spirit, whether you are alive or dead. We teach the dying person that it is not bad to be ill. If we lose our home, our car, or there is an earthquake, these things should not affect us at all. What is important is that we must always have a strong heart or strong spirit. Whenever you give up, whenever you think that you are dead or done for, that is a failure. So we teach them to keep up their strength. Some-times it helps them.

For this monk, in contrast to the physician at the hospital ethics meeting discussed in the previous chapter, refusal to resign oneself to death, while acknowledging that one will ultimately die, is a sign of a strong spirit. When biomedicine has nothing further to offer, patients and families may remain poised between hope and acceptance until the ill person is within a few hours of death or has died. At such times people may arrange rituals (like the Khmer chants of *saut kavada* and *saut pitam*) that are simultaneously oriented toward physical health and spiritual solace. Notice how prevention blurs into prepa-ration in Major Samsuthi's thoughts on fatal illness:

> Talking about birth and death, they are unavoidable. Everybody has to die sometime. . . . In Laos . . . we would have the *su khwan*. We would tie a string on the ill person just to wish for the person, to ask for an extension of life for

the patient from the *thevada*. . . . The relatives of the patient and also the doctors and nurses try to say nice words to the patient to try to comfort and encourage the patient, telling him or her that they will recover very quickly, everything is all right. When the patient is dying, the husband or wife and children and also the parents of the patient would come to the patient and ask the patient what he or she wants to be done, and tell the patient that they will try to carry out that duty or try to satisfy the desire of the patient. . . . Some patients would ask that their body be cremated. Some would ask for their body to be buried. Some would ask, after it is cremated, for the bones to be buried or put next to their loved ones, their parents who had already passed away, or whoever, their cousins, or someone very close to them.

Wondering what might mark the shift from requesting an extension of life to eliciting the patient's last wishes, I asked, "How do you know when it is time to keep assuring the patient that they are going to live, and when it is time to discuss what they want done after they die?" His answer segued into a story of his own first wife's death.

Because the doctor told the relatives that the patient was going to die soon. The relatives of the patient also notice by themselves. So that is the time when you ask the person what things the person has, and how to divide the inheritance among the relatives, the children and grandchildren. . . . [For my wife] we asked the children to come to her and ask her for forgiveness, whenever they did anything wrong to her, so that they don't have any sin. They would come to her with flowers and candles to ask for forgiveness from her, and that is also for her to die peacefully, so that she would not have any sin or sorrow going with her. . . . I knew that death was coming for sure, because she was struggling. She was moving a lot. My son and I were there with her when she was dying, and we took turns watching her. . . . I told my son, she will either go at one in the morning or at five in the morning. And I prayed and I did some chanting, and at one, nothing happened. . . . But then I saw that she was having so much pain and she was suffering so much, and so I prayed . . . to the person who comes to get people who have died, saying, "I think you are anxious to get her. . . . She is suffering so much, so you can go ahead and take her with you. I'm not going to ask her to stay here with me any more. I will let her go." And then I was sleeping, and my son was watching her. But then my son fell asleep at five o'clock, and I woke up, and I saw her stop breathing, and I woke up my son, and then I shook her. I shook her arm. I said, "Oh let me see you for the last time, don't leave me right now." And when I shook her, I also put things in her hand, her favorite things that she liked. And then she breathed again, but she could not say anything. And after that she died. . . . And I called to the nurse, and the nurse came, and then they pushed the red button, and the clock said her last breath was at five o'clock. . . . Because one o'clock in the morning or five o'clock in the morning are the times that usually the worker . . . comes to get people.

Major Samsuthi only physically prepared his wife for death, pressing her favorite possessions into her hands, when he noticed her struggling to breathe. His understanding of death's timing hinged less on a medical assessment of failing bodily systems than on his wife's restlessness and the hours when the dead are usually taken to the next world. He went on,

> We did invite the monk to come over to ask for an extension of life. . . . Right after she passed away I had the monk chant for her. Not many people do this. This was because I already knew in advance that she was dying soon, so I had already made an arrangement, contacted the monk in advance, invite the monk. . . . Right in the hospital. We had already asked permission from the doctors and nurses in the hospital. We told them it was our culture. . . . And they said, "No problem, you can do it, no problem."

Even as Major Samsuthi anticipated his wife's death, he arranged for the ritual that is described by laypeople as a request for an extension of life.[12] Although her death was already clocked, his wife would still absorb the ritual words, encouraging her to accept the cycle of birth and death. A Lao monk told me that the chant he conducted at the time of death sometimes brought people back to life. Healing words cannot always be definitively distinguished from words to ease the transition from life into death.

This imbrication of cure and comfort suggests a temporality of dying somewhat different from that presumed by hospice discourse. According to current hospice protocol, as discussed earlier, patients are officially dying, and therefore hospice eligible, when a physician determines that they have six months or less to live and that further curative treatment is futile. Yet in Major Samsuthi's story and others, patients do not seem to be dying until they are bedridden and visibly struggling. Hospice workers distinguish this shorter time from the dying that begins with terminal prognosis by saying that the patient is now "actively dying." In Lao, Douang pointed out, to say that a person is dying is to imply that he or she is expected to die very soon, within a few hours or days. "That is the time when the person would tell the family, 'Okay, I'm dying, and this is how I'm going to divide the property.'" When Lao people suspect that a person may die in a few weeks or months they might say to one another (though rarely to the patient herself) that she is "seriously ill" or "waiting to die," but not that she "is dying." The temporality of dying is linked to the dying person's struggles for breath or self-initiated acknowledgement of death, rather than to the long-term course of the illness.

For Kmhmu and Hmong, the temporality of dying is similarly out of synch with temporalities of biomedical prognoses. People reminisce, for instance, about the last-minute revivals of those who are close to death or seemingly dead. The Kmhmu man Lt. Phanha told me:

> This is a true story. Three years ago my cousin died. They said he was dead for nine days. Because his body was still warm they didn't bury him. On the ninth day they put him in the coffin and they were going to cremate him. After they started the fire he woke up. He told his family that he had gone to the spirit realm carrying a letter. When the *róoy* read the letter, they said, "Oh, it's not you. You're not coming this year. In three years you'll come again and we will take you. Right now you have to go back." When he woke up the village was almost ready to place him in the fire. This year the three years were up and he died.

Cheuang said, "Usually when doctors say, 'Okay this person has died,' then they unplug everything, they take him away right away. If possible, if they left that person a couple of hours in the room, there might be a way that he might come back." Pheng told me the story of a Hmong woman who died and was placed in a refrigerator.

> Her husband was a pastor and he prayed to God, "Please save her life. I'm a man; I don't know how to take care of children. If you really need someone, take me instead. Bring her back to life." And then there was a knock from the refrigerator. The guy went to open it and she was awake, she had come back to life. Three months later his car was hit by a truck on the street and he died. Two years ago I saw the wife, and I said, "I heard your story. Is it true?" She said, "Yes, it's true. He asked for me to be sent back."

Stories such as these insert a note of doubt into the finality of death or near death. The prayers and incantations referred to in these stories are not simply communications, but powerful performatives that, with the help of the spirits, might possibly keep the heart beating.

Joanne Lynn writes, "There's no term that is more vacuous and misleading than 'the terminally ill.' The difference between being mortal and being terminally ill is a very hard line to find. The arrogance of establishing a category of 'other' that is called 'terminally ill' is a way of distancing ourselves from the fact that we're all dying" (1996, 98). The stories told here respond to the interpellation of terminal illness with a similar understanding that while death may be inevitable, its timing is unknown. Small wonder that truth-telling can be dangerous when it insists on telling the truth of death to a patient who is not yet thought to be dying, at least no more than the rest of us. Lynn's remark reminds us that a terminal prognosis assumes its primary significance less as medical fact than as a shift in social position.

The practice of truth-telling gains intelligibility from an underlying Christian understanding, mentioned earlier, that the soul suddenly and profoundly separates from the world of the living at death. Christianity, Fenella Cannell writes, is a "religion of discontinuity," which relies on the trope of the "unrepeatable event" both in its imagination of conversion as irreversible personal transformation and in its vision of a transcendent eternity (2006b, 8, 38, 44). The latent Christianity that pervades contemporary bioethics posits death itself as an unrepeatable event, an absolute temporal as well as spatial barrier. The logic of truth-telling therefore rests on the presumption that the weeks before death offer the last opportunity to offer guidance to the dying. Correspondingly, truth-telling becomes an apt supplement to funeral practices that are designed more to console the mourners than to minister to the dead. It dovetails with that implicit eschatology in which the dead are instantly catapulted into a still eternity, while the living remain in linear time. The practice of truth-telling is also, I suspect, allied to a philosophical conception whereby the ability to self-consciously face and testify to one's own death is a distinguishing feature of human (as opposed to animal) existence (Derrida 1993, 35–40). It is, by the same token, potentially foreign to cosmologies where animals also possess souls and where humans may transmigrate to animal existences and back. It furthermore fails to take into account those understandings of language in which words are not so much arbitrary and disembodied, as part of the material world, participating in its tactile effects. Finally, the practice of truth-telling may be an irrelevance if not an interference in social worlds where living and dead meet to feast together, and where the living continue to offer their assistance to those who travel from death to other worlds and finally to rebirth.

Funeral Songs

In coining the term "anticipatory grief," Kübler-Ross wrote that it allowed the dying person and his loved ones to "'finish unfinished business,' something we cannot do after death has occurred" (1974, 99). Etymologically, as Ozge Serin (2012) observes, anticipation refers to taking possession. To anticipate one's own death, then, implies to become its subject. Presaging contemporary disciplines of death, Martin Heidegger (1996) refers to the practice of reassuring dying persons that they were not dying (more prevalent in Europe and North America during his time) as a "tranquillization" that compromised their full subjectivity. Serin points out, however, that one can only be a subject of one's death as imagined possibility, not as actual event, "which is never accessible as such for any subject" (2012, 28). Near-death experiences (NDEs) constitute that genre of stories that attempt to reinstate subjectivity into death. Late in life, Kübler-Ross became deeply interested in such experiences, researching the stories of resuscitated patients and engaging in iatrogenically induced out-of-body experiences of her own. Yet she continued to insist on the importance for the dying of completing their relationships with the living prior to death. A modern Euroamerican scenario in which the soul immediately passes into obscurity seems to have shaped her approach to care of the dying, even as she was recording testimonies of the temporarily dead. It is as if she were caught between conflicting European eschatological storylines, what Gilbert calls "expiration," in which the spirit departs the body like the wispy homunculus depicted in medieval paintings, and "termination," an understanding of death as "absolute annihilation" devoid of any story of continuing spirit (2006, 104–6). It is not that Kübler-Ross simply compartmentalizes her mystical interest in NDEs and her secular psychology of dying. She actually undertook a scientific research program to record and prove near-death experience and to outline its prototypical course. Why, then, did she insist both on anticipatory grief and on the idea of death as simply a transition rather than an end? If death is one more rite of passage, why should it call for grief in advance?

One possible answer might be that contemporary Euroamerican near-death folklore works to replenish a dominant Protestant eschatological vagueness, in which clerical counsel for the afterlife has faded into a lack of specifics (Gilbert 2006, 122). Avid scientific proofs of afterlife may supplement the scarcity of institutionally supported avenues through which to enact relationships with the dead. Through a collusion of confessionalist interiority and resuscitation machinery, NDE research labors to create a Euroamerican Christian or post-Christian testimony of the dead, allowing the miniature spirit escaping from the body to appear out of the corner of the scientific eye. Yet the image of a soul moving toward a blinding light might be said to simply repeat and elaborate the eschatological vagueness. Like funerals oriented toward the living and the urgency to complete emotional "business" before death, Euroamerican NDEs seem to evoke an afterlife that is nebulous, obscure, and largely inaccessible from the world occupied by the living.

When one day I asked Lt. Somsy, "Do people ever talk about dying to a person before they die?" he replied matter-of-factly, "No, after they die." If, for some emigrants, the process of dying begins a few days or hours before death, it may continue for weeks or months afterward. In this temporality of dying, anticipatory grief becomes redundant. The ill person will have ample time later to confront and grieve her death, and to say farewell with the support of family, friends, and spiritual practitioners. Coming to terms with death is less a private matter of subjective emotional stages preceding death than a collective matter of specific transformative teachings and practices that redefine the person's social situation following death. If the idea of anticipatory grief appears to demand that the dying become subjects of their own death, the refusal to participate in such grief might be understood to acknowledge the impossibility, as a still living person, of being a subject of one's own death, the impossibility, in Serin's words, of claiming dying as a "personal experience" (2012, 28). This impossibility is registered in emigrants' suggestion that the dead are not initially aware of their death, as if it hasn't actually happened *to them*. Funeral songs might be said to resubjectivize the dead as dead, to make them conscious of their death, to orient them to the afterlife. Again and again emigrants noted that it was crucial to encourage the dying person to recognize his death, not before he had died, but afterward. Funeral songs negotiate a transition that begins, rather than ends, with the cessation of breath.

In Laos, Lt. Somsy told me, Lao used to keep the body in the home for a few days, placed at a right angle to the direction of the beds of the living. "This was just to confuse him, to make him forget how he slept, how he lived in the house, to make him forget everything about his past." Lao say that the *winyan* continues to hover during the funeral ceremony.[13] Listening to the chants on the transience of life recited by the monks, both the dead and the living come to accept death. After the body was taken to be cremated the house was encircled with a string to keep the spirit from returning home and disturbing the family. Later the string was cut. Major Samsuthi explained,

> That is to separate the dead person from the still living persons, saying that the dead person will go to the world of the spirits. . . . They cannot come back. . . . At that time also the spirit knows that he or she is now dead. . . . Before the monk put the string around the house, the dead spirit still did not know that he is dead.

NDEs related by Lao typically reference the period when the dead are still unaware of their death.[14] In Laos, just before cremation, Douang told me, the coffin is opened and one of the family members cuts open a coconut and splashes the coconut water on the dead person's face to offer him a last chance to revive. "There are many stories of people who come back to life at that time." Douang had heard this story of a man who drowned in Laos.

> He didn't know that he had died. He came home, and he saw the body there, and he saw people crying. And he tried to ask people, "Why are you crying?" And nobody talked to him. So sometimes he would knock on the wood, on the wall or something. And then the people said that his spirit was trying to give them a hard time. But in fact he was just frustrated, trying to ask people, when nobody was answering. And then later he saw strings of fire around the house, when he tried to enter again. . . . So he could not enter the house any more, because of the string around the house, the fire. And then that person was pronounced dead, and then came back to life again, became conscious again, and told this story to people. . . . He didn't talk about going to heaven or hell; he just said he was in the rice fields or somewhere around there.

If the deceased had a living spouse, a white string was also tied from the spouse to the dead body. Later it was cut to force the spirit to leave his loved ones behind. In Laos, as the body was carried to the cremation ground, several precautions were also taken to disorient the deceased so that, even if he had not yet entirely resigned himself to death, he would not be able to return home (Archaimbault 1973, 165–66).

The dead must not only be convinced they are dead but also directed away from the world of the living. Similar to the Khmer chants *saut kavada* and *saut pitam*, the Pali texts recited at Lao funerals (both in Laos and in the United States) discourse on the dissolution of the elements, the laws of karma, and the nature of existence after death (Archaimbault 1973, 158). Douang's father, a monk for many years, told him that the funeral chants taught people: "Where there is birth, there is death also, and you have to accept that. Do not cling to anything on this earth, because one day you're going to die. Just try to do good things for others." Douang went on to note, however, "People do not understand these words. They see these words as secret words that guide the spirit of the deceased to heaven." In Lt. Somsy's understanding, for instance,

> The meaning of the chanting of the monks is to tell the dead person, you are now dead, don't make trouble for the living ones, and also telling the way for the dead person, where he should go. And also telling the dead person not to worry about the family members or the loved ones left behind, but just to go his own way.

In *bangsukol*, a Khmer ceremony conducted for the dead at the funeral and on later occasions, the monks also chant Pali texts, teaching both the living and the dead that, just as they arrived in this world with nothing, so they will also leave with nothing. These texts are similarly understood to advise the spirits of the dead to go to heaven or to reincarnate, while reassuring them that their family will continue to make merit for them. One Khmer woman told Nancy Smith-Hefner, "The text recited by the monks has a meaning like, 'You should not become too attached to your physical body. You have to be aware of the fact that your body is decaying, too, and that you will die eventually, just as your relative has died. So think about that'" (quoted in Smith-Hefner 1999, 61). While the spirit observes his own funeral rites and perhaps attempts to get the attention of family members, he is repeatedly urged to recognize his death and leave the living behind.

Kmhmu recalled that in Laos, the deceased was kept at home for three days after the death. During that time, he or she was specifically directed to the land of the ancestors. Lt. Phanha told me that the family wept loudly as they instructed the dead person to journey to his *éem* (in this case his mother's ancestors). In the family of Kam Raw, the Kmhmu storyteller and folklorist, the dead were told:

> Rise from your sleep, from your bed,
> rise and wash your nose and your eyes!
> Carry your gun and gird on your sword!
> Leave your house and go out of your barn!
> Bid farewell to your barn and village,
> bid farewell to your house and kin,
> bid farewell to your bellows and tools!
> Turn this direction and go down there,
> down to the Cril stream and follow it down,
> down to its mouth, then follow the Cuk stream!
> . . . coming up to the Screwpine Waterpipe, wash your hair and bun and continue up!
> . . . Go up to the level path where the civet cats cry,
> and when the path gets silent go over there!
> . . . Coming up to the wells of the Pook and Cam
> reaching the pools with white fish and white carps
> You will find your father and mother there,
> Then stay with your father and mother there! (Lindell, Swahn, and Tayanin 1977–95, 3:234–36)

The recitation mapped out the precise route to the ancestors, naming the cliffs, valleys, trees, rivers, and animals to be encountered on the way. Like Lao and Khmer, Kmhmu strive to persuade the spirit of the deceased to leave his living relatives. As with the Lao, a living spouse was connected by a string to the corpse. At the appointed time in the funeral, Julie said, the string was cut to tell the dead person, "You go your way, and I'll go my way. Don't think you are my wife or my husband any more. Now we are separate and we go our own ways."

In Laos the in-laws of the deceased were responsible for carrying the body to the gravesite.[15] If they were in the midst of a harvest or house construction, however, they would pay someone else to carry the body in their stead. People who were reaping crops or building a house were not expected to attend a burial lest dangerous spirits from the burial grounds follow them back, destroying the harvest or drawing misfortune on the new house. At any other time, Julie said, it was considered an honor to carry the body. "Then people say that the person who died chose the right time to die, because you are available to take care of them." After a burial, *súu hrmàal* was performed at home to protect the mourners from harm. Kmhmu emigrants remembered the burial grounds in Laos as frightening places that were divided into different sections for those who had died of illness, those who died violently, and those who died in childbirth or as infants. When Kampheang, whose father fought with the CIA, was separated from her family and sent to live in her grandmother's village for her own protection, she hid in the cemetery whenever the Pathet Lao passed through.

> It was in the jungle. When someone died, people sacrificed buffalo or cows. They brought the head of the buffalo and placed it at the person's grave along with clothing and other things. Whatever the dead person was given in the past, people brought it there. It was very scary. But that was the only safe place for me to hide. Sometimes I had to stay there all day and all night without food.

Those whose *hrmàal* was considered weak were cautioned against visiting cemeteries. Although Julie's parents were Christians, when her sister was born they consulted a *móo du* about their child's spirit. The *móo du* told them,

> "Don't ever let her go to the cemetery. If the bad *róoy* see her they will take her at that time." And then when she was fifteen years old my parents were about to build a new house so they couldn't go to the cemetery for someone's funeral and they sent my sister instead. One person from each house had to go. They made my sister go and she got sick the next day, and we knew no matter what we did we wouldn't be able to keep her.

Although they sought help from powerful *po kru* and from a hospital in Hoisai, she died soon after. Julie's sister's death suggests another dimension to

Julie's own vulnerability to contact with death. Such stories again emphasize the performative power of funeral rites and burial sites, which do not simply register death, but in some sense produce it.

The Hmong funeral song *Qhuab Ke* or "Showing the Way" guides the spirit of the deceased back through all the habitations of his life to his place of birth—where he collects the jacket of his placenta that lies buried under the floor the house—and then to the place of his ancestors. The lyrics trace the transformation of living person into spirit, persuading both mourners and deceased that the person is on a journey to the ancestors' village. Of Hmong funerals in the United States Mr. Vangay said, "The person who points the way explains to the dead person that the country was at war and we were brought over here. He shows him each place, each doorway, each city or town, until he gets back to where he was born." In at least one version of the text, the deceased encounters his own spirit (or one of them) on the way to his ancestors:

> Now, ah, your ghost, my brother, a brother richly dressed
> appears on the other slope—tall like you, your spitting image.
> Is it you or not? Cock your ears, turn your head.
> Look: that man, the stranger . . . he sings you a spirit song
> Your ghost takes you by the hand, you cross your arms, you cross your legs.
> You rise up with your ghost, is that not so?
> You can no longer talk with men.
> You have glided into the Beyond, you can talk with spirits.
> Let your feet glide and follow the spirits. (K. White and Lemoine 1982, 12)

The question "Is it you or not?" hauntingly conveys the problem of becoming a subject of one's death, wherein one's own ghost is a stranger. Later the text outlines the reunion with the ancestors.

> Your ancestors will spread their skirt to receive you.
> You will jump into the skirt of the ancestors.
> Your ancestors will stretch their skirt to receive you.
> You will leap without hesitation into the skirt of your ancestors.
> Your ancestors will console you with voices soft as flutes.
> Down here your relatives, your brothers will begin to lament you. (38)

The deceased is instructed that when the ancestors try to pursue the person who has shown the way he must say, "He can hear no call . . . No one can follow in his tracks. The weather was dry when he came, when he left, it was raining / And his tracks were all washed away" (38). Pheng noted that the person who shows the way must be careful to hide himself from the spirits, so that they can neither follow him back nor keep him captive. In Pheng's clan, the one who showed the way would try to deceive the spirits by making nonsensical assertions, such as that the man who showed the way has ears as large as an elephant and eyes as big as cups, and that the man came with him today but left yesterday. Such words are designed to confuse the spirits so that they cannot track the guide back to the world of the living.

At other moments in the song text the deceased meets spirit guards who block his path, or (in another version) ask him why he is so well dressed and where he intends to go.[16] The dead man is instructed:

> You must say: It's because the medicine stayed with the plant in the cleft of the rock.
> My mother went in to call in the plant, but the plant didn't answer.
> The helping spirit stayed in the crevice of the cliff.
> The shaman went to call it but the spirit was slow to come. (K. White and Lemoine 1982, 28)

In this way the funeral song, like the terminal prognosis, acknowledges the failure of healing, but in a postmortem time. "'Showing the way,'" Pao Chang observed, "is similar to a preacher or pastor who sends the soul out of a body to God, to heaven, whatever. But for non-Christians we send it to the ancestors." In this translation of the practice, Christian prayers themselves are reconfigured as performatives, bestowing on the pastor's words a pragmatic usefulness to the dead that few comtemporary pastors might claim.

Following the chanting of the *Qhuab Ke*, the nasal music of the *qeej* is played, wherein particular melodic passages signify particular phrases directed to the dead. One recurring sequence of notes, for instance, addresses the deceased as "beloved dead one" (Falk 2004, 130), making it clear that the speech of the *qeej* is intended only for the dead. Except for the players themselves, it is said that only the dead understand the language of the *qeej*. Pao Chang, himself an accomplished *qeej* player, explained that the musician would first play the song called the "cutting off of the breath" *(tu siav)*. "It's for the moment of the last breath. It's not long, it's about thirty minutes to an hour. But the music playing is not finished then. We blow the music at different times until we carry the body to burial." *Tu siav* is a tune thick with corporeal details, composing a graphic sensorium of death. One translation reads:

> Now [the deceased] is about to die for good, die a complete death
> Die with his life-thread cut and saliva flooding his mouth

Die with his life-breath stopped.
At this time the younger and the elder brothers
Will go fetch cold water, fresh water
And heat water to wash his black-beshitten body. (K. White and
  Lemoine 1982, 7)

Following *tu siav*, the remaining *qeej* music may include the creation story
(including the account of how illness and death entered the world), a story
explaining why humans cannot see ghosts but dogs can, a song for each meal
offered to the deceased, a song to mount him on his "flying horse" (the bier
for his body), songs for the grief of each relative, a song to guide the deceased
in overcoming obstacles on his journey, and finally a song to hide the foot-
steps of the *qeej* player, so that no spirits can follow him back home (Morrison
1997; Thao 1993). While there are seven genres of *qeej* music, including music
for weddings, the New Year, and cultural revival events, it is only the funeral
music that is semantically meaningful. The specificity of this musical address
to the dead is such that the funeral songs played on the *qeej* must not be
played at any other time, not even for purposes of rehearsal. As Catherine
Falk writes, "Its content is regarded as being extremely powerful. If it is performed or learned in a private dwelling not at the time of a funeral, a living
soul may be sent inadvertently into the next world" (1992, 3). Hmong funeral
songs, like Kmhmu cemetery rites, are not simply communications to the
deceased but performatives that deliver her more fully into death. Similar care
is taken with the Hmong funeral drum. The drummer is paid in meat or money
to feed the soul of the drum, and owning a funeral drum is a perilous responsibility since it must be fed regularly. If there are not enough funerals, the
hungry drum may cause the death of someone in the owner's family.

   In Catholic funerals, Mr. Lo told me, the passage in the *Qhuab Ke* that in-
structs the deceased to collect his placenta jacket is typically omitted. "For the
old people who used to be animists, we do it to make them happy," he added.
Protestant Hmong have largely replaced "Showing the Way" altogether with
Christian hymns and prayers translated into Hmong, oriented more to the
mourners than to the deceased. The music of the *qeej* and funeral drum is
generally found at neither Protestant nor Catholic funerals. Christian Hmong
sometimes say that these instruments were created by Ntxwj Nyug who is, in
their cosmological understanding, roughly equivalent to the devil. Mr. Lo, however, told me that Catholic Hmong had begun work on Catholic-appropriate
qeej funeral melodies in which the musical phrases would continue to carry
specific semantic values. While Christian conversion works to pull funeral

songs away from their performative roots and toward a more referential logic, the process may never be complete.

Finally, no aspect of death is neglected in funeral songs. Lao and Khmer chants outline the composition of the body, the inevitability of loss, and the necessity to accept the cycles of life and death. Kmhmu song texts meticulously guide the dead to the ancestors. Hmong funeral songs convey regret at the failure of healing, concern to protect the mourners, and compassion for the one who has died. *Tu siav* details physical death down to the release of bodily waste. There is clearly more at stake here than the disconnect between a consciousness of dying that is negotiated through bedside confessionalism versus a consciousness of dying that is negotiated through funeral songs. There is also an insistently physical intimacy with the body suggested by references to washing skin smeared with feces, dressing the corpse, or pouring coconut water on the face. Death involves not just specific language but also specific physical care. It is to this care, and its embeddedness in a relation of material interchange between living and dead, that I now turn.

I call you, Father,
I call you, Mother,
I call you, Grandfather,
I call you, Grandmother!
Come and eat the sacrificed buffalo,
come and listen to the sound of kettle gongs
which we are beating!
. . . and then the ones we do not recognize,
we have never known.
Come all of you,
come every one of you,
come and eat the sacrificed buffalo!
Today we killed a water-buffalo cow,
and offer riches in plenty.
Bring us potent cures
and the elixir of long life!
Come and pour it out on our forehead,
come and coat our crowns!
Come and look after us,
come and rescue us!
Look after our fields,
look after our houses
and look after both women and men,
look after our domestic animals!

—"Calling the Ancestors," Kmhmu song
    accompanying buffalo sacrifices

Chapter 6 **Postmortem Economies**

ONE DAY I WAS SITTING WITH LT. SOMSY and our interpreter in a small, spare room at a community center. A tape recorder sat on the beige formica-topped table between us. Our conversation had eventually gravitated, like many others with emigrants, to a conjunction between violence and material relations with the dead. The lieutenant was describing how he and his unit in the Royal Lao Army handled the bodies of those killed in combat during the wars of the 1960s and 1970s.

> As quick as possible try to get rid of the body. Try to hide the body from the enemy. We dig a hole and take necklace, identification of the person, out. We would use the ID to report. If we had enough time, we would bury that person. If we didn't have enough time, we put gasoline on the dead person and then burn it. If we didn't have enough gasoline, or didn't have any gasoline, then we would put dynamite on the body of the person, and then blow it up. . . . The thing that we should not do is steal anything from the dead person. If you do that then you'll be in danger. Let's say you want to get something from the dead person. I would tell this person that it is not for me. . . . I have to tell the dead person that this is to give to your wife or to your family member. So they can do the ceremony for you. But if I just take these things away from the dead person for myself maybe the spirit of the dead person may haunt me or do some harm to me. . . . There are many people who got things from the dead person. They got shot. They got killed. Some people didn't get shot in the battlefield, but once they got into a safe place, the village or the city, they would fall ill or something would happen to them, and they die. I've seen many people who have had this experience.

The lieutenant's memory of the injunction not to steal from those who died in battle assumes that the dead are enfolded into a material exchange with the living, characterized by an expectation of gifts, a presumption of debt, a possibility of theft, and an acknowledgement (or, the threat of a nonacknowledgment) of sacrifice. Deprived of the ceremonies that would inform him that he was dead, ask him not to trouble the living, and supply him with money and provisions for his journey, a dead soldier was already disoriented and apt to harass the living. If, in addition, he were robbed, he might extract the very lives of the thieves.

The demands of the dead continue to weigh on emigrants from Laos and Cambodia living in the United States, particularly as these demands come to be mediated by thanatopolitical institutions. As physical connections with the dead have become entangled in welfare rules, medical procedure, and mortuary protocol, survivors sometimes fail to fulfill their material responsibilities to the dead, not because of war, but because of lowered economic means and extreme minority status in relation to the dominant ethos underlying management of death in the United States.[1] While it is difficult anyway for emigrants to settle their debts with those who died violent deaths, it is harder for those who owe their survival, as they say, to the benevolence of their ancestors or to bargains struck with spirits. The difficulty is recast in political exile, when emigrants who have been socially marginalized as immigrants and charity recipients are less able to define the terms through which they relate to the dead.

Thanatopolitics and Reciprocity

The frequent connection, in emigrant stories, between violence and a material responsibility to the dead offers an opportunity to rethink biopolitical theory from the perspective of reciprocity. From the vantage point of many emigrants, the postmortem protocols of hospitals and funeral homes threaten to disturb relations with the dead in subtle (and sometimes not so subtle) ways. These protocols are informed not simply by sciences of sanitation and death causation, but also, as suggested earlier, by latent theological presumptions about matter and spirit that are largely Christian in genealogy. As Cannell (2006a) and others have shown, the commitment to a matter–spirit opposition can vary widely in Christianities around the globe. Certain Christian Hmong and Kmhmu practices discussed later in this chapter are exemplary of that variation. Moreover, as Webb Keane (2007, 2006) perceptively notes, the matter–spirit opposition may be more of an aspiration than an accomplishment. The persistence of relics and the transubstantiation of wine and bread to blood and flesh, no less than a fundamentalist insistence on a literal resurrection of the body, all betray a persistent material engagement with the dead on the part of modern Christians. As Agamben has perceptively noted, the roots of "the idea that a corpse deserves particular respect, that there is something like a dignity of death" extend into "the most archaic stratum of law, which is at every point indistinguishable from magic" (2002, 79). On the other hand, these magical undertones are manifestly refused within that part of Christian ethos that is most prevalently institutionalized in psychologies of mourning, funerals, and public discourse addressing past violence, which all tend to reinforce the view that the value of interactions with the dead lies in cathartic and unilateral consolation of the living, rather than in a bilateral exchange of material care between living and dead. Such exchange may also be denied within doctrinaire Theravada Buddhism and certain Christianized versions of animism, as I show below. Certainly it would be a mistake to consider Euro-Christian and Southeast Asian mourning practices as illustrations of representational and visceral engagements with the dead, respectively. Nonetheless a certain insistence on the separation of matter and spirit implicit both in Euroamerican postmortem procedures and in public memorializing is a sign, I suggest, not of the secular banishment of religious sentiment from public institutions, but rather of the institutional enshrinement of a particular religious sensibility (cf. Keane 2007). An inability to conceive of a material indebtedness to the dead in favor of an abstract obligation to remember them is integral to a biopolitical regime that is not only focused on the management of human life (Foucault 1990), but also based on a division of that life into materiality and spirit.

As touched on earlier, Agamben has glossed the biological aspect of human life as bare life, a purely animal existence stripped of social and political value (1998; cf. 2002). Bare life has proved to be a powerful analytic in grasping the gestures of social exclusion that affect refugees, racially marked minorities, and those hovering at the edge of life and death. However, emigrants' stories problematize this concept in several interrelated ways. If, as I noted earlier, Agamben confuses desubjectification with animalization, allowing no possibility for a productively beastly or bestialized subject, he further glosses desubjectification as a condition of (living) death, thus precluding any subjectivity of the dead. Moreover, in arguing, as I discussed earlier, that those reduced to bare life are unable to testify to their own desubjectification (or death), Agamben (2002) forecloses the imagination of a communicative interface between living and dead. Finally, Agamben's critique of biopolitics, although insightful about the devaluation of the living, precludes the imagination of either concrete socialities of living and dead or the violation of those socialities. Emigrants' stories, however, suggest that participation in such socialities affords powerful possibilities for addressing a thanatopolitical violence that pursues the dead into their very afterlives, scarring them in ways that materially wound and rend social worlds in the present.

In his memoir of life under Pol Pot, Pin Yathay recalled his first experience of Khmer Rouge contempt for the dead. He and others were being transported to a work site packed tightly in trucks with no food or water. When two women died en route, the driver ordered their bodies to be dumped at the side of the road, over the weeping and protests of their families. "The idea of leaving them there by the roadside was unthinkable, sacrilegious. I thought: Now I must not hope any longer" (1987, 73). Until then, Yathay had struggled to perceive the cruelty of the Khmer Rouge as an excess of revolutionary fervor. It was the willingness to negate the dead as social beings that exposed the radical devaluation of both living and dead. In the United States, survivors of the covert war in Laos or the Khmer Rouge regime in Cambodia are no longer asked to dump bodies by the roadside. Nonetheless, as the presence of the dead is forcibly translated into the representational economies of medical and mortuary institutions, it is similarly eviscerated. Wartime devaluation of the dead therefore finds an uncanny counterpart in autopsy labs, cemeteries, and crematoria where bodies are handled as inanimate matter with only an intermittent and symbolic relation to spirit, interrupting the material enactment of social relations with the dead.

While the Theravada Buddhism of Lao and Khmer and the modern animism of Kmhmu and Hmong offer a dynamic range of conflicting eschatological possibilities, their death rites share a presupposition that the spirits tangibly receive the care given to the body. Robert Hertz (1960), in his early studies of death practices, noted that in many communities the state of the corpse is parallel to the fate of the soul. Subsequent anthropologies of death have most often interpreted this connection as a symbolic and/or social one whereby the condition of the body works as a metaphor for the condition of the spirit and for the adjustment of the community to the absence of one of their members (e.g., J. Watson 1982; Bloch and Parry 1982; Metcalf and Huntington 1991). The care for the body enacted by emigrants, however, evokes a relationship between body and soul that is less metaphorical than metonymic or indexical (cf. Keane 2006, 311). After death, body and spirit are related less through allegory than through contiguity, still participating in one another's substance.

Even as white Europeans and North Americans, when asked, imagine an eclectic range of afterlives "peopled with ancestors, ghosts and even 'cells of the dead' which, apparently, circulate in the ether" (Bradbury 1999, 2), they appear to adhere to certain parameters of a Christian soul. Unlike the Lao *khwan*, the Khmer *praloeng*, the Kmhmu *hrmàal*, or the Hmong *plig*, this Christian soul is not known to leave the body before death, even during severe illness, shock, or fright. After death, however, it effects a complete and almost instantaneous departure, assuming an apparently immediate indifference to the body it leaves behind.[2] It is a singular and immaterial soul, which, unlike *khwan*, *praloeng*, *hrmàal*, or *plig*, cannot be used to refer to the spirits of various body parts (or, for that matter, the spirits of animals, plants, or houses).[3] Douang recalled that when he was ill as a child, his grandmother used to walk around the house, carrying a bamboo torch and calling for the *khwan* of his eyes, ears, and other body parts to return, coaxing them with promises of eggs and chicken.[4] Some Hmong used to say that when a person dies, the spirits of the ears, nose, and mouth remain in the grave, while the spirits of the eyes and heart go the spirit world (Chindarsi 1976, 30). Of *praloeng* Ashley Thompson writes,

> This concept . . . is the equivalent of neither the [French] *ame*, nor the *soul*, nor the [Pali] *vinnan* [equivalent to Lao *winyan*]. Rather than an individual, immaterial principle animating the human body, the Khmer *bralin* [an alternative romanization of *praloeng*] are multiple, material, and independent entities which animate not only humans but also certain objects, plants, and animals. (1996, 2)

Such physical souls require physical gifts that thanatopolitical regimes necessarily intercept. If the contractual death of contemporary bioethics can startle the spirits out of the living, the scientificity of contemporary postmortem procedures can similarly alienate the spirits of the dead. In the first instance, the spirit is driven from the body through the invocation of an interior self who must confess to her own death. In the second instance the spirit is threatened in her afterlife by the treatment of her body as a scientific object. Loss of *khwan*, *praloeng*, *hrmàal*, or *plig* can be seen as a partial death, a metonym of death, one of its gradations, an event where death seeps into life, demonstrating that the separation between the two is never absolute. These gradations, as is clear from funeral songs, continue after the death that produces a corpse, such that life also seeps into death in the form of persistent needs for food and shelter and friendship.[5] The possibility, therefore, that relatives' bodies have been inadequately tended, whether because of war or emigration, starvation or dependence on public assistance, evokes that "bad death" discussed earlier in which violated or neglected dead are poised to become restless spirits. This bad death, which I return to in the final chapter, must be understood in light of emigrant economies of material care for the dead.

Karmic Investment

The most immediate way of caring for the dead is to send items along with them for cremation or burial. Lao and Khmer place jewelry in their mouths to enable them to bribe the immigration officers who police the border between hell and heaven. As one Lao put it, "If you have money outside your body, then maybe other bad spirits would rob you. But if you put it in a safer place, then when you get to hell, you can try to bribe the guard of hell: 'I have this piece of gold; send me to heaven instead.'" One Lao woman put a pack of favorite cigarettes on her dead husband's bed and was reassured of his happiness when she saw him smoking contentedly in her dreams. Major Samsuthi talked of placing cash, ID cards, and passports by the side of the dying for their journeys into death. Back in Laos, Douang recalled, "For somebody who likes to gamble, they put playing cards in the coffin. For someone who likes women they might draw a picture of a woman's genitals on the coffin. Everyone laughs. It's considered an acceptable joke." In Laos the body was typically kept at home for three days, while guests brought gifts and offered entertainment such as music, videos, and games. Until the cremation, Major Samsuthi said, the spirit "would still come and go in the house. And people would come to visit and play cards, and he would come and play cards with you." As Klima noted for Thai funerals, "The dead are lonely. . . . Indeed, the entire funeral casino is a gift to the dead, the gift of camaraderie. . . . What the family wants above all, and what the funeral gamblers feel morally comfortable in providing, is company for the deceased spirit" (2002, 251).

When Khmer and Lao are visited in dreams by dead relatives requesting things, they take the things to the *wat* where monks deliver them in etheric form to the spirit. Douang recalled this story told to him by his grandmother:

> There was a man who drowned. His wife had a dream that he came home to her and was upset, asking for her help. "Can you send me some clothes? I have no clothes to wear." And she said, "Yeah, I'll send you some clothing." She did a ceremony and made an offering to the monks, of clothing and whatever he needed. Later, she had another dream. He was smiling and thanking her, and wearing the clothes.

Chean Rithy Men tells of a man whose mother appeared in a dream and slapped his face because he had neglected to offer her incense and food after her death (2002, 230). Dreams or not, most Lao and Khmer continue to offer gifts to the dead through monks at their local *wat*. As Major Samsuthi put it, "For those dead who have families, the monk acts as the postman. We send things to the dead person. The spirit knows, the spirit hears us."

In Laos people sifted through the bones after cremation, keeping jewelry or teeth as good luck charms, a trace of the gift to the dead returned as a talisman for the living. In Cambodia, when the cremation fires had cooled, relatives gathered the bone fragments and washed them with coconut water. "The reason coconut water was used," Mr. Chea explained, "was because it is pure. It has not been touched. Not even the wind has touched it. We washed and dried the bones, silently praying that the washing would purify the person in the next life, help them live longer, be wealthy, be pure as the water." Both Lao and Khmer place the remains in urns, which used to be kept on the grounds of a *wat* where they could be cared for in an ongoing way. As one Khmer elder said: "The more often you can visit them the better. At least do it at Pchum Ben, the regular yearly ceremony to feed the dead spirits."

When I spoke with a Lao monk about the miniature houses I saw outside of a *wat* in the United States, he downplayed the dead's need for a dwelling, emphasizing instead the need of the living for a place to enact their continued relationship with the dead.

> It makes it convenient for people to do a ceremony. People build a house instead of a stupa, to have a small place to keep the bones in memory of the deceased. They come and worship them or talk to them. It also reminds the living person of what kind of life the person led. They think about the good things he or she did and reflect that they should do the same.

In the monk's account the little houses work like modern Christian gravesites, where the living remember the dead, at times repaying their care, and more rarely confiding in them or seeking their intercession. Lt. Somsy, on the other hand, remembered similar houses built by Northern Lao and furnished with household goods as fully equipped homes for the spirit: "We have a little house covered with a white sheet of cloth for the roof. It is about the size of a dollhouse for children. In there you put pots and pans, and other things that you want to give to the spirit. That is to ensure that the dead person has a house to live in and the things that he needs for everyday life." In this understanding, what is at stake is not the mnemonic practice of the living, but the material prosperity of the dead. Once, when an ancestral spirit was harassing Douang's family in Laos, they built him a tiny house on their property to appease him.

In a second ceremony that is held in both Southeast Asia and the United States a hundred days after the funeral, Khmer and Lao offer household items such as cooking utensils, clothing, and even beds to the *wat*. "Let's say you have offered more than enough for the person to use," Major Samsuthi explained.

"Then the person will also reserve some things for you when you die." In this circulation of gifts, then, a surplus returns to the giver in her afterlife. "To me as a Buddhist," Major Samsuthi continued, "when I make offerings to the monks, it is like investing—, well, let's say putting money in the bank. I wouldn't say it is like the stock market. Stocks go up and down and you can lose. With this one you never lose. It's just like putting it in the bank, and then you can cash it out when you die." A Lao monk carefully detailed the circumstances under which dead could receive the household gifts brought to the *wat* and the process by which the giver would receive a return on her gift.

> What's happening is that things offered to the monks and the *wat* go to the spirits of the deceased persons who are still wandering around the earth. The deceased person who is in hell can't receive anything, and a person who is already in heaven will not receive the offering either. They have enough. So things that you offer come back to you. It's like if you send mail to the wrong address and then it returns to you.

During Boun Khau Padab Din (or, for Khmer, Pchum Ben), the annual feast for the dead, still celebrated in the United States, during which spirits residing in hell are temporarily released, families again bring specific foods to the *wat* and give them to the monks.[6] "It's for all spirits," Lt. Somsy said. "First for the closest relatives and then for any spirit who is starved out there, like a homeless person." The vagrant dead include those for whom full ceremonies were never performed, like Lao soldiers who died in battle or Khmer civilians dumped in mass graves under Pol Pot.[7] As Major Samsuthi reflected, "The spirit of someone who has died and has no relatives to do the ceremony will wander around like a bird without any tree branches on which to perch." Wandering dead may also include those whose store of merit is uncertain due to their own possible participation in violence (cf. Holt 2012). Khmer in Cambodia often say that they make offerings to vagrant ghosts during Pchum Ben just in case any of their relatives are among them. One text recited in the ceremony describes these ghosts as follows:

> Returning to their old homes, they wait at thresholds. . . .
> Those who feel pity therefore, at the right time
> Give truly pure food and drink to their relatives. . . .
> Dead *preta* [hungry ghosts] survive there on what is given from here. . . .
> The weeping, mourning, and laments of relatives are useless
> To those who remain in such a way.
> But proper gifts dedicated to the *sangha* become useful to them
> Immediately, and for a long time. (E. Davis 2009, 167)

About Boun Khau Padab Din Douang elaborated:

> The spirits who are released from hell join the spirits that have never gone
> anywhere and just roam around freely. All these spirits are hungry. In Laos
> we used to leave the food on fences and under trees and anywhere the spirits
> could get access to it.[8] There were poor people too who ate the food. The poor
> people came and took the chicken or the pork. We didn't like that. We felt that
> the spirits would get offended. But I don't know, I personally think that is a
> good thing.

In Douang's reformed understanding, the offering spilled over to feed not only
the hungry spirits, but the poorest of the living as well. Patrice Ladwig notes
that during Boun Khau Padab Din celebrations in Laos hungry ghosts consume the offerings by "absorbing the vapours" (2012, S92). He further observes
that Lao occasionally mention that ghosts are given not only food but substance for a new body, citing Ang Choulean's suggestion that in the Khmer
ceremony of Pchum Ben, the sticky rice forms a "bodily envelope" for the
dead (cited in Ladwig 2012, S97).

The names of both the Khmer and the Lao festivals refer specifically to
these sticky rice balls and packets that are offered to the dead during the celebration (E. Davis 2009, 160; Ladwig 2012, S91). Yet like other ceremonies,
Pchum Ben and Boun Khau Padab Din are times not only to feed ghosts but
also to produce *boun* (Khmer, *bon*) or merit, which is doubly offered to the dead
and rebounded back to the living, as an investment in improved afterlives and
future incarnations.[9] In a celebration of Boun Khau Padab Din observed by
Penny Van Esterik in Canada, a monk read a story in which Buddha pronounced the benefits of making *boun* on this holiday. "The givers would be
free of danger and gain happiness, their relatives and other beings would gain
shelter, and merit would be shared with other relatives" (Van Esterik 1992,
74). Sodoeung described the U.S. celebration of Pchum Ben in this way:

> People cook a particular dish, sweet, sticky rice with mung bean and pork in
> it. We offer it to the monks. We write down the names of family members
> who have died and put money with the names and give them to the monk.[10]
> The monks take the money for the *wat*. Then they give teachings and bless-
> ings and call the names of the dead to come and be reunited. "Come, because
> the family has offered you food and money, and all kinds of supplies, what-
> ever you can think of. After you eat you have to go and reincarnate." That's
> what the monks say in the ceremony. Some people believe that after you die,
> if you have killed or murdered, you probably become a wandering ghost. Or
> you might reincarnate as a dog or a cat or a wild animal. The monks tell the

spirits to listen to Buddhist advice, to be determined to have a pure mind. Afterward it will bring them merit, and then the merit will bring them to heaven, so they can reincarnate again.

In this account the gifts to the dead are wrapped in Buddhist counsel in such a way that the dead are provisioned for daily existence even as they are guided to purify their minds. The gift of material goods is intertwined with the gift of merit. Erik Davis recounts a story told in Cambodia as the origin of this festival in which a king heard the ghosts of the dead screaming in a forest near his palace. He left food for them, but the next night they were still wailing. The Buddha told him that ghosts could not receive food directly and that he should make merit by giving the food to the *sangham*, and then the ghosts would eat. Davis (2009) suggests that what Khmer ghosts actually eat is the merit itself. In Sodoeung's view, however, the spirits receive merit less as a transfer from the living than as the fruit of their own mental discipline. As in the death ceremonies themselves, during Pchum Ben the munificence of the living is reflected back to them from the world of the dead. Mrs. Sann highlighted the negative potentiality of failing to observe Pchum Ben, saying, "That is when the souls come looking for their relatives. One has to show respect and pay them back. If you don't, then your ancestor or relative's soul will curse you and bring you bad luck."

Lao and Khmer continue to care for their dead relatives, not to mention nameless restless spirits, throughout their lives. During New Year celebrations, which fall in the spring, everyone honors parents (both living and dead), asking their forgiveness for any wrong they have done during the previous year. Douang recalled the New Year festivities in Laos:

> Everybody, family members, relatives used to sit down and pay their respects to the dead person. We poured perfumed water on the bones and prayed that the spirit would stay in heaven. Or, if he was not already in heaven, we would pray for him to go to heaven and live happily there. . . . People say that because it is hot in April, the cool water is to keep them cool. But coolness in Lao means more than just temperature. It also means joy. We wanted them to live with joy. Everybody celebrated the New Year by throwing water at each other in Laos, even Christians and animists.

On such occasions, the dead are included in the festivities of the living and share in the bounty. Many Lao and Khmer also keep small altars or shrines to deceased relatives in their homes where they pray and make offerings.

Those who understand death practices strictly in accordance with Buddhist doctrine say that money placed in the mouth of the deceased at the funeral is not to bribe the border guards of the next world, but to demonstrate that no earthly possessions can be taken into death. They say that the coins that remain among the ashes after cremation are evidence that merit is the only gift that circulates between the living and the dead. Richard Gombrich has argued that the practice of transferring merit to the dead developed as a Buddhist accommodation of a prior practice of feeding the dead by offering food to the monks. "Sensible Theravadin monks decided that food being visibly consumed by a monk could not possibly be eaten by someone else, so that, if people persisted in their habit of feeding dead relatives, the custom required reinterpretation. What the relatives were really getting was something else—merit" (1971, 213–14). Here Theravadin ideology almost approaches the "semiotic ideology" of certain modern Christians (Keane 2007) wherein the difficulty of imagining spirits in need of nutrition necessitates a more symbolic reading of physical offerings. (Note, however, that in Gombrich's representation of Theravadin reasoning, the problem lies less in the inability of spirits to digest food than in the inability of food to be ingested twice.) Nonetheless, in defiance of the illogic detected by Gombrich's hypothetical monks, Lao and Khmer emigrants suggest that food and goods offered to monks are transformed into both merit *and* gifts consumed by the dead. A Lao monk specified that the chants at rites for the dead "teach these Buddhist followers while they are alive, to do good things, to donate, to make offerings to one another, so that when you die in the future you will receive good things." He added, however, that most laypeople, not knowing Pali, interpreted the chants differently.

> They think that it is chanting for the deceased person. . . . The spirit of the deceased person also does receive these good things that you offer to them. . . . But we focus on teaching people to do good things, so that they themselves, when they pass away, can receive these good things that they have done for themselves.

While underscoring karma, whereby the generosity of the mourners returns to them in future incarnations, he deemphasized gift exchange, but did not quite debunk it.

The Khmer ceremony of *bangsukol*, performed at the funeral, the ceremony a hundred days after the death, and then again at Pchum Ben, transfers the merit of the living to the dead, even while, through the very beneficence of that gesture, it simultaneously produces more merit for the living. Yet *bangsukol* transmits not only merit but also matter, sending ethereal forms of food and money to the dead, while leaving visible forms for the monks, and retaining a karmic residue, the good intention motivating the gift, as merit for the giver.[11]

Theravadin funeral exchange, as Klima (2002, 269) points out, always involves gifts that, by their very nature, exist in more than one place at once. The ambiguity of these gifts prompts reflection, but not necessarily rational foreclosure. As one Khmer woman mused, "According to Buddhist doctrine, when someone dies, there is nothing left—no soul, no spirit—so how can they [the deceased] accept something like that [objects such as stoves and refrigerators]? But we believe those dead souls are suffering and we need to help them" (quoted in Smith-Hefner 1999, 61). Here empathy with the distress of the dead overcomes any logical objections to material reciprocity with the dead, as if they are dragged into existence or recoalescence by their own physical needs.

Gombrich further argues that Buddhist laypersons permit merit to take on the character of a medium of exchange, in order to further their social and familial relationships, rather than simply build their own personal virtue or insure their own personal benefit.[12] As is often the case, however, this resolution of a seeming contradiction of doctrine suggests further problems. For Theravada Buddhist doctrine, in at least some of its versions, questions not only the persistence of personal identity beyond death, but even the reality of personal identity, as noted by Smith-Hefner's respondent above. For whom, then, does one accrue merit? Klima perceptively traces the problematics of a gift when there is no fixed subjectivity to fill the role of either giver or receiver: "Generosity brings a return for someone else, a stranger, some other person in the future, to whom you might habitually refer to as 'yourself.' . . . one cannot even rightly say that the gift is for someone else, either. What one is ultimately left with is the acts themselves" (2002, 272). A karmic economy is one "where the gift is already being given to no one in particular, or, alternately, where it can be said, in a relative sense that it is given to all others, of which the self is one" (273). Klima suggests that the mindful observance of such an economy is found not only among the mental discipline of Buddhist renunciants, but in the everyday practices of funerary exchange, where every gift generates a return of merit for everyone involved. Moreover, beyond the circulation of merit, there are persistent stories of magical surplus, such as the dead who might offer lottery numbers in dreams. The social scientific habit of separating out social and individual interests might be unhelpful for understanding the parabolic paths of merit (or, incidentally, as I will consider below, of debt).[13] Even as *boun* passes from giver to receiver it simultaneously doubles back. It binds the community of living and dead as loosely and securely as the white threads winding from monks and mourners around the piles of offerings at funeral ceremonies. It is for this reason perhaps that when I made my own small offering and received the monk's blessing at the Lao *wat*, kneeling before the golden Buddha, my personal history seemed to momentarily flicker out as if in an intimation of that circular karmic current where giver and receiver dissolve.

Beyond Barter

For Hmong and Kmhmu, the material assistance offered to the dead is unmediated by a formal notion of merit. Hmong dress the deceased in the distinctively embroidered burial clothes that will identify him to the ancestors, placing a chicken or rooster (to shelter the spirit from the weather, people say), a bottle of alcohol, a crossbow, and other provisions near the body for the journey.[14] Even Christian Hmong, Mr. Lo said, are not buried in Western clothes. "You wear [the burial clothes] into the spirit world, so that your ancestors can understand or know who you are. If you don't wear that, they will think you are foreign, not Hmong." As the Qhuab Ke ("Showing the Way") is sung, directing the dead to the place of the ancestors, rice wine is offered to sustain them on their journey.[15] They are continually questioned about whether they accept the gifts or have arrived at a particular destination, the answers being read through the position of the *kuam*, the same divination tool used in shamanic healings, either a split buffalo horn or two halves of a piece of bamboo that are tossed on the ground. "The bamboo is a way of communicating with the spirit," Mrs. Vangay told me. "People might ask, 'Are you happy? If you are happy then turn the wood this way. If not, then turn it the other way.' They keep asking until they hear yes or no."

Even as the dead receive gifts from the living, they are obligated to offer them in turn to others on the thoroughfare of death. "We give [the deceased] money to get a boat across the river to where he came from," Mr. Vangay said.

> We tell him to show his appreciation to the country he is living in right now, to the lord or whoever controls the country, to the water, to the woods, to the fire that he used, before he goes. Like he has used so much water, he needs to say thank you for the water . . . to the lord of the water. And for the wood, to the lord of the wood, who let him burn this much wood. To the city, whoever owns the city . . . or to the house, for the use of the house.[16]

The spirit repays the landscape that has sustained him with incense and spirit money (specially fashioned paper money that is burned and in that way sent with the dead) offered by funeral guests. In one version of Qhuab Ke the deceased is told to use the money and incense to engage the assistance of the spirits of the land and villages to build bridges and construct lamps for his journey. Some Hmong refer to a marketplace on the bridge between the world of the living and the world of the dead, where the two communities "trade, deal, and bargain with each other" (Tapp 1989, 64).

Guests stay at the home of the deceased for several days, playing cards and gambling until early morning to "keep the family warm," as one man said. It is said that ghosts may hover around these homes, causing the family to feel cold and afraid. Mourners sometimes hear a door opening and shutting or a voice uttering nonsense words. One woman felt her deceased mother grab at her blanket in the night. As they each tugged the woman insisted, "Mother, you're supposed to leave now." Pheng told me of one bereaved family who felt grateful to the teenage gang members who stayed the night to drink beer and eat the food prepared by the family. As with the Lao, the all-night gambling offers companionship not only to the living but to the dead (cf. Symonds 2004, 138).

If the deceased Hmong is a revered older man, the day before the burial is devoted to the settlement of debts to assure that he is not so poor in the next world that he demands assistance from the living by making them ill. The immediate family of the deceased is responsible for giving an account of the man's life to his lineage. An opposite-gender sibling of the deceased (brother if the deceased is a woman, sister if the deceased is a man) asks his family a series of questions: How many children did he father? Did he feed the ancestors throughout his life? Did he bury his own parents in a proper location? What animals will be killed and sent with him? What articles of clothing were given to him? What property has been left behind, and how will it be distributed? "We need to state how much money everyone is getting and clarify that," Mrs. Vangay said, "so there will be no problems afterwards." That night, messages are delivered to the living through the *txiv xaiv*, the "father of words" (Symonds 2004, 142–44), instructing the descendants to be kind to one another and remember to feed the ancestors. "If you do not want to remain healthy and prosperous," one translation of this song specifies, "it does not matter, but if you want to, you must give charity to your father by giving him three joss sticks, and three amounts of paper money. . . . You must take your father and bury him in a good place and then you will have a lot of children. They will live together as crowded as the bamboo clump" (Chindarsi 1976, 156–57). As the song indicates, an essential gift to the Hmong dead in Asia is the correct orientation of the gravesite, which derives from principles of geomancy *(loojmem)*, but is explained by some emigrants as the dead person's desire for a "good view."[17]

On the day of burial, animals are given to the dead by an opposite-gender sibling of the deceased.[18] A song the night before informs the descendants:

"Tomorrow morning the oxen and pigs will be killed for your father but your father can have only their souls, so you divide the meat and pork among the people who have come to help work in the mortuary rite" (Chindarsi 1976, 156–57). The dual form of the gift is explicit here: the deceased eats the souls of the animals, while the mourners consume the flesh. Consulting with his wife Mai, Pao Chang emphasized, "That sacrifice, its meaning is for love. . . . 'I'm your brother, you're my sister and we love together. I'm not going to leave you alone even though you die.' It's support, a strong, strong support. Let's say the brother dies, and the sister brings a cow to offer, that is only a kindness of her, it's not a demand." Seemingly fending off anthropological or Christian interpretations of animist rites, the Changs insist that gift exchanges with the dead are not rote cultural rules or self-interested transactions, but communications of love. Has the living's fear of the dead and the dead's jealousy of the living made famous in so many ethnographies of animist mourning been edited out here (by the interpreter or by Mai and Pao themselves), swept away by a backwash of Christianity, with its emphasis on love? Perhaps. Or might love have been overlooked over the years in the ethnographic fascination with techniques and taboos to protect the living? How intermixed with fear the love of the dead might be (and no less for Christians) is left unspoken. All that is clear is that in this conversational moment love is insisted upon like a militant reinsertion against a possible Christianity that might tend to reserve love for itself. Moreover, this reinsertion constitutes some delicate backtalk to the division between love and social obligation reinforced by what Povinelli (2006) calls the autological and genealogical, those twin forms of postcolonial discipline into which modern subjects are interpellated: the exercise of autonomous selfhood, on the one hand, and obeisance to social constraint, on the other. In a moment when they feel called upon to explain themselves within the logic of this division, it is difficult to unravel the extent to which the Changs are defying the separation of mandatory reciprocity and love (since the funeral sacrifice is both) or insisting, against anthropological and Christian presumptions, that the sacrifice is primarily autological, an exercise of that love that "belongs properly to the free subject" (Povinelli in Venkatsan et al. 2011, 225–26).

Hmong dead continue to be offered food for several days following the death. Some conjecture that by the fifth day the dead "may be able to find his own food" (Thao 1993, 67). Hmong speak of three *plig* of the deceased: one who travels to the land of the ancestors, another who remains with the body, and a third who is reborn (Johnson 1992, 60; Symonds 2004, 20–21; Lemoine 1996).[19] By directly referring to a spirit that remains with the corpse, Hmong lore formalizes a contiguity of body and spirit, which, for Khmer and Lao Buddhists, is simply ritually enacted. Mr. Vangay's family invited his dead father's spirit to the ceremonial meal known as *xi plig* on the thirteenth day after the burial. Until this meal at least one soul is said to still wander between the previous home and the grave, uncertain where to reside. Mr. Vangay drove to the cemetery, picked up a handful of dirt, called the spirit, and brought the dirt home for an offering of chicken, water, and liquor. "We sat beside him," Mrs. Vangay recalled, "beside the dirt." The intermingling of the soul with the soil of the grave accentuated the physicality of his presence. Again, as in the rite immediately following death, the spirit must communicate to the living his acceptance of the meal and then his willingness to depart after eating. "We actually asked one of the relatives to come and help [toss the *kuam*]," Mrs. Vangay related. "It is very sad for the family member to talk to the soul. They feel sympathy for the dead one. It is very hard to feel that grief. It's easier to get an outsider to do it." The family's avoidance of the anguish of speaking to the spirit through the *kuam* underscores the palpable presence of the deceased. "We pretty much follow the same steps as the time after he died," Mr. Vangay added. "We sacrifice an animal, we play the pipes, we play the drum, we cry. . . . If that is never done then the soul will never be reborn." Even after *tso plig*, a later ceremony to release the soul for rebirth, the possibility remains that the spirit may become restless and make further claim on the living, especially on the anniversary of the death. In Laos, Mrs. Vangay said, "When the calendar comes back to the day a person passed away, when the moon is closest to where it was on that day . . . we have to *caiv*, which means we are supposed to rest. We don't go out. We don't chop wood or anything. Guests are not allowed in the house." At the New Year, when people call one another's souls to stay close to their bodies, they also call the dead to share the feast of chicken and (in Laos) newly harvested rice.

While even Christian converts butcher animals at such times, one Catholic leader, Mr. Lo, explained, "We just kill it for a celebration for the ones who are living. We do not believe that we give the animal to the dead person. In the Christian teachings you don't need to take anything with you. So we as Christians do not really feed our ancestors." Note that Mr. Lo's understanding of Christianity, like doctrinaire Theravada Buddhism, works against the possibility that the dead participate in a material gift exchange with the living. Yet even Christians may feel a lingering responsibility to the dead. Mr. Lo went on to say:

> Some people still do something to make the ancestors happy. When they celebrate the New Year, they still call the ancestors, but they call them in a different

way. They just pray before they eat and say the person's name. "Come and eat with us. Today is a special day. We are celebrating the New Year. We know that you will be with us in spirit. So you can come and eat with us."

As Christian converts, most Kmhmu in the United States are also careful to dissociate themselves from material reciprocity with the dead. "We don't pray to ghosts," one man assured me. "We pray for the person to get into heaven. We take the things to the church. During the mass the priest names the things that people are offering. The diocese allows us to do that." Yet the hybridity of this practice is suggested by other accounts. "We know what kind of food our ancestor likes," Julie Prachitham said, "so we buy that kind of food and offer it to him. If someone offers that and eats that, then the ancestor will receive it." The materiality of the gift to the dead still haunts this Christian offertory. As someone uniquely vulnerable to contact with the dead, Julie used to abstain from eating the food consecrated to the dead.

> I could never eat that. I don't know if I was afraid or if my mom said I couldn't eat it or what. But since I've started coming to this church, I eat it. Because the catechists say, "Oh here's some food. Eat it." And then later they tell me, "You know where that was from?" And I say, "Where?" And they say, "That was from the offertory." And I say, "Oh my God."

Even in Julie's Christianized practice the food retains physical traces of its contact with the dead.

In Laos, Kmhmu, like Hmong, kept the deceased at home for several days, during which the entire village gathered, bringing gifts of food, playing games, and consoling the family. This support for the family continues in the United States, although the deceased now lies in a funeral home. "We still carry that on," Kampheang said, "support each other, help them with things they need." Cheuang, a Kmhmu healer, whose conversion to Christianity did not prevent his pursuit of pre-Christian rites, described the preparation of his mother's body after her death.

> We said, "Here's some money. Whatever you want, you take, and leave us what you don't want." We wrapped the coins in black and white cloth and put them in her hand. In one hand we put sticky rice, and in the other meat. We put other coins in her mouth for her to buy her way to *mìang róoy* [the spirit town]. If we put them in a pocket we'd worry that somebody would steal them. In her mouth we know they're safe.

His story signals again the concreteness of the gift, the return of part of the gift to the giver, and the care taken to avoid any interference in the exchange with the dead. Reflecting on these practices Kampheang mused, "Some people put the money in the mouth. And if you ask why do you do that, [it's] because he needs to have that money to go buy a new place for himself. That's how we translate it out." Safe passage or spiritual real estate, the gift of money slides from a visible capitalist economy into a shadow economy of the dead, one currency translated to another.

This material reciprocity is referenced in a Kmhmu folktale told by Kam Raw about two brothers whose mother was seriously ill (Lindell, Swahn, and Tayanin 1977–95, 3:83–88). The younger son cared attentively for his mother, but the older son did not. When the mother died, and the youngest son asked his brother to help with the burial, he refused, saying, "Oh no, I won't go to bury mother because I have work to do. I am still feeding my children, I won't go bury her. You go alone!" After the burial, the younger son offered rice to his mother each morning at the burial site. One day he found a stone at the gravesite. The next day he heard the stone singing and whistling. Eventually he took the stone home with him where the stone began to sing at his command. When he boasted to some merchants about the stone, they wagered everything they owned that the stone could not sing. Winning the bet, the son became rich. When his older brother learned about the stone he asked the younger brother to let him borrow the stone to get wealthy as well. The younger brother refused, saying, "It is something mother gave to me to return [my] kindness and good care. I cannot give it to you!" So the older brother stole the stone and made a bet with another group of merchants that the stone would sing at his command. He agreed to enslave himself to the merchants if he lost. Of course, the stone would not sing for him, and he became their slave. Kam Raw concludes,

> He did not love his parents. When his mother was ill and going to die he did nothing to cure her. When she died and he was asked to go and bury her he did not go. It was only his brother who took care of her all alone. Thus the younger brother received his mother's blessing, while he did not get any blessing from her. (88)

It is tempting to imagine that the materiality of such relations with the dead is in tension with their emotional charge. Exchange with the dead, as Mai and Pao Chang emphasized, is rooted less in utilitarian obligation than in persistent connection and love. However, once again, an expressivist witnessing is not what the dead primarily ask of that love (cf. Foucault 1990). They ask instead that it be manifest in physical gifts and actions. They require companionship, hospitality, a good view from their burial sites. This materiality signals not a narrowly self-interested exchange, but a continuous current of care flowing in several directions at once, defying the split between autology and genealogy.

Drawing Heidegger's and Georges Bataille's thoughts on the gift into dialogue, Rebecca Comay (1990) writes of an indebtedness that is simultaneously an infinite gratitude (for time, for other beings, for being itself).[20] Comay suggests that this indebtedness marks a sociality prior to exchange and a responsibility prior to law. It is gratitude so profound in the face of generosity so extravagant that no payback can be thought.[21] Within the limits of European philosophy such an exuberant gift, and the infinite gratitude it provokes, is imagined as a gesture toward immaterial abstraction, rather than a moment of material exchange. Although the gift exchanges with the dead that are traced here hold some of the resonance of that radical Heideggerian gift, they simultaneously exhibit a gritty physical existence: mung beans, rice wine, the washing of the bones, or polishing of the urn. Jean-Luc Nancy and Richard Livingston (1991) note that for "Western" thinkers, the concept of sacrifice is "spiritualized" such that true sacrifice is necessarily figurative rather than literal. They point out that philosophers from the Greeks through Bataille consider the more literal sacrifice practiced by peoples around the world a vulgar economism. Yet they observe:

> When someone says to his gods: "Here is the butter. Where are the gifts?" it may be that we do not know what he is saying, since we know nothing of the community in which he lives with his gods. . . . We need to admit that what we consider as mercenary exchange ("here is the butter . . .") sustained and gave meaning to billions of individual and collective existences, and we do not know how to think about what founds this gesture. (We can only guess, confusedly, that this barter in itself goes beyond barter.) (26, 35)

For "gods," in this statement, we might substitute "the dead." The parenthetical caution that barter may go beyond barter is provocative. Yet, rather than resign ourselves to the absolute foreignness of a more literal sacrifice imagined by "billions" of humans, might we learn to sense what is at stake in a material reciprocity with the dead?[22]

The stories above are not told in an innocence of a more figurative interchange between living and dead, but rather in the face of it. But if a modern reason tends to constrain the dead to a metaphorical existence where they are only symbols for the grief of the living, the dead themselves insist on a more bodily presence. Charles recalled that once, as a young man living in the Cambodian countryside with his family, he fell ill after a visit to the city.

Having tried several remedies to no effect, his mother consulted a *krou teay* who ascertained that Charles's dead great-grandmother was angry with him. "Her spirit was upset because I went away from her without letting her know. My mom did a ritual, and the next day I got better. Maybe I should have gone to the grave and said, 'Grandma I'm going to go away.'" He laughed. "I don't really believe in it, but it happened." His skeptical comment registers his journey not only away from the burial site where his grandmother lingered, but also toward a civil society swept relatively clean of spirits, where relations with the dead are subject to a more symbolic status. With such a seismic shift in the terms of reality, his great-grandmother demanded of him not just the sticky rice, cooked with mung beans and pork, presented at Pchum Ben, but an acknowledgement of her capacity to participate in impromptu (and not only prescribed) physical exchanges with the living.

In a discussion of Japanese mediums who contact the dead for troubled mourners, Marilyn Ivy suggests that it is the very slippage in the physical encounter with the dead (the way the voice of the dead speaking through the medium differs from the voice mourners remember) that facilitates an outpouring of grief (1995, 180). It is possible that slippages in the material exchange with the dead in the stories told above—the dirt that is not quite the body, the dream image that is not quite the person, the coin that remains in the ashes after cremation, the answers of the deceased that must be read through the split buffalo horn—evoke grief in a similar way. Physical encounters with the dead—whether through burning spirit money or inscribing slips of paper with names of the dead and passing them into monks' hands, whether through stripping rotten flesh from bones or inhaling the smoke of a cremation fire—intensify mourning by simultaneously accentuating and assuaging absence. To intercept these material encounters, then, might be to foreclose mourning, and in the process aggravate a sense of mounting and unaddressed debt.

O grasses, your grandson begs you—
if the grandfather grasses know
the whereabouts of my father's grave,
I shall shave my head in thanks.

O grass of thickets, grass
of sticking burrs, where is
the skeleton concealed?
Tell—and I shall ask no more of you.

—U Sam Oeur, from "Searching for Dad"

The ranger in khaki shorts and Smokey-the-Bear hat said
"You have to know someone who died there"
I stood my ground
Letting the emotions clog my throat, sting my eyes

What had I expected him to say
"Your father Tooj Cib Muas is right over here?"
My mute tongue could not scream
"But I do know someone who died there"
I know six who died there
. . . .
The white man had moved on
To other people—tourists gathered
Around the memorial as if
It was an exotic exhibit
. . . .
I stood my ground

—Mai Neng Moua, from "D.C."

Chapter 7   **Spirit Debt**

THESE POEMS BY THE CAMBODIAN POET U Sam Oeur and the Hmong
poet Mai Neng Moua track the relationship between mourning and physical
traces of the dead, lamenting and protesting the loss of remains within a
landscape and the missing names on a monument. In different ways, the
poems register longing and anger related to an absence of physical connection with the dead. This connection has been broken, the poets infer, by state
terror that separated families and destroyed villages and temples; by state-
sponsored bombs and landmines that tore up landscapes; and by state memo-
rials that honor soldiers in the U.S. armed services while excluding foreign
operatives or civilians. What is at stake in this rupture of material engagement with the dead is a break in the reciprocity with ancestors that is understood as essential to life itself.

Ironically, just as the ranks of the dead swelled in wartime Laos and Cambodia, reciprocity with their spirits was severely disrupted. In Laos, soldiers
were hastily buried or burned by their comrades in the place where they had
died. In Cambodia under the Khmer Rouge, fabric was so scarce that gravesites were raided for the cloth wrapping the bodies.[1] With the destruction of
the *wats* and the murder and forced defrocking of monks by the Khmer
Rouge, the dead received scant mourning. Those who were clandestinely exe-
cuted were simply thrown in mass graves. Even the ashes of those who had
been cremated earlier were lost when *wats* were destroyed. "When the Vietnamese took over," Sodoeung recalled, "people were supposed to look for their
relatives' bodies and bones. But how could they look?" One young woman,
like many others, had lost her entire family. "She didn't do any ceremony,"
Sodoeung said. Then one day her family sent a message through a neighbor's
dream. "'If you don't go to the *wat*, we won't have any food or clothes to wear.'
She didn't believe it, because she was one of the kids who grew up under the
communists. Later on she got sick." Although the Khmer Rouge officially

nullified all responsibilities to the dead, their violence, like the violence of the relentless U.S. bombing campaigns that preceded it, simply inflated the debt, prompting the dead to request recompense through bodily forms of haunting.

There is still public discussion in Cambodia of whether to cremate the anonymous remains of those who were summarily piled in mass graves. Meanwhile the unsettled dead pull at emigrants in the United States. "They have regrets," Sodoeung said. "Every time they go to the *wat* they say, 'I wish I could find where my parents' grave is, or their ashes, so I could put them in the *wat*.'" Sodoeung described the loss of her grandmother's remains under the Khmer Rouge. "We left her ash in the temple," she said. "But then in 1975 we didn't know where her ashes went. The temple was destroyed. My mother thought that maybe we should find my grandmother's urn, but it was impossible to find." During the Khmer Rouge regime those very temple grounds had been used as a torture site. The disturbing possibility went unspoken that Sodoeung's grandmother's ashes now intermingled with this blood-soaked earth, her spirit lost among the hungry ghosts of tortured prisoners.

Debts for Survival

Yet it was also the dead, submerged in the landscape or emerging from it, who offered a haphazard protection during war or state terror. In his memoir of life under the Khmer Rouge the musician Daran Kravanh wrote: "I cannot tell you why or how I survived; I do not know myself. It is like this: love and music and invisible hands, and something that comes out of the society of the living and the dead, for which there are no words" (LaFreniere 2000, 3). In Kravanh's rumination, the debt to the dead emerges as a form of sociality, less a specific transaction to be completed than a relationship to be cultivated. Even if no words can capture this sociality, stories offer glimpses and approximations, singular moments in the interchange of living and dead. When Kravanh first heard his brother play a certain song, he watched his spirit drift out of his body "like steam rising from a bowl of rice"(15). Long after his brother had died, when Kravanh was in trouble, he heard the song again and sensed his brother nearby, offering him protection.

As a soldier in the Cambodian army, Charles's brother sought protection from a spirit known simply as Yeimao (grandma). According to legend, Yeimao had declared, when living, that she would only marry a man who could defeat her in combat. After several men perished in the attempt, she herself eventually died, still chaste, on the mountain where she lived. "Hundreds of people cross the mountain," Charles said, "and before they cross they buy some fruit and offer it to her spirit, so that they can pass safely. Otherwise they end up in a car accident or falling off the mountain." Charles's brother took a rock from the mountain. "He went down on his knees and asked for it. Now even a bullet can't hit him. During the war, people would shell him, his clothes would burn, be all ripped, and no bullet touched his body. He brought this rock when he visited and showed me. It's black. It changes color according to the temperature." Again Charles's skepticism wavered in the face of the physicality of the rock and his brother's survival. Human dead whose essence can enter minerals confound an ontological division between animate and inanimate, geological and social. Through such situational sharing of substance, objects such as the protective rock embody both everyday ordinariness and ontological alterity. The power inhering in such objects extends the indebtedness to the dead into nonhuman realms, as articulated in the Hmong funeral song in which the deceased is directed to compensate the landscape with the spirit money supplied by the living.

In addition to the rock, Charles's brother carried a human skull in his backpack. He told Charles, "That skull protects me. When I go to sleep I just put the skull on a stick standing next to me. I tell it, 'Please protect me, any harm that comes, please wake me up.'" "He's been in the army for ten years, fighting in combat," Charles marveled. "And he still survives."[2] In her memoir of life under the Khmer Rouge, Rouen Sam relates finding some duck eggs nestled in a human skull. "One egg was stuck close to the mouthful of teeth. I thought that the dead person wanted to eat this egg. I took it, then put it back. I told the dead body, 'Don't let me see you in my mind.' . . . Later I went to a pond that was used for bathing and pretended to be bathing so that I could eat my eggs" (quoted in Pran and DePaul 1997, 79). This story evokes the sharing of food between living and dead in Buddhist ceremonies, while also suggesting how those struggling to live were pressed to continually negotiate with unsettled dead. During an escape from her work unit under the Khmer Rouge, Sodoeung also sought protection from human remains. "I saw a monk's body in a stupa, sitting close to the Buddha's foot. I slept next to the monk's body. By that time it was just bones. I didn't smell anything. I saw the Buddha's picture and the monk, and they both are very gentle people. I thought they would protect me." Here the lack of odor works against the swampy muck of the killing fields, indicating the auspiciousness of the dead. The spirit's purity and merit is evidenced by the cleanliness of the bones. The homology of spirit and corpse evoke a tangible sense of protection. Douang's safe passage out of Laos was arranged not only with a saleswoman for an import-export business, but also with a guardian spirit of Vieng Chan, Chao Mae Simeuang (Honorable Mother Simeuang). According to legend, when Simeuang was making offerings for a new *wat*, she fell into the construction site and died. Because she was pregnant at the time, her death was charged with an extra-ordinary power. Since her merit had mingled with the earth, her benevolence sheltered all those who made offerings there. Douang's mother promised Simeuang gifts if he crossed safely into Thailand.

Hmong and Kmhmu emigrants also speak of debts to and protection from the dead under conditions of violence and displacement. Mysterious death in sleep among Hmong and Lao men (common enough to have earned a diag-nosis, Sudden Unexpected Nocturnal Death Syndrome, SUNDS) is associated with nightmares of a suffocating spirit who sits on the sleeper's chest. Hmong say that those who have been deserted by their ancestors are particularly vul-nerable to such attack (Adler 1991, 59). "[My brother and I] are suscepti-ble," one man said, "because we didn't follow all of the mourning rituals we should have when our parents died. . . . We have lost contact with their spir-its, and thus we are left with no one to protect us from evil spirits. . . . I had hoped flying so far in a plane to come to America would protect me, but it turns out spirits can follow even this far" (quoted in Tobin and Friedman 1983, 444).[3] Historian Mai Na Lee (2009) corroborates that many Hmong attribute sudden nocturnal death to the curses of family members who died during war without gravesites or funeral rites. Elders credit the decrease of incidents in the first decade of the twenty-first century to the numerous rit-uals that have been conducted for war dead. Pao Chang related the story of a man who returned to Thailand to tend his great-grandfather's grave.

> When he got home, not too long after he became sick. The doctor found out that it was cancer. Later on some radiation treatment and it was gone. But still the ill condition did not get any better. And the doctors said, "We can't find anything else. And we can't treat you any more. That's it." So they had no choice. They went and called the *txiv neeb*. The son was Catholic since thirty years ago. . . . And the guy diagnosed that "Somehow your people have been Christian for a long time. You never *laig dab*, feed your ancestors any more for this time, thirty years. And somehow one of you went back and messed up the house and damaged the house of the ancestors and they're not happy so they punished you for it."

After this, the family performed *laig dab* belatedly, but the man did not recover.[4] When physician Robert Putsch suggested the possibility of ancestor illness in a young Hmong woman suffering from severe headaches and nightmares, she and her husband insisted, "We're Catholic; we went to Catholic school, we don't know about these things" (1988, 17). Nonetheless they agreed to consult Hmong elders, who traced the illness to the woman's failure to seek permission to marry from her dead parents. After a meal was hosted for the parents to request their blessing, the dreams and headaches ceased.[5] In such stories, efforts to assimilate to more symbolic recognitions of the dead are subverted by a physical haunting that initially goes unrecognized. More recently Hmong have been haunted by the 2005 exhumations of Hmong bodies at Wat Tham Krabok in Thailand, where Hmong fleeing Laos in 2003 were temporarily housed.[6] The disinterred dead have appeared in Hmong dreams demanding, "Where is my home?" Hmong children have also fallen ill. Mai Na Lee (2009) suggests that it would be difficult to calculate the ritual expense needed to satisfy those homeless spirits. Hmong still remember the desecration of Hmong graves in China as an attempt to eradicate "the Hmong soul." Such accounts suggest that part of what is at stake in the shift to a more representational economy of relationships with the dead is the loss of means to materially address the past as embodied in the present.

When Julie Prachitham's sister fell ill in Laos, her family first consulted a *po kru*, and then, when he was unable to heal her, took her to the nearest city, Hoisai, a day's walk away. "There was supposed to be a hospital there," Julie said, "but the hospital was really poor. So she died." Having no way to transport her back to the village, the family was forced to bury her in the hospital plot. "The funeral didn't have a very good appearance," Julie recalled.

> In our village we could have made a coffin or bamboo covering to wrap her body. But because we were on the road, we just wrapped her in some white cloth. I don't think my mother was happy about that. She felt that what she had done was not enough. When we went home I had a dream in which my sister was saying, "I'm not dead yet. I don't know why you buried me." I interpret that to mean that we did a poor job of burying her. Twenty years later I still feel bad about what happened. If there were a way, I would like to go back. I don't think I could ever find out where her grave is. I would just know the area but I wouldn't know which grave because they didn't put the names. My mother has never gotten over it. Every day she talks about it and cries.

Although Kmhmu village cemeteries were described as fearsome places where no one wanted to linger, in this story the city hospital is an even more upsetting burial site. "In that hospital place," Julie said, "we were so poor. We were poor in that place." She might easily have spoken in the same breath of how poor Kmhmu are in U.S. hospitals. Her story foreshadows the frustration many feel over postmortem practices in the United States.

When I asked Lt. Phanha how he protected himself during battle, he replied, "I just believed in *róoy kàan.* Whenever there was danger ahead I always had a dream." In prison camp, for instance, a woman appeared in a dream to warn him that he was about to be killed. Because of the dream he decided to flee the camp the next day. When a guard shot at him, the gun misfired. Although, at the time of our conversations, he was contemplating converting to Christianity, he was unwilling to abandon his ancestors until he could make arrangements for their well-being. "If I ever have the opportunity to go back to Laos," he said, "I will have a big Buddhist ceremony for my parents and tell them, 'If you want to find me, look for me at the church.' I want to inform them in a kind way. Otherwise they will be waiting for me to make an offering every so often."[7] When I asked why he would choose to do a Buddhist rather than Kmhmu ceremony for *róoy kàan,* he answered, "Kmhmu don't have a place for our ancestors. We just bury them anywhere. In my family we used to say the dead went to a certain lake. But now I see that some people have a place where they keep their ancestors. For instance, Buddhists keep the ashes in a temple. I want my ancestors to have a place to stay. That's why I have been keeping two *rit, rit* Kmhmu and Buddhism." In Laos, Lt. Phanha's debt to his ancestors would have been paid by dressing and acting in specific ways— handling the rice pot gently for instance—on the anniversary of the day that *róoy kàan* had died. Such practices have been replaced in his community by the offertory made to a Catholic parish in the name of the dead. Meanwhile the mountain landscape where *róoy kàan* were once said to reside was reordered for Lt. Phanha by the war operations in which he spent his early adult life.[8] For years he has not crossed the distance to that place of ancestors, either in imagination or in funeral songs. No one in his local community today chants the soul of the deceased along such a route. Lt. Phanha therefore contemplates transferring his ancestors to a Lao *wat,* after telling them how to find him in a U.S church. In this way he hopes that he can continue to pay his debt to the dead.

Derrida has explored that inherent paradox of the gift, that in the very instant it is recognized as a gift, it is no longer a gift as such, but rather an exchange, or to put it another way, the establishment of a debt. The giver develops the expectation of a countergift, even as the receiver becomes conscious of the call for a countergift (1992; cf. Derrida 1995).[9] In the exchange with the dead, however, there is never any certainty regarding whether a gift to the dead was received, or whether the value of a gift exceeds or falls short of a prior gift traveling in the reverse direction. It is impossible to erase the risk of dangling and unclaimed gifts, unknowingly accepted gifts, and mysterious remainders of debt that, being beyond calculation, might be neither repaid nor repayable. Gifts offered to the dead, therefore, might take on some of the exteriority of a pure gift in relation to political economy. The exchange quickly falls into darkness, unfolding in a time out of time, exaggerating the quality of incommensurability that is already inherent to the gift (Comay 1990, 67), the mystery, for instance, of trading fruit or rice for survival. There is, finally, a bottomless quality to reciprocity with the dead, gifts mirroring gifts into an infinite distance, signifying the immeasurable debt owed to the dead.

Two days before her twenty-one-year-old daughter died in the United States, Mrs. Sann heard a voice in a dream say, "For the past twenty-one years I have left you something to take care of for me. Now I am going to take it back." In the dream Mrs. Sann directed her son, "Whatever belongs to them, give it back." Her son retrieved a briefcase and put it by the front door of the house. "In Khmer," Mrs. Sann explained, "we have a word for somebody who allows you to come into this world and then at a certain time takes your spirit back. I believe that my daughter passed away so quickly and so easily because I was too willing to give the briefcase away. I don't like to keep other people's belongings." Mrs. Sann understood her daughter's death as a return of her soul to her spirit family. Her mistake, she thought in retrospect, was in being too quick to settle the accounts, mishandling the temporal negotiation of gift and countergift.[10]

The story resonates sharply with another story she told, of losing another daughter in Cambodia. While she was away working on a Khmer Rouge collective farm, her mother sent one of her daughters to a relative for safekeeping.

> I was so sad. I asked her why she did that. She said, "Another woman's family was already killed. I gave her away in case they found out you are a wife of a soldier too. They would have killed you also. At least one of your daughters will live." My daughter lived with them for a year and then she died. I thought I killed her. . . . I would have paid whatever I could to get my daughter back. If I had decided to give up my necklace, maybe they would have given my daughter back. But after I found out she was dead, I felt so sad. I thought I had committed a sin and I had killed my daughter.

"Why do you think you sinned?" I asked. "You were taking care of your daughter as well as you could at the time." She replied, "Sometimes I don't think I sinned because at the time I knew the couple who had taken my daughter were poorer than me. I knew that when the country became stable I could give them some gold and I could have my daughter back. I knew that for sure." These stories trace a heartbreaking parallel between the daughter Mrs. Sann's mother gave up too easily and the second daughter Mrs. Sann fears she her-self gave away too soon, between the daughter who died before Mrs. Sann could offer gold for her return and the daughter who died when Mrs. Sann was too hasty to repay the spirits. Each daughter's life seems to have been lost in a mistiming of a gift. As Derrida comments in response to Marcel Mauss, "The gift is not a gift, the gift only gives to the extent it *gives time*" (Derrida 1992, 41). An inherent risk of gift exchange, in which the return is posited but placed in indefinite suspension, is that the exchange will misfire for giver or taker, when the temporal dimension is collapsed or interrupted. This risk was intensified for Mrs. Sann as gift exchanges unfolded in the shadow of death, during encounters with spirits or under conditions of state terror.

In another story Mrs. Sann recounted how she had purchased survival for herself and her remaining children from a Khmer Rouge cadre who was ques-tioning her closely about her husband.

> I felt so scared, I felt like my soul was not with me anymore. I told her my hus-band worked as a mine laborer. All along I had been thinking that when she asked me, I would give her the real answer, which was that my husband was a former government officer. If I had told the truth I would not be here any-more. She asked if I had any gold. I said "I've already exchanged it for rice for my children. This is all I have." I gave her a pack of uncut gemstones.

If the deaths of two of her children occurred through mistimed gift exchanges, the survival of her other children was secured through trades of gold for rice and semiprecious stones for silence. Despite a terror in which she sensed her soul leaving her body, a life-threatening event in itself, Mrs. Sann was able to strike a deal that evaded death for herself and her children.

For Mrs. Sann, the living receive their very lives from the dead, not only through ancestral bloodlines, but also through the permission of spirits for (re)birth. Since the repayment of this debt, the countergift of life (or death) can only be deferred, never finally avoided; all other gifts offered to the spirits are supplements but also postponements of this gift of death. Specifying the dead as the first group with whom humans entered into a contract, Marcel Mauss commented, "Indeed, it is they who are the true owners of the things and possessions of this world" (1990, 16; cf. Willerslev 2009). The circula-tion of gifts can only have been set in motion from beyond the world of living humans (cf. Siegel 2006, 5). That is not to say, however, that the gift of death ends the exchange either, since the dead remain both debtors and themselves frequently indebted.[11] In such a gift cycle, the ethical necessity might be less to give without guarantee of return (already a given in exchanges with the dead) than to participate in an open-ended reciprocity. Jonathan Parry (1986) points out that Mauss himself suggested that the purity of the gift is only a problem for social worlds where a clear distinction is drawn between obligation and gift. Similarly, Klima argues that the problem of the pure gift evaporates within a Buddhist economy of karma. He asks, "What if the 'gift without exchange' already was the state of affairs? What if the practice of exchange were seen through different moral eyes, ones not so full of an unfulfilled desire for the absence of interest, hierarchy, asymmetry, or—and this is forceful—not haunted by the deep cosmological tradition of the 'evil' of money?" (2002, 269). Arguably Derrida (1995) himself locates the problem of the pure gift in European ethics, linking the valorization of the gift to a Christianity marked by solitude, interiority, and a private contract with God.

Nonetheless, following Klima, we might contemplate further the difference between what Derrida termed the "terrestrial" and "celestial" economies of Christianity, and what Klima calls the material–spiritual exchange of Buddhism. In the Christian contract, God sacrifices himself to pay off human debts, but only for those who "believe," becoming investors or creditors of God, giving alms for the sake of a heavenly reward (Derrida 1995, 114–15; cf. Cannell 2006b, 21). In the Buddhist exchange, the living offer gifts not only to known ancestors but also to anonymous crowds of dead, including the hungry, derelict, or abandoned. In this gift cycle, as in the sacrifices theorized by Bataille (1989, 43–49), gifts surpass mere productive utility, as the distinction between giving and receiving dissolves in the possibility of abundant, redoubling, perennially flowering gifts, or in the danger of gifts gone awry. The sociality of living and dead is characterized by a gift exchange that might be said to operate symbiotically, nourishing everyone's well-being. Perhaps the most extreme danger in this sociality today is the danger of institutional disavowal, an official ostracism of the dead amounting to contempt for their gifts, for their sacrifice.

Death's Bureaucracy

In the United States, the disavowal of the gifts of the dead is interwoven with the disavowal of the sacrifices of those who died or nearly died in U.S.-sponsored wars and their aftermath in Laos and Cambodia. The sacrifices of Kmhmu, Hmong, Lao, and Khmer in the covert wars and their attendant theaters of operation still largely goes unrecognized, even though displacement and diaspora was a direct consequence of U.S. military involvement, which changed the field of regional politics with its capital and armies, as much as it altered the landscape with its bombing campaigns and defoliants.[12] After

U.S. withdrawal, those who supported the U.S. efforts found themselves not only without compensation for their sacrifice, but also without governmental protection. As refugees they became quintessential figures of social exile, recognized citizens of no national community, with no political rights unless to humanitarian charity. Of his time spent in a Thai refugee camp Lt. Phanha said, "If they saw that someone's wife was beautiful they would kill him and abuse his wife. Probably whoever did it didn't actually get an order to do it but they did it anyway, because we were refugees. Who cares if you kill them?" The sense of being dispensable, without being explicitly targeted, did not end with arrival in the United States. As one Lao man asked, "What good to come here, USA, if nobody knows my name? Is this not the same as the dead ones?" (quoted in Proudfoot 1990, 112).

Emigrants speak, therefore, not just of their own debts to spirits, but of the U.S. people's debts to them. "They say the Americans 'lost' the war," one Lao commented, "but really we lost because everything we knew was destroyed. . . . Really they have won because they haven't been made to pay the damage" (quoted in Proudfoot 1990, 117). Mercenaries in the covert war remember that the CIA promised to compensate them for loss of families and homes. Lt. Phanha voiced his bitterness that Kmhmu veterans are seldom recognized for the services they rendered to the United States. What refugees receive from the U.S. government is less recognition of their sacrifice than the humiliations of public assistance. The injury is often registered less as a broken contract than as a broken promise, a betrayal of friendship that is less possible to calculate or repay. "Why did the United States invite us here with promises," asked one Lao, "and then make us feel very low when we ask for these promises?" (quoted in Proudfoot 1990, 117).

When such promises are ignored, falling outside of a national accounting, it is left to the dead to demand compensation, maybe because only such a demand, coming from beyond the reach of worldly economy, can register the immeasurability of what is owed. Consider those Thai deaths by political violence that, in Klima's account, enabled, through their material, photographically reiterated horror, the ousting of a military dictatorship and the establishment of a liberal democracy. Then, by contrast, consider those other Thai deaths, not recognized as sacrifice since they led to no regime change, which resulted only in restless ghosts, reminders of the bloody violence hidden at the foundations of the modern democratic state and the structural violence that still sustains it. The ghosts of the forgotten, Klima writes, watch "from the outside," the outside, that is, of the cycle of exchange in its politically sanctioned and patriotically intelligible versions

(2002, 86). It is in a similar environment of unresolvable debt that U.S. institutions for managing death become critical sites for the disruption of gift exchange and the discounting of sacrifice.

There is a pervasive concern, for instance, about the engagement of medicine in bodily dismemberment (cf. Scheper-Hughes 2000, 2005). When elderly Khmer hear that a baby has been born without lungs, Charles told me, they say she must be the reincarnation of someone whose lungs were removed in a funeral home. Among Lao, anxieties about organ removal in medical or mortuary contexts invoke stories of bad spirits who eat the internal organs of others, while among Khmer they invoke stories of soldiers who ate the livers of their enemies (Hinton 2005). As might be expected, organ removal, like money given to the dead, is viewed differently by monks than by laypeople engaged in reciprocal relationships with ancestors. A Lao monk, for instance, assured me that organ donation in no way violated Buddhist dharma:

> Buddhist religion does not stop you from giving away these things. When you give your organs to somebody else, it is like taking spare parts from one car and putting them in another car, or taking parts from one house and putting them in another house. There's nothing wrong with that. In fact, donating things to someone is doing a good deed, so that a person will be healthier or have a happy life. Maybe the spirit of the dead person will receive good merit from doing that.

Doctrinal Buddhism notwithstanding, however, many elderly Lao and Khmer Buddhists are reluctant to risk the integrity of a new incarnation by cutting up the old one. "If you had an eye missing," Lt. Somsy reasoned, "you would be afraid that when you were born in the next life you would have only one eye." When Douang countered, "I'm a donor. I have a different philosophy," Lt. Somsy responded, "You are speaking only for yourself, not for your relatives. If you died and you had something missing in your body, they would be very, very sad."

Hmong and Kmhmu voiced similar wariness of incomplete bodies. "When the spirit finds that he is missing some parts of his body," one man said, "he will come back to get replacements from people who are still alive." Like many Lao, Hmong say that the deceased will be unable to reincarnate if any body part has been lost. Even Christian Hmong are opposed to autopsy, insofar as it treats the dead as experimental objects. Mr. Lo elaborated, "People complain that the doctors just use [autopsy] to study the body. They are angry about it. They don't like to have the body cut. They think that an autopsy is just for the doctor to learn more, but not any good for the family or for the

dead person." In the Kmhmu community, stories circulated of a hospital jan-
itor who every day reportedly disposed of buckets of livers, hearts, and intes-
tines removed during autopsies.

As if to compensate for possible violations to dead bodies, people organize
elaborate funerals. Yet even these fail to shield the dead from institutional disregard. "Here, even though we have everything," Sodoeung said, "food, cars,
VCR, all hi-tech, material things, still something is not complete. We do a lot
of big ceremonies, and spend a lot of money, but people feel like they still need
something else to add to it." When Sodoeung's father died, ceremonies were
arranged at the *wat*, but her mother longed for a ceremony at home as well.
"She really wanted to do a big ceremony," Sodoeung said, "because she loved
my father so much."

> We told the manager, and he was okay about it. But the neighbors were not.
> People who live in housing projects don't have space inside the house. So we
> had to do the ceremony outside with a green plastic tarp and a mat on the
> ground. We were loud, because the monks came, and friends and guests.
> When someone dies in the community, you don't need to know them, you
> come forward to support the family, everybody comes. The monks were chant-
> ing for about two hours in the morning. After that about fifteen monks stood
> in line, held their bowls, and everybody offered them food. It was from nine
> o'clock to noon, and in the evening from six to eight-thirty. It's very hard if
> your neighbors are not understanding. In our case, they called the police. It
> bothered my mom a lot. That's what made her upset, when she saw the police
> come.

The neighbors' opposition and the arrival of the police created an atmosphere
of harassment, cramping an event intended as an act of lavish generosity to
the dead.

Some Khmer are philosophical about the alterations of death rites, even
as they are acutely aware of them. Mr. Chea minutely listed for me each gap
in U.S. ceremonies, from the failure to take the temporary vows of monkhood
by relatives who are afraid to show up at work with shaved heads, to the inability to play the eerie funeral music known as *klorng khaek*, which might be
offensive to non-Khmer,[13] to the impossibility of circumambulating a cremation site that is enclosed in a funeral home. In Cambodia, he specified, the
achar, a lay spiritual leader, lit the cremation fire, while in the United States
the cremation switch is controlled by funeral home staff. "But in Buddhism," he
insisted, "nothing is fixed. If you can't do something, it is still okay." Amidst
this complacency about incomplete ceremonies he introduced only one note

of discontent, saying, "I wish that the funeral home would allow the monks to go into the funeral home every evening to chant until the body is cremated. But it depends on the relatives' schedule, and the money, whether you have the money." Even if funeral home protocol does not interfere in the flow of gifts and merit between living and dead, poverty often prevents mourners from fully caring for the dead.

Whatever the flexibility of Buddhist doctrine, many Khmer and Lao are less complacent about ceremonial changes than Mr. Chea. Before cremation, for instance, funeral home staff remove candles and flowers from the body and take the coins out of the mouth. Later Khmer families argue about whether the spirit will have enough money. "Younger people think it's just symbolic," Sodoeung said. "'Just put it on and then take it off. He's not going to know.' But my mom said, 'No, if you take it off that means you've lied. You didn't do it honestly.'" Those educated in the United States learn to understand the offerings to the dead as symbols, in accordance with Christian theology and anthropology.[14] For them a focus on "what something signifies" rather than "how it works . . . expels haunting" (Morris 2000, 162). Elders, on the other hand, understand the offerings as gifts that secure the comfort of the deceased and the prosperity of the family. Nonetheless, Sodoeung noted that few Khmer openly protest funeral home protocol, explaining, "When we try to do something and they say, 'No, you cannot,' it's in the middle of when we're really grieving. . . . We don't want to argue. So we all just come home and get upset among ourselves. We get mad about everything we cannot do for the loved one."

It was difficult for people to articulate the amorphous absence they sensed at the heart of ceremonies in the United States. These days, Major Samsuthi told me, people can return to Laos to perform a ceremony for their dead parents. "It is true that you can do it here also," he added, "but it is not as good as when you do it over there. . . . Everything there is just done correctly, the way it has been done since our ancestors' time." When I pressed him for the differences he amended,

> In fact, there is not really anything different between here and there. Because we're talking about spirits. When we talk about spirits, we talk about things that we don't see, and these spirits can go around in the world, any time, anywhere. Like for example, when we talk about spirits from Laos, we can call the spirits and they can be here right away.

Yet when it came to a certain austerity he planned to perform, he intended to return to Laos. He had promised the guardians of the land that if he survived the reeducation camp he would take monk's vows for three months. "But I have not had any chance to do as I promised, like after I was saved out of there." Ethnographic questions seemed to force an awareness of the possibility of spirits as generic entities, distributed across nations and religions. Such spirits might be cosmopolitan travelers. Major Samsuthi's promise had not been made to such abstract spirits, however, but to place-specific spirits who had been critical to his survival.

Even people on public assistance, one Khmer woman emphasized, try to save money to conduct ceremonies for the dead in Cambodia. When they perform ceremonies in Cambodia, she said, they feel immense relief. "This is why some of the elders want to die in Cambodia," Sheila confirmed. "The funerals there are more complete. . . . Because we understand that this is the United States, we do not try to enforce things we believe. But the older generation always feels that they have not done their part for their loved ones." Douang speculated that because of ceremonial lapses, people earn less merit making offerings to the dead in the United States than they would in Laos. He had not heard, however, of any hauntings in North America outside of dreams. "Back home it is a big deal," he said. "The spirit will come back and haunt you if you don't do [the funeral] right." Lt. Somsy reasoned that spirits of the dead are so familiar with U.S. customs that they are probably tolerant of inadequate ceremonies. Anyway, he added, most spirits probably return to Laos. "They would think there's nothing here for them," he said. "No place for them to live with their family, no place to be comfortable." Working against the apparent complacence of the spirits about changing traditions is the strong sense that this is no place for a Lao soul. The dead members of the community vote with their ethereal feet, returning to Laos, reversing the exile of the living. In every instance of spirit illness in the United States of which Lt. Somsy was aware, the *moh phi* consulted in Laos reported that the spirit also was from Laos. Lt. Somsy speculated that *phi* (spirits) might follow visiting Lao-Americans from Laos back to the United States, haunting them only after they had again placed themselves in a Lao landscape, under the jurisdiction of its spirit powers. In their tendency to drift, spirits may be aptly shaped to embody diasporic experiences of displacement. At the same time, however, spirits of the dead, like spirits of the land, sustain relationships to place, reactivating senses of belonging and responsibility, enacting return without the political difficulties of repatriation.

When his wife died, Lt. Somsy asked the funeral home to put her clothes on backwards as would have been done in Laos. They obliged him with the underwear, but put her other clothes on the usual way. "They said they had to do it according to their own rules. They could not do it exactly according to my wish. That means she will be in two cultures." Even as Lt. Somsy imagined that Lao souls want to return to Laos, he noted that his deceased wife, like he himself, was caught between worlds, her forward-facing blouse a sign of her persistent limbo, a warning that her confused spirit will continue to wander.[15] Douang faulted such funeral homes for their rigid protocol. "If they do not let a family put the shirt on backwards, there are some who will feel very bitter. They will worry that the spirit will not go away and will still be roaming around the house. If you don't put the clothing on in the reverse way, they say that the spirit still knows how to come back home."

Major Samsuthi noted that some funeral homes refuse to allow the relatives to initiate the cremation. "We want to witness the cremation with our five senses," he said, "to touch the button, to see the burning. We want to see the body going in the oven, and see the smoke going up. When we don't get to do that, we don't feel good." Those who still remember washing their deceased loved ones, wrapping them in cloth, carrying them to the pyres or the cemetery, splashing coconut water on their faces, or cleaning their bones want at least to press the cremation switch with their own fingertips. They seek out a sensory and tactile participation in the passage of the dead, which might work to concretize the continued relationship with the spirit. "When you're there with the dead person," Major Samsuthi went on, "doing the ceremonies with your own hands, you gain a lot of merit, more than you would by donating money. . . . There are times when you cannot help it, you cannot do the funeral properly, like for soldiers in a war. . . . But in this case, when there is something that you can do, you really must do your best." In war, when dangerous spirits were everywhere, an incomplete funeral was nonetheless understandable, while in North America, where no spirits want to linger, it is not. Here Major Samsuthi evoked the desecrations of war only to index a still more unforgivable violation.

When we spoke about the death of her daughter in the United States, Mrs. Sann at first downplayed the differences between U.S. and Cambodian funerals. A little later, however, she worried about the impossibility of performing the disinterment ceremony for her daughter that she had performed for her mother.

> I asked the person at the cemetery if we would be able to do a second burial and he didn't know. He said that if I wanted to do that, I would have to ask the welfare office. Now I feel bad that I had to bury her. If I had known that I couldn't do a second burial, I would have burned her. A second burial would probably cost a lot of money too. The graves are so close to each other it seems impossible. . . . When I get older, there will probably be no one to bring flowers

to her grave. Bringing flowers to the grave is not the Khmer way, but when I have a chance to bring flowers to her grave, it makes me feel better. Back home, we had a house and land, so we could do whatever we wanted. For some people we put another little house outside in a place they liked. Every mealtime, we brought a little bit of rice and soup or whatever we were eating to that little house.

The contrast between Mrs. Sann's reminiscences of caring for the dead in Cambodia and her uncertainty of how she will care for her daughter in a U.S. cemetery registers a relative emptiness of gestures of hospitality toward the dead in this country. In Cambodia, it is not just flowers her daughter would have received, but food and shelter. "My friend's son was shot to death," Mrs. Sann recounted.

He was getting into the car and they just shot him in the head. She decided to put his bones inside the house. Every mealtime she would offer him a little bit of food. My children were scared of the bones. I told his mother to put them elsewhere, but she didn't want to. . . . Here, if you want to put the ashes in the temple, you have to know the monk. And it is difficult to build a *chedey* [stupa]. In Cambodia you can build it as high as you want, but here they only allow you to build it to a certain height.

Sodoeung related a similar dilemma about her father's remains.

It is very hard to find a place to put the urns. . . . My mother didn't think the *wat* was a safe place for my father's ashes in case of fire. She didn't want to lose his ashes. When he died she said, "Oh, I wish there was a place to put the ashes." We said, "Do you want to bury him here?" and she said, "No, we will take him home." So now his ashes are in the *wat*. He told me to take them home when I can, and bury them over there. Build a stupa for him. But now my mom says not to take him because she will feel lonely.

Such anxieties echo the ongoing distress over the dislocation of war dead in Asia. Diaspora stirs up the wartime dread that the dead will be permanently displaced.[16]

One Lao monk spoke of the importance of holding ceremonies in the home of the deceased or, failing that, in the *wat*.

The guests come to pay respects to the deceased and give warmth to the relatives. . . . But here in the United States we cannot do the same thing, and it is not really okay. People do not feel good like they did when we did the entire ceremony in Laos. We think that death is very important. . . . Anybody who knows that someone has passed away will come right away. But here, because we cannot keep the body at home, and we cannot have a social event in the funeral home, it is not as comfortable or as warm as it should be.

In Minneapolis one funeral home advertises the design of "meaningful events," precisely grasping the longings of many modern Christians and post-Christians. For elderly emigrants who are less concerned with meaningfulness than with warmth, comfort, and physical intimacy with the dead, funeral home events may seem strangely cold and condensed. As one Lao man put it, "The American goes from box to box to do whatever he has to do . . . church, school, home. They don't mix together very much. You can see the new baby in the glass cage . . . and the dead also go into a box. In Laos it was not that way" (quoted in Proudfoot 1990, 212).

Kmhmu and Hmong also commented on institutional interference in care for the dead. "The place that we arranged for my dad was really strict," John Prachitham recalled. "We went there only one time, only for fifteen minutes. That's all they allowed us. And they did not allow many people in." Unable to gather at the funeral home, people congregated at the family's home to offer their gifts. When asked whether the elders worried about the ability of the deceased to receive the gifts at such a distance, John answered with a characteristically Christian presumption of the separation between body and soul: "No. We don't care where the body is. We just make offerings for the spirit." Nonetheless Kampheang negotiated with funeral home staff to be permitted to place rice in her dead husband's hand. "If you don't give him rice," she asked, "what is he going to eat?" And when Cheuang died of cancer, a friend placed the gifts of coins and food in his hands, reciting the route to his ancestors. There was, however, an upsetting incident at his burial. Typically the coffin would have been opened just before burial, to allow mourners to see him once more, and to offer him a last chance to return to life. Cheuang himself had spoken to me two years earlier about the importance of giving the dead a chance to revive: "We made an offering of money, rice, and candles, and said to the *róoy*, 'Tell me if this person is really dead or if he is going to come back.' People will come back or not." But the funeral home personnel refused to open Cheuang's coffin, foreclosing the communication between living and dead, denying any enactment of gradations of death.

As Mrs. Vangay's father-in-law was dying, the family dressed him in the burial garments that would identify him to his ancestors. "We told the funeral home, 'After you clean him up, then you should put the clothes back on.' But they didn't do that. After they finished cleaning him up, they wrapped him in

plastic." At the funeral home the family replaced the plastic with burial garments, laboring to turn a depersonalized corpse back into a spirit's body. In
Laos, Hmong calculated an auspicious day and location for the burial, but
here they can seldom afford that luxury. "Back there," Mr. Vangay recalled,
"the funeral doesn't take much money. We did the ceremony at home and
prepared everything ourselves. Here everything takes money. We have a low
income and couldn't afford life insurance. My father's funeral was all out of
our pockets. Some relatives came from another state and helped out." Those
whose gravesites are paid for by public assistance must sometimes be buried
in layers, which, for non-Christians, can result in a hierarchical conflict among
the dead. "So he or she will come back to the family to cause the members of
the family and the clan serious problems, sickness, even death," Mr. Lo elaborated. "Because that person says, 'You put me in a hard position.' So he or
she would come and get someone to go with him." Such burial practices may
feel as risky to the living as the slipshod burials of wartime.

Since sanitation laws prevent the cow offered to the deceased from being
killed while it is tethered to the corpse, Hmong in the United States arrange
to have the cow slaughtered elsewhere. "Back home we did it at home, in our
own home," Mr. Vangay said. "Here we do everything at the funeral home,
which does not belong to us. We have to kill the cow at a farm or somewhere
else. . . . The elderly don't like it. They feel so sorry about that problem of not
being able to sacrifice the animal with the body."[17] "All we can do then is bring
the head of the animal to the body and sacrifice the head only," Mrs. Vangay
added.

> We put it at the door and then tie the rope to the body and give it to [the de-
> ceased]. . . . After the sacrifice, we bring the head home and put it in the garbage
> or throw it in the dumpster. Back home in Laos, we cooked it and ate it. But
> here we have enough meat and we don't need it. . . . There was one case in
> another state where they gave the head to the body, and he went back to Laos
> and came in a dream to the relatives and said, "The Hmong in America only
> sacrifice the head to the body. There are no feet, no arms and legs, so the ani-
> mal has a very hard time walking. And it is really hard for me to get the ani-
> mal to go with me."

Telling this story Mrs. Vangay laughed, aware of the disjunction between the
United States, where spirits are mostly absent, and Laos, where spirits are
tangibly present. Her laughter registers the irony and risk of recounting ghost
stories in an ambivalently enchanted modern world. Yet her own belief or
lack of belief in the possibility of sending a spirit cow with the deceased does

not diminish the intensity of her story. Images of *plig* dragging legless cows across a spirit landscape forcefully convey the neglect of dead who belong to communities scattered from the mountains of Laos to the urban streets of North America.

Pheng knew of a man who had buried his mother in a Chicago cemetery with her head pointed downhill, violating geomantic principles. When his father saw the gravesite he foretold, "Now your life will go down hill until you die." The son subsequently became an alcoholic, was divorced by his wife, lost his house, and finally sought refuge in a Buddhist monastery in Thailand. His younger brother, who also suffered a divorce and the loss of his house, made plans to rebury their mother. He intended to hire a Buddhist monk to conduct the reburial, in hopes that the monk would prove more powerful than the non-Buddhist ancestors. Pao Chang compared inadequate death rites to abandoning the trail in a forest. The consequences, he cautioned, are sickness and death for those who follow.[18]

For emigrants, then, a litany of lacks hovers around efforts to meet the debts to ancestors in the United States—a lack of correct ingredients, proper gravesites, strict enough monks. The sense of incompleteness, variously explained, and sometimes even explained away, as a lack of smoothness, social support, or appropriate space, is an ellipsis, troubling precisely to the extent that it cannot, like a vague but compounding debt, be decisively settled with the foreign currency of U.S. mortuary practices. The desire for bodily intimacy—to be close to the corpse, to perform rites with your own hands—is difficult to satisfy in U.S. postmortem and mourning practices. The immediate rupturing of the spirit from the body presumed by dominant morgue and funeral home procedures allows little scope for tangible gifts, denying both the materiality and the lapse of time essential to reciprocity. What is missing from diasporic mourning is not so much any specific gift, but rather the enactment of the sociality of living and dead. The incompleteness arises from the tendency of institutional practice to implicitly deny the literal presence of the dead, substituting a symbolic presence that would be satisfied with symbolic gifts. For elderly emigrants especially, this substitution is apt to seem like a counterfeit coin that discounts the dead as social beings. For the dead demand less to be remembered than to be re-membered, reembodied in material practice. The management of death in the United States disturbs this embodiment, implicitly urging emigrants to leave the dead in the past and replace bodily engagement with memorialization, embracing symbolic economies of mourning.

Desecration

In his account of burying the dead who had fallen in battle, Lt. Somsy spoke only of the bodies of his fellow soldiers, saying nothing of the bodies of those he himself had killed. Yet sometimes a debt may be owed not only for survival, but also for murderous acts. Charles spoke of his brother's harassment by ghosts who undoubtedly included not only comrades whose deaths he witnessed but enemy soldiers whose deaths he caused. "He spent a lot of time in the jungle fighting, and he saw a lot of spirits," Charles said. "Ghosts would bother him at night. He would spend the night in his hammock hanging in a big tree, and a spirit would make noise or make the tree branch break." As discussed earlier, he found his most powerful protection in another ghost, the human skull mounted on a stick that guarded him as he slept. One day, when Lt. Phanha was speaking of his intention to convert to Christianity, he said, "In this life I know I'm going to suffer badly because of what I have done, being a leader. I had to kill so many people. I don't think god will ever forgive me." He did not specify what god he meant. Yet surely he referred to the Christian god he expected one day to worship, because whenever he spoke of the spirits who helped him to tend rice fields, heal illness, or escape from prison camp, he referred to *róoy,* the word used for spirits ranging from the ancestral dead *(róoy kàan),* to the spirits of the forest *(róoy pri* or *róoy patay),* to the guardian spirits of a village or a city *(róoy kún* or *róoy mìang),* to the spirits of those who died violent deaths *(róoy he'ép),* and numerous others.[19] In speaking of forgiveness, he evoked Christianity as if it promised (and yet might fail) to assume his debts to those he had killed. Conversion, it appeared, was one way to consolidate his debts to the dead, transferring the debts to a god who might have the power to cancel them.[20]

Dr. Stoltz spoke about the silence of ex-soldiers about the deaths for which they felt responsible.

> If I take care of somebody who was a prisoner and was beaten, and the person is talking about being victimized, it raises the question immediately to me about whether they ever victimized somebody else, but they don't want to talk about that part. . . . People often don't come in and tell you that they murdered somebody or set a place on fire. We do see a lot of people who feel like they were responsible for the death of their child and have taken an unforgiving stance about their culpability for that. People were on the run, somebody died.

Are enemy dead also enfolded into the gift exchange of death? Or are they deliberately and forcefully excluded from it? When Lt. Somsy spoke of "hiding" the body of his comrade, he tacitly acknowledged the risk that the dead could become targets for desecration. Katherine Verdery reports on Serbs who machine-gunned the graves of Croatians in post-Yugoslavia (1999, 107). U.S. soldiers sometimes carry in their wallets the ID cards of those they killed, showing them off to friends, drawing power from the trace of a life they have erased. Alexander Hinton retells a story of a group of Khmer Rouge soldiers who cut out and ate the liver of a man as punishment for stealing cassava roots from the collective (2005, 290–93). In doing so, they intended, Hinton suggests, to strip the man of his membership in the social community, while simultaneously absorbing his vitality. Violation of bodies does more than refer to acts of violence; it reiterates them in mimetic acts of terror. The defaced body is not merely a political symbol, but a trace of violent death, a hauntological presence bearing an intense potency to affect not only mourners, but possibly perpetrators as well.[21] Another word than symbol is called for here, one less enervated by decades of anthropological, psychological, and theological language, one that might convey the material and spiritual intensity of the violated corpse.

Violence to dead bodies appears to position them decisively outside a given community as those to whom nothing is owed, whose deaths are, in Agamben's terms, forbidden to be seen as sacrifice. For Agamben, a sacrificial victim retains his social and political value insofar as his death is consecrated through a relationship to a deity or, in the more modern and ostensibly secular patriotic sacrifice, to a political cause. *Homo sacer*, a term Agamben borrows from ancient Rome, are those, on the other hand, whose deaths are permitted but not meaningful, killable but not sacrificeable. Their dead bodies, purged of personhood, are available as objects for scientific experimentation, commodity extraction, or anonymous disposal. It might be argued that there is surely a difference between the casual treatment of bodies as commodities and intentional desecration, which implicitly recognizes, if only in order to theatrically negate, the body's sacredness for others. Shooting into gravesites or eating body parts suggests an *attack* on the social existence of the dead, while piling bodies into mass graves suggests the *preclusion* of such an existence altogether. Yet mass graves also tend toward ritual excess in their ability to terrorize and horrify. At the very least, anonymous disposition of corpses signals an overt devaluation of the dead.

After calling for an investigation of the "practical and political mystery" of the European separation of body and soul, Agamben, in a rare consideration of the ontological status of the dead, revisits Aquinas's solution to the medieval confusion over the resurrection of the body. Severing animality from spirit, Aquinas asserted that in the Christian paradise there would be no need of food, drink, sex, or sleep (Agamben 2004, 16–19). It is noteworthy that Agamben's compelling discussion, in *The Open*, of the split between matter and spirit at the heart of European definitions of the human is marked by the recurrent phrase "in our culture" (16, 80, 92). With these words he delimits the salience of the matter–spirit dynamic he so carefully examines. It seems strange, however, to confine philosophical attention to "our culture" in a world where U.S. operatives recruit Hmong and Lao to fight North Vietnamese in the jungles of Southeast Asia; where Khmer, Kmhmu, Lao, and Hmong receive education about U.S. culture in Thai refugee camps and cram for examinations for U.S. citizenship in U.S. housing projects; where Hmong grow vegetables to sell in public markets to urban middle-class whites; where Hmong and Kmhmu bury their dead in North American soil and Khmer and Lao burn their dead in U.S. crematoriums; and where everyone forcibly learns the theological lesson of the merely symbolic presence of the dead in U.S. funeral homes and hospitals. In a meditation on humanity as a troubled counterpoint of animality and spirit, what space is left for imagining relations of living and dead in other terms? The radical separation of matter and spirit found necessary by Aquinas, and all but ineluctable by Agamben, is problematized if not absent within stories of dead who return as lizards to watch over their grandsons or dead who are in need of clothes and cookware. In the world imagined by those stories, desecration of dead bodies cannot be defined simply as an attempt to render the dead as debased beasts, void of spirit. The stories gesture to a simultaneously corporeal and spectral power of the dead.

Indeed, for the tellers of these stories, the very effort to radically devalue the dead may have the effect of backhandedly acknowledging their uncanny power. Desacralization involves active ritual effort (collecting the ID card, machine-gunning the grave, carving out the liver) that, as Michael Taussig observed, may stir up "a strange surplus of negative energy . . . from within the defaced thing itself" (1999, 1). Many survivors, including those who themselves dealt death, are wary of that spectral surplus. They sense that those whose deaths are denied a sacrificial dimension are precisely those who return to haunt the living, defying their devaluation, seizing for themselves the mystical power released in their fetishization. Recall John Prachitham's account of the magical measures taken to prevent haunting by a Pathet Lao soldier killed in a shoot-out in John's village. In wartime, those who became dangerous spirits were sometimes those who were killed by virtue of being an enemy, deprived of rights within a particular social regime. Yet in becoming restless spirits, they take on an alternative potency. Ghost narratives make reiterative reference to a dangerous agency that is never dissolved, and may even be intensified through a violent or desecrated death. One way of understanding restless ghosts, Klima suggests, is as those whose sacrifice has not been recognized. "To be a ghost," he writes, "is to be marginal, to have no role to play in the economy of the living" (2002, 163). Yet the exclusion of ghosts, as he also shows, can never be absolute as long as the dead retain the power to haunt from the margins, impressing their material presence on the living. Those uncommemorated or enemy dead, excluded from a given social or political space, whose deaths are denied a sacrificial dimension, often haunt the living more intensely than those who are publicly mourned. The violation of the corpse, whether in a fetishistic seizure of power or a scientific denial of personhood, is prone to backfire. Any negation of the social existence of the dead is apt to recoil on the living in the appearances of ghosts with insatiable demands.

Pemberton (1994) notes that in Java offerings once made for particular spirits are now made simply on behalf of tradition. With the loss of specificity people can never be sure whether the offerings are complete. A similar sense of incompleteness nags at emigrants who struggle to mourn their dead in the United States. When Douang noted that Lao in the United States no longer share their dreams of the dead he went on to say, "People think that they have become more sophisticated. And if you believe in dreams, that is kind of backward." In Laos, spirits were acknowledged members of the everyday world. In the United States, spirits newly excluded from the everyday world make their (absent) presence felt in other ways. If spirits of the living threaten to desert the body at a terminal prognosis, spirits of the dead trouble the mourners with a sense of insufficiency, as the sanitized space of the funeral home prevents them from seizing death with all their senses. It is as if, in the wake of excessive violence and the ascendance of new theological regimes, the dead have lost some of their capacity for benign or pragmatic interventions. Like the desecrated dead of wartime, the diasporic dead seem to be unmoored and remote from a reassuring participation in daily life, too often inconsolable and therefore without the power to console.

What is at stake in the dismantling of reciprocity with the dead? Noting that the Nazi concentration camps are sometimes said to have degraded death even more than life, Agamben notes that death was already degraded by the city and the hospital. Yet even as he aptly traces the idea of respecting the corpse to archaic regimes of magic, he simultaneously asserts that this idea does not belong to ethics. Philosophers, he suggests, would toss the body away like dung (2002, 70–80). In this way he seems to casually disallow the possibility of an ethics rooted in magical thought. Elias Cannetti has suggested, on the other hand, that in certain Chinese ancestor cults, the nature of the relationship between ancestors and a living person "means that any feeling of triumph in his own present existence which comes to tinge his veneration will be of a very mild and moderate kind and carry no temptation to increase the number of the dead" (1984, 272). Could a sensory experience of indebtedness to the dead cultivate a wariness of generating yet more death? Might the recognition of the dead as social beings, rather than symbols of sacrifice to social ideals, invite a sense of responsibility to both the dead and the future dead (the living), enabling a certain caution against creating a heavier burden of debt?

Afterword   **On the Status of Ghosts**

> I would say that there is no politics without an organization of the
> time and space of mourning, without a topolitology of the sepulcher,
> without an anamnesic and thematic relation to the spirit as ghost
> [revenant], without an open hospitality to the guest as ghost [in
> English in the original], whom one holds, just as he holds us, hostage.
>
> —Jacques Derrida, *Aporias*

THE GUEST AS GHOST in one guise might be the emigrant turned immigrant, becoming invisible and disavowed by virtue of being absorbed into a sociological slot. The ghost as guest, in its turn, calls to mind those dead who make demands on the hospitality of the living. One surprise in this formulation might be that the appearance of the ghost calls for hospitality rather than exorcism. Why, one might ask, does this book emphasize consoling, rather than dispelling, the ghost?

Spectrality has been a well-traveled metaphor in recent years, appearing at times in discussions of economy as a metaphor for commodities and speculative forms of value, but even more often in discussions of historical memory and forgetting, as a metaphor for past injustices whose repressed effects persist in the present. In such discussions the ghost flits between metaphor and literality, sometimes referring or partially referring to actual dead, known or anonymous, sometimes remaining more abstract, signifying a hidden or disavowed violence. For such ghosts, the task seems at first to be simply recognition, but eventually there nearly always comes a call for exorcism. Perhaps this call arises from a latent Christian determination to drive out demons, or from a desire, on the part of psychoanalysis in some of its versions, to be done with mourning.

To be sure, the ghosts reconjured in this book insist on recognition as well. But responding to this insistence seems to be less a matter of exorcism than of solace. Furthermore, the spectral quality of relations with the dead, as lived by the emigrant storytellers consulted here, is not itself metaphorical, even if it lends its power to the metaphorical usages outlined above. Ghosts for these emigrants are not simply stand-ins for violated corpses of political citizens or for unremembered victims of violence, but rather the material traces of dead who insist on active relations with the living. Yet, with some crucial and nearly always anthropological exceptions,[1] much of the scholarly conversation about haunting in the wake of violence has been conducted without reference to those in the contemporary world who speak of their own or others' encounters with the dead. What does the literal ghost have to offer to this conversation?

It might be helpful to first ask why the ghost has become such a compelling figure for the embodied aftereffects of violence, even without inspiration from accounts, other than literary ones, of spectral interactions. The ghost is not simply a convenient sign for inchoate memories of violence, and for the horror and dread that suffuse such memories. The ghost also operates as a hinge to draw together two forms of engagement with the dead: haunting, where one is seized involuntarily, and mourning, where one actively strives to give the dead their due. The ghost draws our attention to the way that mourning might necessarily involve a surrender to being haunted, while haunting demands a repeated and performative mourning, which in turn works to shift haunting toward a reciprocity with specters. Moreover, as suggested earlier, the ghost is an undeniably powerful witness. Boreth Ly observes that in contemporary Cambodia it is the dead who maintain the panoptical surveillance once reserved for Angka (the personification of Pol Pot's regime, said to have eyes on all sides like a pineapple), as skulls in the memorial at the killing fields of Cheung Ek are arranged to look in every direction (2008, 122). As in the oracles of a Sri Lankan war zone described by Lawrence, spirits offer a "counterpoint to the muteness of political silencing" (1997, 199). In this book, spirits—whether *dab, róoy, phi,* or ancestors—bear witness not only to war, terror, and displacement, but also to the inhospitableness of North America experienced by both living exiles and their ghostly counterparts. As crucial sites for the mediation of death, the regulation of bodily practices, and the enforcement of regimes of rational truth, U.S. medical and mortuary institutions are often focal points of spirit unrest and censure. Spirits implicitly interrogate modern techniques of thanatopolitics and the metaphysical logics that sustain them. They speak to the violence of managed death in the United States even as they speak to the violence of war and its aftermaths in Southeast Asia.

Many have called attention to the way that modern states and capital are themselves animated by the dead.[2] Consider the spirits of those who died in national sacrifice or national terror in order to initiate and sustain U.S. democracy and capitalism: African slaves; soldiers and civilians in numerous wars; countless early residents of this continent, dead from smallpox, shrinking lands, heartbreak, alcohol, bullets. All these dead, the ones memorialized and the ones not memorialized, the ones buried on this soil or burned in this air, and the ones buried or vaporized elsewhere, belong to a U.S. nation-state of mind; all these uneasy ghosts are part of a repressed story of national freedom. All may be thought of as sacrifices, yet only some of these sacrifices are officially or publicly acknowledged. As Klima writes, it may be "necessary one day to disinter the mass grave of neoliberal economy" (2002, 233).

To enlist or listen to ghosts as witnesses to violence is less a triumphalist move, however, than a tragic one (cf. Scott 2004, 166). If the dead testify, they do so in terms that necessarily exceed modern political rationality. Ghosts do not speak in a discourse of civic rights and obligations. They are irreducible to ex–citizen subjects, medical patients, or even religious practitioners. They do not bear witness in courts of law, war tribunals, or truth-and-reconciliation commissions. Ghosts interrupt the disciplinary shape of stories told about them precisely because they do not speak on law's terms, on history's terms, or even on anthropology's terms. As Heonik Kwon (2008) has shown for the Vietnamese ghosts of the American war, they may be less concerned with political causes than they are with suffering. Their grievances are always demands on our grief (cf. Cheng 2001). Yoneyama (1999) has written of the ways that the voices of Hiroshima dead, evoked by proxy in survivors' stories, possess an originary quality, irreducible to rote narratives of victimization and survival. Similarly, the ghosts in the stories examined in this book are possessed of an uncanny unanswerability that is not resolvable within legalistic, multiculturalist, or bioethical frames.

Nonetheless, this book would not have been written except on a gamble that the encounters with literal spirits recounted in these pages might hold some tenuous counsel about mourning, responsibility to the dead, living with specters, and addressing haunting through rites of hospitality. At stake in the thanatopolitical disruption of a material sociality of living and dead are not only particular imaginations of afterlives, but also particular politics of grief. As Douang mused,

> There [in Laos] you have more freedom in talking about the dead person. Like they talk about dreaming about the person, and the person is ready to believe

you and join you in the conversation, and share experiences. "Oh, I had a dream like that too. My cousin passed away, and this and that." . . . But here about the deceased person, people tend to keep quiet. It's like they try to forget that, leave it behind. . . . Now we are in the decade of the computer, new technology. So for many people, they are afraid that the other person would say, "That's nonsense." I think it is not as good as back home in Laos. It heals, but it takes longer.

The path of mourning and healing Douang imagines is not so much the successful transformation of ghost into memory, but rather the hosting of ghost as potentially benign presence. Such a practice of mourning, like the Yukaghir notions of reincarnation described by Rane Willerslev, "emphasizes the continuity rather than the finality of personal relationships" (2007, 54). Douang's remarks confirm Christopher Nelson's insight that conceptions of mourning must take into account "the maintenance of relationships with the dead" (2008, 25).

Grace Cho writes of summoning ghosts in performance in order "to unravel the haunting silence that generates ghosts" (2008, 46). Following Abraham and Torok (1994), Cho suggests that such performances consist of "staging" the "phantom" and thereby "releasing" it (Cho 2008, 36). Yet rituals that summon ghosts in a more literal sense might ultimately be less a matter of releasing phantoms than assuaging them, gifting them, or soliciting their help. Imagine a summoning of ghosts, then, that is not an exorcism, not a cathartic release of affect, but rather a feasting, a consolation, or sometimes a shamanic effort to harness spectral power. For the idea of catharsis, like the idea of staging, invokes a sense of substitute, the release of affect through vicarious experience. Ghosts, however, are not substitutes for the dead. Rather they might better be understood, following Todd Ramon Ochoa, as versions of the dead (2010, 2007) or, following Deleuze, masks of the dead, where every repetition is a mask that hides nothing but other masks (1994, 17).

Deleuze suggested that the death drive—the source in one of its guises of repetitive nightmare and haunting—be understood not as a "tendency to return to the state of inanimate matter," as Freud hypothesized, but rather "in relation to masks and costumes" (Deleuze 1994, 17; cf. Freud 1922, 47, 80). Freud himself, Deleuze notes, knew it was not enough for one suffering a repetition compulsion to remember without emotion; rather it was necessary "to seek out the memory there where it was, to install oneself directly in the past" (Deleuze 1994, 18). Healing takes place not through memory but through a more "theatrical and dramatic operation" (19). Within psychoanalysis the name of such an operation might be the repetition of transference, as Deleuze claims (19; cf. Freud 1922, 43). But outside of psychology altogether, other repetitions, other masks and costumes, other sources of demonic power, are available through performative encounters with the dead. To dig up bones and clean them, to listen to the requests of the dead in dreams, to feed the dead in annual feasts: all these are theaters for enacting hospitality to the dead.

Such an imagination of the dead, it must be acknowledged, flagrantly defies the structural division that anthropology has classically drawn between ghosts and ancestors, where ghosts are strangers, hungry spirits who injure the living, and ancestors are kin, benevolent spirits who protect them. In all the discussions above I have deliberately blurred this distinction, suggesting that these different versions of the dead are less structural positions than revisions of situation over time. Not only are ghosts and ancestors mutually constitutive categories, as Kwon notes, but the dead's status as one or the other is often indeterminate, unstable, and subject to metamorphosis, perhaps especially in the wake of mass violence (2008, 7, 100, 111). A ghost may shift from stranger to guest to kin, may be a potential ancestor, a fallen ancestor, or someone else's ancestor. Ladwig has observed that, in the Lao context, the vagueness of ancestral lore enables the imagination of all dead as possible ancestors, deserving of Buddhist compassion no less than hospitality (2012, S95). At the same time, one's own kin might not be securely ancestral, sliding toward potential ghostliness at certain apparitional moments. The dead might be conceptualized, ultimately, not only as versions, but also as temporary, if recurring, coalescences, shifting assemblages similar to the Buddhist self, playing loose with time. In different dreams of mine, for instance, a friend who died in 2009 has appeared as a limp form half hidden under a crumpled white sheet and a woman solid in my embrace who seemed either ignorant or unconcerned about her death and intent on a warm bath.

"History eschews simultaneity," Rosalind Morris has written. "The profanity of its line is potent enough to banish ghosts and spirits and all those specters who testify to the folding and possible multiplicity of time (though it is doubtful that any society has ever come completely under its sway)" (2000, 61). As repetitions, encounters with the dead—whether through dreams, rituals, or uncanny sensory events—interfere with progressive and singular timelines. They suggest the need to recognize that past loss, never originary and forever made phantasmal, is deeply embedded in the present. Healing and mourning, only possible if understood as impossible to complete, are not a matter of restoring temporal order in an effort to avoid loss by assigning it to another time. To perennially animate the dead is to allow mourning to approach a melancholy irresolvable by libidinal shifts or letting go, which, in any event, tends to simply send the loss looping back by another route. The dead are not merely representatives of the past as past. They belong both to a past that is still its own present, and to the current present. In what sense, then, can haunting be understood as a mode of memory, as suggested by Cho (2008, 25, 29)? Haunting is not an active memorializing but rather a condition of being accosted by the dead in dreams or immersive memories where temporality no longer maintains its usual points of reference. A phantasmal memory in which the past insists on its own present-ness is distinct from a remembrance that bows to time's arrow; these submersive memories repeat the dead in ways that both cancel and intensify their absence. Can we imagine a mourning that ritually reshapes this repetition, without closing it down?

During one conversation with Dr. Stoltz I attempted (inadequately) to convey Avery Gordon's argument in *Ghostly Matters*. Perhaps taking Gordon (inaccurately) as emblematic of academic discussions of ghostliness, Dr. Stoltz's first response was to say, "One of the problems with Avery Gordon is that she doesn't believe in ghosts." From there the conversation branched in eschatological directions.

DR. STOLTZ: So when the rubber hits the road and your grandfather or whoever it is that's bugging you is in your room at night, and telling you this or that, or trying to eat dinner with you, or giving you advice in a dream—. . . . A British general practitioner in Wales went around and started interviewing widowed people in his practice, and he asks them whether they have ever heard, seen, talked to, been touched by, or felt the presence of their deceased husband or wife. And it turns out that half of the people he talked to said yes. Now he discounted anything that occurred lying down or at night, and he discounted anything that occurred if somebody said, "Well you know I see her, but it's only in my mind's eye." If they psychologized it away, he wouldn't count it. And then he broke it down across boundaries, of laundry workers versus professional people. Any idea how that came out? It happens way more frequently to professionals than it does to lower-paid people. So anyway I thought to myself, if in fact it happens that frequently (a), and (b) it's viewed as abnormal thought process in everything that's been written in psychiatry up until about 1990, what's that all about? Since psychiatry's a Western phenomenon.

J.L.: So it turns out to be "normal."

DR. STOLTZ: Well either that or everybody needs stelazine, or whatever the latest drug is for being psychotic. So that's a pretty interesting commentary about how the West thinks and constructs things. This work has been replicated over and over.

J.L.: You're right: academia does not allow you to admit that the dead are actually present.

DR. STOLTZ: In any way, shape, or form.[3]

J.L.: What Avery Gordon says is, ghosts are a part of our world, they're social figures.

DR. STOLTZ: That's it. I agree with that.

Put another way, ghosts are part of the contemporary world, regardless of belief. "As we social scientists often forget," Chakrabarty writes,

> gods and spirits are not dependent on human beliefs for their own existence; what brings them to presence are our practices. They are parts of the different ways of being through which we make the present manifest. . . . These other ways of being are not without questions of power or justice, but these questions are raised—to the extent that modern public institutions allow them space, for they do cut across one another—on terms other than those of the political-modern. (2000, 112)

As an alternative to "anthropologizing" spirits, bracketing them out as cultural beliefs, Chakrabarty suggests that recognition of spirit agents might be understood as another possibility for living in this world (1998, 24; 2000, 108). Then again, it might further be understood as another possibility for apprehending the world altogether, an alter-ontology. As Willerslev cogently notes in a discussion of animist thought,

> by insisting that what the people themselves are saying about their relations with spiritual beings is nothing but a metaphorical reflection of those relations that obtain within their own human community, the anthropologist effectively prevents his own study of animistic understandings from telling us anything new about what the world is like. (2007, 182)

For Willerslev, to assign spirits and ghosts a metaphorical status is to impose on those who relate to those ghosts a dualistic ontology of reality and dream, actuality and metaphor, whereas for the people themselves there may be "only one reality" involving both living humans and spirits, both dream and waking life (176, 182).[4]

As I have labored to suggest, the literality of the ghost pulls at certain central threads of biopolitical theory, tending to unravel it. These threads include an inability to take account of the social existence of the dead, the reproduction of a theological split between spirit and flesh, and a complicity with the deceptive story of disenchanted secularism. The literality of the ghost also complicates bioethics, inviting a contemplation of the sensitivity of spirits (whether of the seriously ill or the dead) to language and gestures and physical care. Finally, the literality of the ghost stretches psychoanalytic theory, suggesting that persistent relations with the dead are not necessarily pathological, but may enact a necessary relationship of the living with death. As the dead we know by name accumulate, we may feel closer to death ourselves. Imagine, then, a death drive, an orientation or surrendering to death that is not a desire to return to the inanimate, but a desire to reanimate and reunite with the dead.[5] This movement toward death would not be opposed to an impulse toward connection and change but would be another version of it. Rather than letting go of the dead, and rather than turning them into lessons of history or prescriptions for the future, imagine acknowledging them as part of our social world, insubstantial, shifting elusively from individual phantoms to faceless crowds, but pressing on us, jostling us, calling to us. Death, after all, is a populated, well-worn road. If the melancholic repetition that allows the dead to return in ever-changing masks is not pathological, then a death drive might not undermine our capacity to live but enrich it (cf. Edelman 2004).[6]

The Tuol Sleng compound, site of Khmer Rouge torture of political prisoners, remains a haunted site. Both staff and visitors report seeing ghosts wandering the buildings after dark. In 1999, as I conducted fieldwork for this book in the United States, monks were invited to the museum memorializing the prison in order to offer food to propitiate the restless ghosts. Reciting sutras, the *bikkhu* (monks) sprinkled holy water onto the bare skulls to calm the angry souls of the dead. In such ways material engagement with the dead can be critical to inhabiting the prevading grief of political violence. But of course interactions with ghosts may be integral to more ordinary grief as well. Charles knew of one deceased Khmer woman in the United States who was seen walking in and out of her house in the middle of the day. At night her friend who had worked alongside her as a seamstress at a local clothing factory felt someone tickling the soles of her feet; and sometimes when she answered the ringing telephone, she heard nothing except the sound of a sewing machine. Eventually she organized a ceremony with the help of an *achar* to soothe the ghost.

The night after my mother died, I slept in my old second-story bedroom. In my dream she flew by the window, flashing me a radiant smile, waving. When I heard her voice in the kitchen talking to one of my brothers, I raced downstairs and threw my arms around her. But she unwrapped my hands, telling me we couldn't communicate that way any more. How then? I asked. Her answer was careful and specific, like the steps of a ritual. But on waking, I could make no sense of it. The Welsh doctor's research notwithstanding, this dream with its nonsensical recipe for communicating with the dead signifies for me the erosion of Euroamerican relations with the dead, as they become increasingly displaced by incitements to memorialize. A few months after the friend's death that most recently cast its shadow on this book, I descended in a dream along an open stairwell and saw her one level down, dressed in a blue jacket I know well, holding her dog, who had died many years before, by a red leash. His face was blurred; hers was still clear. She met my eyes with a familiar contemplative gaze, neither evaluating nor emotional. Stay where you are, I commanded, I'm coming right down. But I found myself wedged between two wooden beams, unable to slide through, and she faded away.

Acknowledgments

Many hands helped to shape this book. My greatest debt is to the people of Lao, Khmer, Hmong, and Kmhmu descent who shared their stories with courage, patience, and insight, and to Sompasong Keohavong, Rouen Sam, Paularita Seng, Linda Chulaparn, and Yakobo Xiong for their skillful interpretation (in all its senses) and for a generous assistance that went way beyond their job descriptions.

The initial fieldwork for this project was conducted under the auspices of the Cross-Cultural Health Care Program, with financial support from the Kaiser, Cumming, and Swedish Foundations. I thank the staff of CCHCP at that time, especially Robert Putsch for his friendship and provocative conversation; my co-investigator Naima Solomon for her methodological intuition; James Heng, Ira Sengupta, and Leng Taing for invaluable consultation; and Bookda Gheisar and Tom Lonner for their faith in the haphazard unfolding of ethnographic process. I also thank the CCHCP research advisory group (Noel Chrisman, Barbara McGrath, Jane Peterson, Jim Green, and Helene Starks) and medical advisory group (Sharon Geist, Erika Goldstein, and Robert Putsch) for crucial advice. I am grateful to Rodney Smith, Katie Gillespie, Pat Jordan, and Rita Click for glimpses into the grief, frustration, humor, commitment, and quandaries involved in care for the dying. I thank Dr. Carey Jackson, Kevin Wilhelmsen, Mamae Teklemarian, Max Chan, Marilyn Castine, Grant Hiraoka, Chia Moua, Lea Vang, Pang Chang, Kampha Chantharangsy, Nancy Donnelly, Frank Proschan, and Jip Chitnarong for graciously sharing from their wealth of knowledge and experience.

Subsequent fieldwork, library research, thinking, and writing were supported by the University of Minnesota, the McKnight Foundation, the School for Advanced Research in the Human Experience, the Salus Mundi Foundation, and the Institute for Advanced Study at the University of Minnesota. I am especially grateful to SAR and IAS for offering intellectually capacious spaces where ideas had room to breathe and interweave, and for the perceptive commentary of colleagues at both of these places, especially Carolyn Yezer, Micaela di Leonardo, James Brooks, Rebecca Allahyari, Catherine Cox, Ivan Karp, and Cori Kratz at SAR, and Nancy Luxon, Teresa Gowan, Mark Pedelty, Leena Neng Her, Ann Waltner, and Juliana Hu Pegues at IAS. At SAR I thank Jean Schaumberg and Leslie Shipman for their warm hospitality and librarian Laura Holt for locating numerous articles and dissertations.

This work has been enriched and complicated over the years by thoughtful responses and questions from many scholars, including Lorna Rhodes (still my most essential mentor), Karen Ho, David Valentine, Karen-Sue Taussig, John Ingham, Gloria Raheja, the late Daphne Berdahl, Jennifer Gunn, Rebecca Klenk, Celia Lowe, Mike Fortun, John Kelly, Ann Mongoven, Todd Ochoa, Margaret Weiner, Matei Candea, Veena Das, Naveeda Khan, Tim Dunnigan, David Lipset, Stephen Gudeman, Bill Beeman, and the students in my Haunting seminars, as well as participants and audiences at conferences and colloquia. Most of all, Hoon Song and Stuart McLean have been incomparably gentle and astute readers and listeners for several pieces of this book.

I owe a debt to those scholars and artists, too numerous to list, who have dedicated their professional lives to exploring the histories and cultural practices of Lao, Khmer, Hmong, or Kmhmu peoples. Whatever comprehension I have of the stories recounted in this book rests on their work.

I am immensely grateful to the staff of the University of Minnesota Press, especially to Jason Weidemann for his persistent faith in this work and also to two anonymous reviewers (one of whom understood the manuscript in the way I imagine every scholar dreams of being understood), and Andrew Willford, whose incisive suggestions infused the revision process with an unusual joy.

Outside academia friends and family listened to many articulations of this project or shared their thoughts on death, among them James Langford, Judy Augustson, Gail Smith, Gina Ryken, Kathy Ross, Pam Churchill, June Gabriel, Andi Scott-Dumas, Francesca Profiri, Connie Palmore, the late Carol Nockold, Marianne Turnbull, Spike Squire, Katharine Lee, Leanne Chattey, Justin Leaf, Yvonne and Johnny Palka, and the late Judith Clarke. Special thanks to Gail Smith for her inspired photo magic.

This book owes its center of gravity to my own relationships with the dead, especially with my brother John Langford, passionate activist for peace, and with my mother, Naomi Justina Hess Langford, who first introduced me to stories, poetry, social justice, spirits, solace, and death.

Finally, this book was deeply nourished (not to mention repeatedly read) by Sharon Kaylen, artist in the kitchen and on the page, whose poetry reminds me that it is possible and necessary to create beauty out of loss, and that the ancestors (human and nonhuman) encompass the dead we acknowledge or fail to acknowledge and the dead we will become.

Notes

Introduction

1. Emigrants and health-care providers consulted for this project have been given pseudonyms to honor promises of confidentiality. For the same reason the exact locations of fieldwork have been kept vague.

2. I use the term Lao as shorthand for Lao Loum, also known as ethnic or lowland Lao.

3. See Didier Fassin and Richard Rechtman for an illuminating discussion of the changing valence of "immigrant" and "emigrant" in French social services (2009, 237).

4. The distinction drawn here resembles the difference in orientation Macarena Gómez-Barris delineates between the identity of immigrant and the identity of exile (2010, 251–52).

5. The various fictional works of W. G. Sebald (e.g. 1996, 1998) offer a striking illustration of this image of the European emigrant.

6. Klima (2006) makes a similar point in relation to multiple vantage points on global finance.

7. In Thailand, for instance, Rosalind Morris suggests that certain sword dances pay tribute to a medium's most important spirits by fighting off competitors (2000, 114).

8. This shift is visible in Laos as well where Kmhmu sword dancers and drummers from a newly established village of intermigrants displaced by the American war have been participating in a procession for Lao New Year (which falls at a different time than Kmhmu New Year), right behind the Buddhist monks, in the northern city of Luang Prabang (Trankell 1999, 197).

9. Relevant here is Louisa Schein's discussion of the way that Hmong in China (known there as Miao) perform their modernity by making "culture" an "object of reflection," disembedded from "everyday or ritual life" (1999, 372, 380).

10. This not to say, however, that ideas of social difference organized around language, customs, and artifacts are simply an invention of anthropology and the

colonial classificatory disciplines with which it is complicit. See, for instance, Frank Proschan's fine-grained discussion of Kmhmu conceptions of social difference (closely resembling the idea of "ethnicity") that arguably predate European colonial regimes, reflecting other regional hierarchies (Proschan 2001; cf. Proschan 1997).

11. Arguably, the effects of minoritization are intensified in the United States even for Hmong and Kmhmu due to a more pronounced dissonance with dominant cosmological frameworks.

12. Relevant here is Jacques Derrida's (2001) forceful argument that hospitality is not merely one ethic or one cultural practice among others.

13. It seems, for instance, that the love that satisfied my father in this dream is not the same love that is practiced by the Tamil family with whom Margaret Trawick (1992) lived and worked, nor the love sought by nineteenth-century Bengali widows from their in-laws (Chakrabarty 2000, 118–48).

14. Ghosts, Morris cogently suggests, only become uncanny when death has become "naturalized" (2000, 195–96).

15. See Elizabeth Hallam, Jenny Hockey, and Glennys Howarth (1999) for a thoughtful interrogation of the sociological status of the dead through consideration of those who occupy the border zones of life and death.

1. Violent Traces

1. See Stanley Tambiah (1984) for an account of the use of such amulets in Thailand.

2. In *Black Sun*, Julia Kristeva suggests that both mourning and melancholy are characterized by an inability to find any symbolic compensation for loss. To the extent that she proposes a therapeutic intervention for melancholy it is literary (or, she adds parenthetically, "religious") and operates as a cathartic reenactment of relations with the lost (1989, 24). The encounters with the dead I relate below, however, refuse to collapse into catharsis insofar as they are conceived not as reenactments of a past relation but as enactments of a current (if intermittent) relation and are designed less to vent feelings abreactively than to extend concrete assistance to the dead.

3. This shift in Freud's thoughts on melancholy parallels his shift in thinking about trauma, whereby trauma attributed to a singular childhood event eventually came to be understood as trauma inherent in the structure of the self. Yet this view of trauma, as Fassin and Rechtman note, is not sustained in contemporary conceptions of trauma in medical and humanitarian contexts (2009, 34).

4. For some of the problems with Caruth's argument, see Leys's finely tuned critique (2000, 266–97).

5. See also the work of Susan Brison (1999), for whom the remaking of the self after trauma involves a shift from being the object of another's speech to being the subject of one's own.

6. Ernst Van Alphen (1999), commenting on the book from which this testimony is taken, separates desubjectification and its associated loss of voice into four distinct linguistic situations: an undecidable limbo between being an active subject and a passive object; an utter lack of subjectivity; an absence of meaningful narrative frame for one's experience; and the impossibility of the narrative frames offered by history.

7. As Grace Cho comments, some violence has been so disavowed that it seems as though it can only be observed by the spirits of the dead (2008, 173).

8. Fassin and Rechtman note that one of the entailments of the traumatological narrative is to enable an account of war as suffering rather than politics, as cause rather than consequence (2009, 197).

9. By juxtaposing these terms here, I do not mean to suggest that they are equivalents of each other, but only that each of them tends to be recruited as the imprecise gloss for a "globalatinised" notion of the Christian soul (Derrida 2001, 32).

10. During this time there was a total collapse of rice production and distribution in Cambodia (Keyes 1994, 58).

11. Michael Vickery (1990) notes that the Khmer refugee camps set up along the Thai border were maintained partly to facilitate black-market trade across the border. After 1979, he argues, the camp system drew many thousands of people who might have been able to find livelihood in Cambodia itself. He further suggests that no one who left Cambodia after the destruction of the Khmer Rouge regime was in danger of political persecution except for Khmer Rouge cadres themselves. He makes clear the extent to which both Thai and U.S. governments encouraged the use of refugee camps to tempt skilled and educated persons away from Cambodia in order to weaken the Vietnamese-backed regime in Phnom Penh, and to serve as military bases for insurgents, including those loyal to Pol Pot. While Vickery's assessment is both compelling and chilling, it cannot speak to the range of feelings, reasoning, rumors, and loyalties that led individual families to leave Cambodia. In the situation of Sodoeung's family, the loss of the family home, a desire to reunite with her elder sisters, a wish to be reunited with her brother (whom she later found in the United States), along with a shell-shocked uncertainty about the future, were among the forces that persuaded them to leave.

12. Noting that many of his Khmer patients are unable to abandon their dead, psychiatrist and anthropologist Richard Rechtman understands his clinical task as facilitating memories of the dead when living (as the "departed" rather than the dead) so that his patients will no longer be "living in the same world as the dead" (Rechtman and Gée 2009). Dr. Stoltz's work, however, suggests a third alternative: that the dead qua dead might be solicited to address the suffering of the living.

13. The erasure is all the more striking given the massive numbers of dead concerned: for instance, thirty-five thousand Hmong soldiers killed in battle, and nearly one-third of all Laotian Hmong dead from disease and starvation as a result of the war (Quincy 2000, 5).

14. Young's argument draws on Ian Hacking's (1986) insight that psychological diagnoses and the syndromes they describe develop in tandem, as typologies of persons organize possibilities of enacting those typologies, which further shape the typologies in a feedback loop.

15. Boreth Ly (2008), for instance, describes hysterical blindness in Cambodian women who witnessed family members being killed.

16. In the context of Chile, Lessie Jo Frazier notes that certain political activists have engaged in "countermourning," refusing official rites of reconciliation or memorial and "allowing themselves to be haunted" by dialoguing with the dead killed during the military dictatorship at the now-empty site of their original mass grave (1999, 105). See Antonius C. G. M. Robben (2000) for a similar argument about the refusal of official mourning of the disappeared by the Madres de Plaza de Mayo in Argentina. While the emigrants discussed here are not refusing to forget the dead out of an overt call for justice, their continuing dialogue and gift exchange with the dead has the effect of keeping the injustice suffered by the dead in view.

17. On a related note Fassin and Rechtman observe that as the focus of French psychiatrists working with recent immigrants has shifted over time from the mourning of exile to the trauma of violence, the first model still underlies the second (2009, 237).

18. Barbara Frye and Carol D'Avanzo gloss *koucharang* as "a state of rumination over and preoccupation with intrusive thoughts or memories" (1994, 90).

19. See, for instance, the compelling memoirs of Molyda Szymusiak, born Buth Keo (1999), Chanrithy Him (2000), Daran Kravanh (LaFreniere 2000), Ly Y (2000), U Sam Oeur (Oeur and McCullough 2005), Loung Ung (2000), Pin Yathay (1987), Haing Ngor (Ngor and Warner 2003), and Someth May (1986).

20. Mrs. Sann's mother was living in a Vietnamese village at the time of her death and was buried and disinterred according to local custom.

21. While these younger male relatives were described as nephews they were at a further remove than the nephews of European kinship networks.

2. Displacements

1. For accounts of the wars and political regimes of late twentieth-century Laos, see Martin Stuart-Fox (1997), Jane Hamilton-Merritt (1992), Grant Evans (1998, 1990), and Carol Ireson-Doolittle and Geraldine Moreno-Black (2004), among others.

2. Penny Van Esterik notes that people left Laos both out of fear for their "personal safety" and out of an inability to subsist after the 1977 droughts and the 1978 efforts to collectivize farms (1992, 11).

3. For accounts of events in Cambodia in the 1970s and beyond, see David Chandler (1999, 2000, 2002), Ben Kiernan (1993a, 1993b, 1996), Judith Banister and Paige Johnson (1993), Chanthou Boua (1993), May Ebihara (1993, 2002),

Kate Frieson (1993), Gregory Stanton (1993), Serge Thion (1993), John Marston (2002), Judy Ledgerwood and John Vijghen (2002), and Alexander Hinton (2002, 2005), among others.

4. See Ebihara (1990) on the range of situations endured by different social classes under the Khmer Rouge.

5. In Thailand it is said that if tiny dwellings are not built for the "lords" of a place they could be "dislocated and thus rendered dangerous when the land is taken up by humans" (Morris 2000, 117).

6. The Khmer festival of *loeng neak ta* ("raising the ancestors") is celebrated at the beginning of the growing season, by inviting monks to say prayers for the dead at the places where particular *neak ta* are thought to reside (Chandler 1996, 129; cf. Harris 2005, 54). Ian Harris separates *neak ta* into three categories, the first associated with natural features such as mountains, rivers, and trees, the second associated with ancestors, and the third with gods and mythical heroes (2005, 53).

7. I am grateful to Andrew Willford for this insight.

8. "Doubt," Morris comments, "is the condition in which spirits acquire their full mysteriousness" (2000, 196).

9. In contrast to European folktales, Edwards observes, transformation into animals within Cambodian tales often signifies not imprisonment but release (2008, 146).

10. See George Condominas (1975) on *phi ban* cults in Laos.

11. This spelling reflects a common romanization of this term when appearing in Lao. It differs from the romanization *(móo du)* used earlier for the Kmhmu usage of this term.

12. See Tambiah (1970) for a discussion of *moh du* in northeast Thailand.

13. *Sai bat* is the practice of giving alms to Buddhist monks.

3. Disciplines of Dying

1. Marilyn Strathern identifies a "conceptual collapse" in the distinction between nature and culture insofar as nature, whether understood as nonhuman aspects of the planet or biological aspects of the human, can no longer exist without "cultural intervention" (1992, 174). Yet arguably "nature" has always been entangled with "culture" insofar as it is both a cultural category and an ambiguous assemblage of entities and processes that include human knowledge practices, history, and mischief.

2. Mary Bradbury notes that in Great Britain, the movement for natural death was created in the image of the movement for natural childbirth (1999, 161).

3. Even such lives may be socially engaged, however. Long after her pediatricians considered her brain-dead, the Hmong child made famous by *The Spirit Catches You and You Fall Down* (Fadiman 1997) lay on a bed centrally placed in her family's house while nieces and nephews tumbled over her body (Fadiman, lecture). See Sharon Kaufman (2000) for insightful ethnography of long-term care of patients in a persistant vegetative state (PVS).

4. Kaufman acknowledges the salience of this popular representation of technology as the "primary culprit" behind prolonged dying, even as she justly contests its accuracy (2005, 237).

5. At the time of the publication of Mitford's book, only 3 to 4 percent of dead bodies in the United States were cremated; some thirty years later the percentage was over 20 percent (Mitford 1998, 111).

6. For a consideration of the ambiguities of the term "life support," see Kaufman (2005, 236–42).

7. For the most part, it is permitted to treat the patient for pain to the point of death as long as the intent is to relieve suffering and not to end the patient's life. The exception is in those states, like Oregon, where physician-assisted death is legal for patients diagnosed with a terminal disease who have not been determined to be suffering from untreated depression.

8. Modern tools of detection allow a finer and finer analysis of this ambiguity, dividing human death into the breakdown of specific cells, organs, and systems.

9. Disciplines of dying unfold within a broader set of bodily disciplines enacted on emigrant bodies. As Ong details for Khmer communities, such disciplines range from containment of Asian contagion and Asian reproduction to training in hygiene and offhand diagnoses of PTSD (2003, 91–121).

10. On the reading of rumor, see Veena Das (2001), Ranajit Guha (1983), and David Arnold (1988).

11. The studies most often cited are those conducted by SUPPORT (Study to Understand Prognosis and Preferences for Outcomes and Risks of Treatment) (Kaufman 2005, 31; Webb 1997, 51; Drought and Koenig 2002, 119). In one experimental program where advance directives did indirectly influence the eventual decisions, the influence was attributed less to the directives themselves than to the conversations they prompted (Gawande 2010, 46).

12. Each translation of this booklet is identically formatted, with the same number of sentences in each section occupying the same amount of space. In order to create a useful translation in Lao or Khmer, it would have been necessary to avoid Lao or Khmer equivalents of technical phrases, narrating them instead in colloquial language illustrated by specific scenarios, no matter how many extra sentences that entailed.

13. Families who participated in a pilot program allowing them to be present at resuscitation efforts said that they found it easier to accept the death, having observed how hard the doctors tried to prevent it. They believed that the patient also appreciated their presence. Participating physicians noted that if they failed to revive the patient they at least were able to satisfy some of the emotional needs of the family (Timmermans 1997).

14. These lines are excerpted from the poem "Litany" (Pereira 2003, 20–22).

15. Although viewings at home with the body on dry ice have begun to be possible in the United States, they have not lodged in the popular imagination. In the UK, on the other hand, a movement to bypass funeral homes distributes information on do-it-yourself funerals, including instructions for building a coffin and laying out the body (Bradbury 1999, 155).

16. As Stacy Pigg (1996) points out, belief itself is defined by and depends on the possibility of selectively directed skepticism.

17. See also Jean Baudrillard's discussion of the modern erosion of exchange with the dead (1993, 125–94).

18. I have changed several identifying details of this story.

19. Ceremoniously placing the loved one's ashes in the Ganges is a common practice. See Jonathan Parry (1995) and Ann Grodzins Gold (1988) for accounts of Hindu mourning practices in India, and Stephen White (1997) and Shirley Firth (2001) for accounts of Hindu mourning in diaspora.

20. Kaufman notes that hospital staff consider unsuccessful CPR the antithesis of "death with dignity" (2005, 166).

4. Dangerous Language

1. The modern hospice movement began in the UK in 1967. The first North American hospice was established in 1974.

2. It was not until 1992 that all fifty states had legalized some form of advance directive, of which living wills were the earliest example.

3. Kübler-Ross (1969) differentiates five psychological stages of confronting death: denial, anger, bargaining, depression, and acceptance.

4. Laurie Lyckholm (2004) suggests that establishing a program for dying was less of a priority for Kübler-Ross than instilling skills of compassionate listening in caregivers.

5. As Derrida writes, Ariès and authors of similar histories of death "both *deplore* and *denounce* what, according to them, they must record: a sort of disappearance of death in the modern West and in industrialized societies. They even *declare* their disapproval and denunciation, they put it forth, they recognize therein a determinant motivation of their research" (1993, 57).

6. Studies suggest that the practice of disclosure is much less frequent in southern Europe, Asia, the Middle East, and Africa than in northern Europe and the United States (Mystakidou et al. 2004; M. Gold 2004).

7. See the next chapter for discussion of the more precise senses of *khwan*.

8. Some studies suggest that AIDS patients who accept their death may live a shorter time than those who do not (Webb 1997).

9. Julie elaborated that even Christian converts asked the *móo du* to check their newborn babies. "He would check the child and say, 'Oh, this is good. It is a blessing to have this child. And he's this kind of baby.' There were different kinds of babies.

People might have a ground baby or a grass baby. If you're a grass baby you live, because you eat grass. But if you're a ground baby then they believe that you will go back to being dirt again." According to lore, if a ground baby passed the age of one she would live to be fifteen, if she passed the age of fifteen she would live to be thirty-five, if she passed the age of thirty-five she would live to be sixty-five, and if she lived past that age she would live to be one hundred and twenty.

10. For discussion of the linguistic status of mantra, see the collection edited by Harvey Alper (1989), and also Langford (2003).

5. Syllables of Power

The epigraph opening the chapter is from Lindell, Swahn, and Tayanin 1984, 233.

1. This was unusual. Under the Khmer Rouge most monks left alive were forced to defrock.

2. See Ashley Thompson (1996) for a comprehensive discussion of *hav praloeng*.

3. Thompson writes of healing ceremonies designed to deceive spirit parents about a child's identity so that they do not attempt to take it back to the spirit world (1996, 18). See Ang Choulean (1986) for further discussion of spirit families.

4. *Bai si* refers to this carefully arranged offering. See Phra Anuman Rajadhon (1946) for an account of ritual contexts for which *bai si* were used in Thailand in the mid-twentieth century.

5. I have been unable to confirm whether *saut kavada* corresponds to the Buddhist text *sutta kevaddha*. If so, it is interesting that that text largely dismantles the credibility of any miraculous powers other than the powers of mental detachment.

6. These four aspects of awareness are known in Sanskrit or Pali as *vedana, samjña, samskara,* and *vijñana.*

7. Illness may also be divined by inspecting a raw egg.

8. See Anne Fadiman (1997, 277–88), Nusit Chindarsi (1976, 52–55), and Robert Cooper et al. (1996, 60–71) for descriptions of Hmong shamanic healings.

9. According to Hmong legend, sicknesses entered the world from an egg laid by the wife of Ntxwj Nyug, the younger son of the first man, Lou Tou, who emerged from a vein of rock on a mountain. Ntxwj Nyug's older brother was already in charge of the earth and sky, so Ntxwj Nyug was put in charge of plants and animals. Ntxwj Nyug's father, realizing that the egg laid by Ntxwj Nyug's wife was full of *dab*, cautioned him to destroy it, but Ntxwj Nyug refused. After describing the various evil spirits that emerged from the egg, the story goes on to tell how the hero Siv Yis learned sorcery to kill them off. Later, however, the illnesses which had come out of Ntxwj Nyug's strange egg brought death into the world of humans (Johnson 1992, 58–59).

10. See in particular Thomas Pearson's (2009) compelling analysis of the interweaving of Christian, biomedical, ethnonationalist, and anticommunist missionizing of the Montagnard Dega in Vietnam through the coordinated efforts of U.S. religious and military aid.

11. Lindell et al. (1982, 7), following the usage of Damrong Tayanin, uses the term *móo róoy* (spirit healer), translating it as "shaman." According to Kampheang *po kru* and *móo kru* are essentially the same.

12. Erik Davis notes that certain Pali chants are performed both for extension of life and at Cambodian funerals (2009, 78–80).

13. The term *winyan* refers to the spirit of the person as it passes from one life to the next. The term *khwan* refers to the spirits of the living person that are vulnerable to being separated from the body (Tambiah 1970; Keyes 1982). In the Khmer context, John Holt refers to *vinnana* (equivalent to Lao *winyan*) as "the quality of the mental conditioning process that is consciously in play at the moment of death" (2012, 6).

14. James McClenon (1991) argues for several consistent features between East Asian and Euroamerican NDEs including a stage of not knowing one is dead, contact with spiritual guides, and a life evaluation. There are, however, significant differences between the Southeast Asian stories I heard, of frustrated attempts to get the attention of the living, and Euroamerican stories of walking toward the light.

15. If the deceased were a woman this would be the *khuy*, or "wife-receivers" in anthropological terms. If the deceased were a man this would be the *éem* or "wife-givers."

16. White's (in K. White and Lemoine 1982) and Chindarsi's (1976) translations of "Showing the Way" are from Green Hmong and Blue Hmong, respectively. Though differing in some details, they contain roughly the same stories and instructions.

6. Postmortem Economies

The epigraph opening the chapter is from Lindell, Swahn, and Tayanin 1977–95, 3:232.

1. As an example, in 2001, more than 54 percent of Cambodian families in one U.S. city (higher than that of any other group) lived below the federal poverty level.

2. As Margaret Lock astutely notes, the brain takes the place of the soul in certain contemporary medical contexts, enabling the definition of death as brain death (2001, 107).

3. As Rane Willerslev writes, "The notion of soul in Christian discourse is part and parcel of an ontological opposition of spirit and matter, which implies that souls are immaterial" (2007, 57).

4. On the *khwan* of body parts, see Rajadhon (1946, 124).

5. Although Siegel suggests that the purpose of funeral rites is to separate life and death (2006, 53–54), it strikes me that they could just as well be understood in the opposite way, as specifying the terms according to which life and death can bleed into one another.

6. Both of these festivals are held on the new moon of the ninth lunar month, which falls in August or September. For accounts of *Pchum Ben* celebrations in the

United States, see Thomas J. Douglas (2005, 132–34) and Nancy J. Smith-Hefner (1999, 58–59). For accounts of *Pchum Ben* in Cambodia, see Erik Davis (2009) and John Holt (2012). For an account of *Boun Khau Padab Din* in Laos, see Ladwig (2012).

7. Holt suggests that *Pchum Ben* has become increasingly important in contemporary Cambodia as a way to restore familial relations and console restless ghosts in the wake of the Khmer Rouge regime. One elderly woman told him that she had been celebrating *Pchum Ben* devotedly ever since "she encountered many ghosts while hiking in the mountains following the Pol Pot era" (2012, 49).

8. In a celebration in Laos observed by Patrice Ladwig (2012), the packets of sticky rice and fruit were left on the grounds of the *wat*.

9. It is no mere metaphor when Charles Keyes uses economic language to describe one of the two meanings of karma in Theravada Buddhism: "First, merit is seen as a form of spiritual insurance, an investment made with the expectation that in the future—and probably in a future existence—one will enjoy a relatively prolonged state without suffering" (1983, 267).

10. Erik Davis writes that in Cambodia there is a daytime celebration in the *wat*, in which offerings are made for specific named dead, and another celebration at night where monks play no role and rice packets are left on the ground for anonymous ghosts, as Douang described for Laos (2009, 180).

11. In a Thai context Morris observes that merit for the giver is made possible by the monk's lack of acknowledgment for the gift: the "fiction" of forgetting the gift purifies it (2000, 31).

12. Wrestling with the apparent contradiction between transference of merit and individual karmic responsibility, Keyes concludes that merit is a form of "spiritual currency" that works to strengthen social community (1983, 282–83).

13. As David Graeber points out in his discussion of "primordial debt," any debt to the universe should logically disappear, given that no one is separate from the universe in the first place. To speak of circulations of incalculable debt or merit might then be one way of dramatizing this lack of separation (2011, 68–69).

14. For accounts of Hmong death rites of various clans in various locales, see Nusit Chindarsi (1976), Catherine Falk (1996), Jacques Lemoine (1979), Patricia Symonds (2004), Nicholas Tapp (1989), and Cziasarh Neng Yang (2002).

15. In one ceremony Symonds witnessed, the wine was poured into the ground by the dead person's head at intervals during the chant (2004, 118–19).

16. In one translation, this passage reads: "You have come to live at [place of death] and you have consumed an area of [the local spirits'] forests, used a section of their firewood, and have drunk a volume of their water. Now you will go and the spirits of the land and the spirits of the town will open their arms to block your path. . . . Since you have consumed an area of their forests, used a section of their firewood, and have drunk a volume of their water, you will have to thank them and repay them with paper money and incense sticks" (Yang 2002, 119–20).

17. For further accounts of Hmong geomancy, see Roberta Julian (2004, 38), Nicholas Tapp (1989, 86; 1988; 1986), Bruce Thowpaou Bliatout (1993), and Robert Cooper et al. (1996). Tapp relates that one who is buried in the perfect place along the *loojmem*—the "veins of the dragon," rivers that flow in a certain way down a mountain toward a pool where rebirth begins—is able to catch the *loojmem* and ride it to the otherworld (1986, 90).

18. The cow's soul serves to replace one of the souls of the deceased, which has been consumed by Ntxwj Nyug, the Hmong spirit responsible for sickness and death (Quincy 1988, 108).

19. While these different souls are key to the complexities of mourning practice, many hesitate to identify them as taxonomic categories (Tapp 1989, 87). Timothy Dunnigan (personal communication) suggests that it is a mistake to place these souls in a classificatory scheme; they are more appropriately understood as different situations of spirit arising in different discursive contexts. In at least some versions of the funeral chant *Qhuab Ke*, one stanza specifies, "Since you have gone, your body is dead / But not your souls. / One of your souls will go to put on the rebirth shirt." The chant also refers to "one person, three souls" and later to "one body, three souls" (Symonds 2004, 228).

20. Heidegger speaks of this indebtedness as "guilt," casting it in a distinctively Christian light (1996, 284).

21. Graeber reasons that if we might be said to "owe an infinite debt to humanity, society, nature, or the cosmos (however one prefers to frame it)," no one could "possibly tell us how we are to pay it," in which case all established authorities who delineated amounts of debt would be presuming "to calculate what cannot be calculated" (2011, 68–69).

22. See also Chakrabarty (1998) on the persistence of gods and spirits in modern practices.

7. Spirit Debt

1. In Cambodia, victims of violent death are usually buried rather than cremated. In addition, some Cambodians, such as the Muslim Cham and Sino-Khmer, routinely bury the dead.

2. See Harris on occult powers used by the Cambodian military during the 1970s (2005, 168).

3. SUNDS, also diagnosed among Filipino men, is nearly always associated with social displacement (cf. Munger and Booton 1998).

4. For additional discussion of ancestor illness among the Hmong, see Lillian Faderman and Ghia Xiong (1998, 115).

5. Frank Proschan tells a story of a Catholic Kmhmu family in the United States who insisted they had abandoned their beliefs in spirits, but then accused a neighboring family of witchcraft when one of their elders fell ill (1992, 153–54).

6. The exhumations were reportedly undertaken to allow the land to be used for a different purpose.

7. Mary Steedly found that a recent addition to the spirit world in Indonesia were those spirits whose Christian kin no longer provided for them (1993, 145).

8. According to Kam Raw, there were two spirit villages in Northern Laos, one where a large ficus tree grew, and another at a vast lake, also described as a "quagmire." Both were actual geographical locations that were not visited by living Kmhmu (Lindell, Swahn, and Tayanin 1977–95, 3:11, 313).

9. This is an insight variously articulated by Bataille (1988, 70), as well as Marx, Hegel, and Nietzsche (Comay 1990, 66).

10. The story brings to mind Pierre Bourdieu's comment that countergifts must be deferred in order to not be insulting. The strategy of the gift, he points out, lies in that interval between gift and countergift (1977, 6).

11. In the Thai context Morris notes that the indebtedness of the dead is one reason they require the living to make merit for them (2000, 172).

12. On the war in Laos and its effects, see Martin Stuart-Fox (1997), Grant Evans (1998), Carol Ireson-Dolittle and Geraldine Moreno-Black (2004), and Keith Quincy (2000). On the war in Cambodia and the Khmer Rouge regime, see Elizabeth Becker (1986), David Chandler (2000), Ben Kiernan (1996), Karl Jackson (1989), and David Chandler and Ben Kiernan (1983).

13. *Klorng khaek* is played with drums, an instrument similar to an oboe, and a *korng*, a circular instrument played by striking metal discs to produce various tones. In Cambodia *klorng khaek* was played in the home just after a person had died, partly to announce the death to the neighbors. It was described to me as frightening music that brought chills to its listeners. Mr. Chea said that when *klorng khaek* is played, "those who are afraid of ghosts are very, very scared. They cover themselves up and have goose bumps."

14. See Talal Asad (1988) for a genealogy of ritual as symbolic action.

15. Similarly, after the hybrid funeral of a Muslim convert in Thailand, his relatives worried, "His legs are torn in two directions; one towards Islam, the other towards Buddhism. He cannot get into either a temple or a mosque. We do not know how to make merit for him" (Nishii 2002, 238).

16. See Milada Kalab (1994) for a relevant account of Khmer ceremonies for the dead in Paris, France.

17. In Mr. Vangay's city, at that time, there were no Hmong-owned funeral homes.

18. Many Hmong say that rituals for warding off *dab* and returning lost *plig* are less effective in the United States also (Mouanoutoua 2003, 218).

19. Kmhmu referred also to spirits that occupy the bodies of living humans, who emanate light from their eyes or head and have the ability to fly *(róoy yun)*, spirits who monitor and punish incestuous marriages *(róoy rklàk)*, and lightning spirits *(róoy saungpa)*. For a description of various *róoy*, see Damrong Tayanin (1994, 20–28).

20. See Derrida (1995, 114) on Friedrich Nietzche's discussion of Christ's assumption of debt.

21. For Derrida, hauntology or the "logic of haunting" refers to the irreducible power of that which—and those who—are not technically present (1994, 10, 51, 161).

Afterword

1. See, for example, Kwon (2008), Siegel (2006), Klima (2002), Mueggler (2001), Taussig (1987), and McLean (2004).

2. See, among others, Taussig (1997), Klima (2002), Comaroff and Comaroff (1999), and Verdery (1999).

3. Our exchange here is reminiscent of Derrida's comment that "There has never been a scholar who really, and as a scholar, deals with ghosts" (1994, 12). As Matthew Watson (2012) points out, however, that may not be entirely true, at least within anthropology.

4. See also Siegel's comment that when we assert that association with the dead, without banishing them to the past, ought to induce cognitive disorder, it may be that we are simply insisting on our own ontology (2011, 115).

5. See Morris on Southeast Asian ghosts as a manifestation of the death drive (2008, 232).

6. Citing a number of bereavement studies, psychologist George Bonanno (2009) suggests that ongoing relationships with the dead may be nonpathological in certain situations or according to cultural contexts. Yet his own story of the powerful effect of offering paper money to his father in China emphasizes the power of interactions with the dead across cultural borders.

Bibliography

Abraham, Nicolas, and Maria Torok. 1994. *The Shell and the Kernel.* Translated by Nicholas T. Rand. Vol. 1. Chicago: University of Chicago Press.

Adler, Shelley R. 1991. "Sudden Unexpected Nocturnal Death Syndrome among Hmong Immigrants: Examining the Role of the 'Nightmare.'" *Journal of American Folklore* 104:54–71.

Agamben, Giorgio. 1998. *Homo Sacer: Sovereign Power and Bare Life.* Translated by Daniel Heller-Roazen. Stanford: Stanford University Press.

———. 2002. *Remnants of Auschwitz: The Witness and the Archive.* Translated by Daniel Heller-Roazen. New York: Zone.

———. 2004. *The Open: Man and Animal.* Translated by Kevin Attell. Stanford: Stanford University Press.

Alper, Harvey P. 1989. *Understanding Mantras.* Albany: State University of New York Press.

Althusser, Louis. 1971. "Ideology and Ideological State Apparatuses." In *Lenin and Philosophy,* 170–86. New York: Monthly Review.

Anderson, Elizabeth C. Walker, and Patricia F. Walker. 2003. "Strategies for Health Care Providers and Institutions to Deliver Culturally Competent Care." In Culhane-Pera et al. 2003, 273–79.

Archaimbault, Charles. 1973. *Structures religieuses Lao rites et mythes.* Vientiane, Laos: Vithagna.

Ariès, Philippe. 1974. *Western Attitudes toward Death: From the Middle Ages to the Present.* Translated by Patricia M. Ranum. Baltimore: Johns Hopkins University Press.

———. 1982. *The Hour of Our Death.* Translated by Helen Weaver. New York: Vintage.

Armstrong, David. 1987a. "Bodies of Knowledge: Foucault and the Problem of Human Anatomy." In *Sociological Theory and Medical Sociology,* edited by Graham Scambler, 59–76. London: Tavistock Publishers.

———. 1987b. "Silence and Truth in Death and Dying." *Social Science and Medicine* 24 (8):651–57.

Arney, William Ray, and Bernard J. Bergen. 1984. *Medicine and the Management of Living: Taming the Last Great Beast.* Chicago: University of Chicago Press.

Arnold, David. 1988. "Touching the Body: Perspectives on the Indian Plague, 1896–1900." In *Subaltern Studies V,* edited by V. Ranajit Guha, 55–90. New Delhi: Oxford University Press.

Asad, Talal. 1988. "Towards a Genealogy of the Concept of Ritual." In *Vernacular Christianity: Essays in the Social Anthropology of Religion,* edited by Wendy James and Douglas H. Johnson, 73–87. Oxford: Jaso.

———. 2000. "Muslims and European Identity: Can Europe Represent Islam?" In *Cultural Encounters: Representing "Otherness,"* edited by Elizabeth Hallam and Brian V. Street, 11–27. New York: Routledge.

Austin, J. L. 1965. *How to Do Things with Words.* New York: Oxford University Press.

Banister, Judith, and E. Paige Johnson. 1993. "After the Nightmare: The Population of Cambodia." In *Genocide and Democracy in Cambodia: The Khmer Rouge, the United Nations, and the International Community,* edited by Ben Kiernan, 65–139. New Haven: Yale University Southeast Asian Studies.

Barley, Nigel. 1995. *Grave Matters: Encounters with Death Around the World.* Long Grove, Ill.: Waveland.

Bataille, Georges. 1988. *The Accursed Share: An Essay on General Economy.* Vol. 1: *Consumption.* New York: Zone.

———. 1989. *Theory of Religion.* New York: Zone.

Battin, Margaret Pabst. 1994. *The Least Worst Death: Essays in Bioethics on the End of Life.* New York: Oxford University Press.

Baudrillard, Jean. 1993. *Symbolic Exchange and Death.* Translated by Iain Hamilton Grant. London: Sage.

Becker, Elizabeth. 1986. *When the War Was Over: Cambodia and the Khmer Rouge Revolution.* New York: PublicAffairs.

Benjamin, Walter. 1968. "The Storyteller: Reflections on the Work of Nokolai Leskov." In *Illuminations,* edited by Hannah Arendt, 83–109. New York: Schocken Books.

Berger, Jeffrey T. 2005. "Ignorance Is Bliss? Ethical Considerations in Therapeutic Nondisclosure." *Cancer Investigation* 23 (1):94–98.

Beste, Jennifer. 2005. "Instilling Hope and Respecting Patient Autonomy: Reconciling Apparently Conflicting Duties." *Bioethics* 19 (3):215–31.

Bhabha, Homi. 1990. "DissemiNation: Time, Narrative, and the Margins of the Modern Nation." In *Nation and Narration,* edited by Homi Bhabha, 291–322. New York: Routledge.

Blackhall, Leslie J., Sheila T. Murphy, Gelya Frank, Vicki Michel, and Stanley Azen. 1995. "Ethnicity and Attitudes Toward Patient Autonomy." *Journal of American Medical Association* 274 (10):820–25.

Bliatout, Bruce Thowpaou. 1993. "Hmong Death Customs: Traditional and Acculturated." In *Ethnic Variations in Death, Dying, and Grief: Diversity in Universality,* edited by Donald P. Irish, Kathleen F. Lundquist, and Vivian Jenkins Nelsen, 79–100. Washington D.C.: Taylor and Frances.

Bloch, Maurice, and Jonathan Parry. 1982. "Introduction: Death and the Regeneration of Life." In *Death and the Regeneration of Life*, edited by Maurice Bloch and Jonathan Parry, 1–44. Cambridge: Cambridge University Press.

Bonanno, George A. 2009. *The Other Side of Sadness: What the New Science of Bereavement Tells Us about Life after Loss*. New York: Basic Books.

Boua, Chanthou. 1993. "Development Aid and Democracy in Cambodia." In *Genocide and Democracy in Cambodia: The Khmer Rouge, the United Nations, and the International Community*, edited by Ben Kiernan, 273–83. New Haven: Yale University Southeast Asian Studies.

Bourdieu, Pierre. 1977. *Outline for a Theory of Practice*. Translated by Richard Nice. Cambridge: Cambridge University Press.

Bourke, Joanne. 1996. *Dismembering the Male: Men's Bodies, Britain, and the Great War*. London: Reaktion.

Bradbury, Mary. 1999. *Representations of Death: A Social Psychological Perspective*. London: Routledge.

Brison, Susan J. 1999. "Trauma Narratives and the Remaking of the Self." In *Acts of Memory: Cultural Recall in the Present*, edited by Mieke Bal, Jonathan Crewe, and Leo Spitzer, 39–54. Hanover, N.H.: University of New England Press.

Butler, Judith. 1997a. *Excitable Speech: A Politics of the Performative*. New York: Routledge.

———. 1997b. *The Psychic Life of Power: Theories in Subjection*. Stanford: Stanford University Press.

Cain, J., L. Stacy, K. Jusenius, and D. Figge. 1990. "The Quality of Dying: Financial, Psychological, and Ethical Dilemmas." *Obstetrics and Gynecology* 76 (1):149–52.

Candea, Matei, and Giovanni Da Col. 2012. "The Return to Hospitality." *Journal of the Royal Anthropological Institute* 18 (S1):S1–S19.

Cannell, Fenella, ed. 2006a. *The Anthropology of Christianity*. Durham, N.C.: Duke University Press.

———. 2006b. "Introduction: The Anthropology of Christianity." In Cannell 2006a, 1–50.

Cannetti, Elias. 1984. *Crowds and Power*. New York: Farrar, Strauss and Giroux.

Carrese, Joseph A., and Lorna A. Rhodes. 1995. "Western Bioethics on the Navajo Reservation." *Journal of American Medical Association* 274 (10):826–29.

Caruth, Cathy. 1995a. "Recapturing the Past: Introduction." In *Trauma: Explorations in Memory*, edited by Cathy Caruth, 151–57. Baltimore: Johns Hopkins University Press.

———. 1995b. "Trauma and Experience: Introduction." In *Trauma: Explorations in Memory*, edited by Cathy Caruth, 3–12. Baltimore: Johns Hopkins University Press.

―――. 1996. *Unclaimed Experience: Trauma, Narrative, and History.* Baltimore: Johns Hopkins University Press.

Chakrabarty, Dipesh. 1998. "Minority Histories, Subaltern Pasts." *Postcolonial Studies* 1 (1):15–29.

―――. 2000. *Provincializing Europe: Postcolonial Thought and Historical Difference.* Princeton: Princeton University Press.

Chandler, David. 1996. *Facing the Cambodian Past: Selected Essays 1971–1994.* Chiangmai, Thailand: Silkworm Books.

―――. 1999. *Voices from S-21: Terror and History in Pol Pot's Secret Prison.* Berkeley: University of California Press.

―――. 2000. *A History of Cambodia.* Boulder, Colo.: Westview.

―――. 2002. "S-21, the Wheel of History, and the Pathology of Terror in Democratic Kampuchea." In *Cambodia Emerges from the Past: Eight Essays,* edited by Judy Ledgerwood and Kheang Un, 16–37. DeKalb: Southeast Asia Publications, Northern Illinois University.

―――. 2008. "Songs at the Edge of the Forest: Perceptions of Order in Three Cambodian Texts." In *At the Edge of the Forest: Essays on Cambodia, History, and Narrative in Honor of David Chandler,* edited by Anne Ruth Hansen and Judy Ledgerwood, 31–46. Ithaca: Southeast Asia Program, Cornell University.

Chandler, David, and Ben Kiernan. 1983. *Revolution and Its Aftermath in Kampuchea: Eight Essays.* New Haven: Yale University Southeast Asian Studies.

Cheng, Anne Anlin. 2001. *The Melancholy of Race.* New York: Oxford University Press.

Chindarsi, Nusit. 1976. *The Religion of the Hmong Njua.* Bangkok: Siam Society.

Cho, Grace M. 2008. *Haunting the Korean Diaspora: Shame, Secrecy, and the Forgotten War.* Minneapolis: University of Minnesota Press.

Choulean, Ang. 1986. *Les êtres surnaturels dans la religion populaire Khmere.* Paris: Cedoreck.

―――. 2004. *Brah Ling.* Phnom Penh: Reyum.

Comaroff, Jean, and John L. Comaroff. 1999. "Occult Economies and the Violence of Abstraction: Notes from the South African Postcolony." *American Ethnologist* 26 (2):279–303.

Comay, Rebecca. 1990. "Gifts without Presents: Economies of 'Experience' in Bataille and Heidegger." In "On Bataille," edited by Allan Stoekl, special issue, *Yale French Studies* 78:66–89.

Condominas, George. 1975. "Phiban Cults in Rural Laos." In *Change and Persistence in Thai Society,* edited by G. William Skinner, 252–73. Ithaca: Cornell University Press.

Cooper, Robert, Nicholas Tapp, Gary Yia Lee, and Gretel Schwoer-Kohl. 1996. *The Hmong.* Bangkok: Artasia.

Culhane-Pera, Kathleen A., Dorothy E. Vawter, Phua Xiong, Barbara Babbitt, and Mary M. Solberg, eds. 2003. *Healing by Heart: Clinical and Ethical Case Stories of Hmong Families and Western Providers.* Nashville: Vanderbilt University.

Da Silva, Carlos Henrique Martins, Renato Luiz Guerino Cunha, Ronaldo Borges Tonaco, Thulio Marquez Cunha, Ana Carolina Boaventura Diniz, Gustavo Gontijo Domingos, Juliana Diniz Silva, Marcelo Vitral Vitorino Santos, Melissa Ganam Antoun, and Rodrigo Lobato de Paula. 2003. "Not Telling the Truth in the Patient–Physician Relationship." *Bioethics* 17 (5–6):417–24.

Daniel, E. Valentine. 1996. *Charred Lullabies: Chapters in an Anthropography of Violence.* Princeton: Princeton University Press.

Das, Veena. 1996. "Language and Body: Transactions in the Construction of Pain." *Daedalus* 125 (1):67–89.

———. 2001. "Crisis and Representation: Rumor and the Circulation of Hate." In *Disturbing Remains: Memory, History, and Crisis in the Twentieth Century,* edited by Michael S. Roth and Charles G. Salas, 37–62. Los Angles: Getty Research Institute

———. 2007. *Life and Words: Violence and the Descent into the Ordinary.* Berkeley: University of California Press.

Davis, Erik. 2009. "Treasures of the Buddha: Imagining Death and Life in Contemporary Cambodia." PhD diss., Divinity School, University of Chicago, Chicago.

Davis, Richard. 1984. *Muang Metaphysics: A Study of Northern Thai Myth and Ritual.* Bangkok: Pandora.

de la Cadena, Marisol. 2010. "Indigenous Cosmopolitics in the Andes: Conceptual Reflections Beyond 'Politics.'" *Cultural Anthropology* 25 (2):334–70.

Deleuze, Gilles. 1994. *Difference and Repetition.* Translated by Paul Patton. New York: Columbia University Press.

Deleuze, Gilles, and Felix Guattari. 1987. *A Thousand Plateaus: Capitalism and Schizophrenia.* Translated by Brian Massumi. Minneapolis: University of Minnesota Press.

Derrida, Jacques. 1981. "Plato's Pharmacy." In *Dissemination,* 61–171. Chicago: University of Chicago Press.

———. 1992. *Given Time.* Vol. 1: *Counterfeit Money.* Translated by Peggy Kamuf. Chicago: University of Chicago Press.

———. 1993. *Aporias.* Translated by Thomas Dutoit. Stanford: Stanford University Press.

———. 1994. *Specters of Marx: The State of the Debt, the Work of Mourning, and the New International.* Translated by Peggy Kamuf. New York: Routledge.

———. 1995. *The Gift of Death.* Translated by David Wills. Chicago: University of Chicago Press.

———. 2001. *On Cosmopolitanism and Forgiveness.* Translated by Mark Dooley and Michael Hughes. London: Routledge.

———. 2009. *The Beast and the Sovereign.* Translated by Geoffrey Bennington. 2 vols. Chicago: University of Chicago Press.

Desan, Christine. 1983. "A Change of Faith for Hmong Refugees." *Cultural Survival Quarterly* 7 (3). Available from www.culturalsurvival.org/ourpublications/csq/article/a-change-faith-hmong-refugees.

Devereux, George. 1967. *From Anxiety to Method in the Behavioral Sciences*. New York: Humanities Press.

Douglas, Thomas J. 2005. "Changing Religious Practices among Cambodian Immigrants in Long Beach and Seattle." In *Immigrant Faiths: Transforming Religious Life in America*, edited by Karen I. Leonard, Alex Stepick, Manuel A. Vasquez, and Jennifer Holdaway, 123–44. Walnut Creek, Calif.: Altamira.

Drought, Theresa S., and Barbara A. Koenig. 2002. "'Choice' in End-of-life Decision Making: Researching Fact or Fiction?" *Gerontologist* 42 (suppl. 3):114–28.

Dumit, Joseph. 1998. "A Digital Image of the Category of the Person: PET Scanning and Objective Self-Fashioning." In *Cyborgs and Citadels: Anthropological Interventions in Emerging Sciences and Technologies*, edited by Gary Lee Downey and Joseph Dumit, 83–102. Santa Fe, N.M.: School of American Research.

Ebihara, May. 1990. "Revolution and Reformulation in Kampuchean Village Culture." In *The Cambodian Agony*, edited by David A. Ablin and Marlowe Hood, 16–61. Armonk, N.Y.: M. E. Sharpe Publishers.

———. 1993. "A Cambodian Village under the Khmer Rouge, 1975–1979." In *Genocide and Democracy in Cambodia: The Khmer Rouge, the United Nations, and the International Community*, edited by Ben Kiernan, 51–63. New Haven: Yale University Southeast Asian Studies.

———. 2002. "Memories of the Pol Pot Era in a Cambodian Village." In *Cambodia Emerges from the Past: Eight Essays*, edited by Judy Ledgerwood and Kheang Un, 91–108. DeKalb: Southeast Asia Publications, Northern Illinois University.

Edelman, Lee. 2004. *No Future: Queer Theory and the Death Drive*. Durham, N.C.: Duke University Press.

Edwards, Penny. 2008. "Between a Song and a Prei: Tracking Cambodian History and Cosmology through the Forest." In *At the Edge of the Forest: Essays on Cambodia, History, and Narrative in Honor of David Chandler*, edited by Anne Ruth Hansen and Judy Ledgerwood, 137–62. Ithaca: Southeast Asia Program, Cornell University.

Eng, David L. 2002. "The Value of Silence." *Theatre Journal* 54:85–94.

Evans, Grant. 1990. *Lao Peasants Under Socialism*. New Haven: Yale University Press.

———. 1998. *The Politics of Ritual and Remembrance: Laos since 1975*. Honolulu: University of Hawai'i Press.

Fabian, Johannes. 1983. *Time and the Other: How Anthropology Makes its Object*. New York: Columbia University Press.

Faderman, Lillian, and Ghia Xiong. 1998. *I Begin My Life All Over: The Hmong and the American Immigrant Experience*. Boston: Beacon.

Fadiman, Anne. 1997. *The Spirit Catches You and You Fall Down: A Hmong Child, Her American Doctors, and the Collision of Two Cultures*. New York: Noonday.

Falk, Catherine. 1992. *Hmong Funeral in Australia in 1992*. Available from http://www.hmongnet.org/hmong-au/funeral.htm.

———. 1996. "Upon Meeting the Ancestors: The Hmong Funeral Ritual in Asia and Australia." *Hmong Studies Journal* 1 (1), at www.hmongstudies.org/Hmong StudiesJournal.html.

———. 2004. "The Private and Public Lives of the Hmong *Qeej* and Miao *Lusheng.*" In *The Hmong of Australia: Culture and Diaspora,* edited by Nicholas Tapp and Gary Yia Lee, 123–52. Canberra: Pandanus Books.

Fan, Ruiping, and Benfu Li. 2004. "Truth Telling in Medicine: The Confucian View." *Journal of Medicine & Philosophy* 29 (2):179–93.

Fan, Ruiping, and Julia Tao. 2004. "Consent to Medical Treatment: The Complex Interplay of Patients, Families, and Physicians." *Journal of Medicine & Philosophy* 29 (2):139–48.

Fassin, Didier, and Richard Rechtman. 2009. *The Empire of Trauma: An Inquiry in the Condition of Victimhood.* Princeton: Princeton University Press.

Firth, Shirley. 2001. "Hindu Death and Mourning Rituals: The Impact of Geographic Mobility." In *Grief, Mourning, and Death Ritual,* edited by Jenny Hockey, Jeanne Katz, and Neil Small, 237–46. Buckingham: Open University.

Foucault, Michel. 1973. *The Birth of the Clinic: An Archaeology of Medical Perception.* Translated by A. M. Sheridan. New York: Vintage.

———. 1982. "The Subject and Power." In *Michel Foucault: Beyond Structuralism and Hermeneutics,* edited by Hubert J. Dreyfus and Paul Rabinow, 208–26. Chicago: University of Chicago Press.

———. 1990. *The History of Sexuality.* Vol. 1: *An Introduction.* Translated by Robert Hurley. New York: Vintage.

Francis, Doris, Leonie Kellaher, and Georgina Neophytou. 2005. *The Secret Cemetery.* Oxford: Berg.

Frazier, Lessie Jo. 1999. "'Subverted Memories': Countermourning as Political Action in Chile." In *Acts of Memory: Cultural Recall in the Present,* edited by Mieke Bal, Jonathan Crewe, and Leo Spitzer, 105–19. Hanover, N.H.: University of New England Press.

Freud, Sigmund. 1922. *Beyond the Pleasure Principle.* Translated by C. J. M. Hubback. London: International Psycho-Analytical Press.

———. 1955a. "Mourning and Melancholia." In *Standard Edition of the Complete Psychological Works of Sigmund Freud,* edited by James Strachey, 14:243–58. London: Hogarth.

———. 1955b. "The 'Uncanny.'" In *Standard Edition of the Complete Psychological Works of Sigmund Freud,* edited by James Strachey, 17:219–56. London: Hogarth.

———. 1962. "Screen Memories." In *Standard Edition of the Complete Psychological Works of Sigmund Freud,* edited by James Strachey, 3:301–22. London: Hogarth.

Frieson, Kate. 1993. "Revolution and Rural Response in Cambodia, 1970–1975." In *Genocide and Democracy in Cambodia: The Khmer Rouge, the United Nations, and the International Community,* edited by Ben Kiernan, 33–50. New Haven: Yale University Southeast Asian Studies.

Frye, Barbara A., and Carolyn D'Avanzo. 1994. "Themes in Managing Culturally Defined Illness in the Cambodian Refugee Family." *Journal of Community Health Nursing* 11 (2):89–98.

Gagliardi, Jason. 2002. "Behind the Secret of the Naga's Fire." *Time*, November 17. Available from www.time.com/time/magazine/article/0,9171,391567,00.html.

Gawande, Atul. 2010. "Letting Go: What Should Medicine Do When It Can't Save Your Life?" *The New Yorker* (August): 36–49.

Gilbert, Sandra. 2006. *Death's Door: Modern Dying and the Ways We Grieve.* New York: W. W. Norton.

Gleeson, Kevin, and Scott Wise. 1990. "The Do-Not-Resuscitate Order: Still Too Little Too Late." *Archives of Internal Medicine* 150:1057–60.

Gold, Ann Grodzins. 1988. *Fruitful Journeys: The Ways of Rajasthani Pilgrims.* Berkeley: University of California Press.

Gold, Michelle. 2004. "Is Honesty Always the Best Policy? Ethical Aspects of Truth Telling." *Internal Medicine Journal* 34 (9–10):578–80.

Gombrich, Richard. 1971. "Merit-Transference in Sinhalese Buddhism: A Case Study of the Interaction between Doctrine and Practice." *History of Religions* 11:203–19.

Gómez-Barris, Macarena. 2010. "Reinscribing Memory through the Other 9/11." In *Toward a Sociology of the Trace*, edited by Herman Gray and Macarena Gómez-Barris, 235–56. Minneapolis: University of Minnesota Press.

Gómez-Barris, Macarena, and Herman Gray. 2010. "Toward a Sociology of the Trace." In *Toward a Sociology of the Trace*, edited by Herman Gray and Macarena Gómez-Barris, 1–14. Minneapolis: University of Minnesota Press.

Gordon, Avery. 1997. *Ghostly Matters: Haunting and the Sociological Imagination.* Minneapolis: University of Minnesota Press.

Gordon, Elisa J., and Christopher K. Daugherty. 2003. "'Hitting You over the Head': Oncologists' Disclosure of Prognosis to Advanced Cancer Patients." *Bioethics* 17 (2):142–68.

Graeber, David. 2011. *Debt: The First 5000 Years.* New York: Melville House.

Gray, Herman, and Macarena Gómez-Barris. 2010. "Prologue: Traces in the Social World." In *Toward a Sociology of the Trace*, edited by Herman Gray and Macarena Gómez-Barris, vii–xvi. Minneapolis: University of Minnesota Press.

Guha, Ranajit. 1983. *Elementary Aspects of Peasant Insurgency in Colonial India.* New Delhi: Oxford University Press.

Guillon, Anne Y. "Medicine in Cambodia during the Pol Pot Regime (1975–1979): Foreign and Cambodian Influences." Paper presented at the symposium on "East Asian Medicine under Communism" at the City University of New York. Available from hal.archives-onverles.fr/docs/00/32/77/11/PDF/04_Paper_CUNY_juillet.pdf.

Guneratnam, Yasmin. 1997. "Culture Is Not Enough: A Critique of Multi-Culturalism in Palliative Care." In *Death, Gender, and Ethnicity*, edited by David Field, Jenny Hockey, and Neil Small, 166–86. London: Routledge.

Hacking, Ian. 1986. "Making Up People." In *Reconstructing Individualism: Autonomy, Individuality, and the Self in Western Thought*, edited by Thomas C. Heller, Morton Sosna, and David E. Wellbery, 222–36. Stanford: Stanford University Press.

Hallam, Elizabeth, Jenny Hockey, and Glennys Howarth. 1999. *Beyond the Body: Death and Social Identity*. London: Routledge.

Hamilton-Merritt, Jane. 1992. *Tragic Mountains: The Hmong, the Americans, and the Secret Wars for Laos, 1942–1992*. Bloomington: University of Indiana Press.

Haraway, Donna. 1991. *Simians, Cyborgs, and Women: The Reinvention of Nature*. New York: Routledge.

Harris, Ian. 2005. *Cambodian Buddhism: History and Practice*. Honolulu: University of Hawai'i Press.

Hartman, Rebecca L. 1996. "To Tell or Not to Tell, Part 2: Ethical Comment." *Dimensions of Critical Care Nursing* 15 (6):319–23.

Heidegger, Martin. 1996. *Being and Time: A Translation of Sein und Zeit* [1953]. Translated by Joan Stambaugh. Albany: State University of New York Press.

Hern, H. Eugene, Jr., B. A. Koenig, Lisa Jean Moore, and P. A. Marshall. 1998. "The Difference that Culture Can Make in End-of-Life Decisionmaking." *Cambridge Quarterly of Healthcare Ethics* 7 (1):27–40.

Hertz, Robert. 1960. "A Contribution to the Study of the Collective Representation of Death." In *Death and the Right Hand*, 27–154. Glencoe, Ill.: Free Press.

Him, Chanrithy. 2000. *When Broken Glass Floats: Growing Up under the Khmer Rouge*. New York: W. W. Norton.

Hinton, Alexander Laban. 2002. "Purity and Contamination in the Cambodian Genocide." In *Cambodia Emerges from the Past: Eight Essays*, edited by Judy Ledgerwood and Kheang Un, 60–90. DeKalb: Southeast Asia Publications, Northern Illinois University.

———. 2005. *Why Did They Kill? Cambodia in the Shadow of Genocide*. Berkeley: University of California Press.

Hockey, Jenny. 1996. "The View from the West: Reading the Anthropology of Non-Western Death Ritual." In *Contemporary Issues in the Sociology of Death, Dying, and Disposal*, edited by Glennys Howarth and Peter Jupp, 3–16. London: Macmillan.

Holt, John Clifford. 2012. "Caring for the Dead Ritually in Cambodia." *Southeast Asian Studies* 1 (1):3–75.

Ireson-Doolittle, Carol, and Geraldine Moreno-Black. 2004. *The Lao: Gender, Power, and Livelihood*. Boulder, Colo.: Westview.

Ivy, Marilyn. 1995. *Discourses of the Vanishing: Modernity, Phantasm, Japan*. Chicago: University of Chicago Press.

Jackson, Karl D. 1989. *Cambodia 1975–1978: Rendezvous with Death*. Princeton: Princeton University Press.

Jeganathan, Pradeep. 1998. "'Violence' as an Analytical Problem: Sri Lankanist

Anthropology after July, '83." *Nethra: Journal of the International Centre for Ethnic Studies* 2 (4):7–47.

———. 1999. "On the Anticipation of Violence: Modernity and Identity in Southern Sri Lanka." In *Anthropology, Development and Minorities: Exploring Discourses, Counter-Tendencies, and Violence,* edited by Alberto Arce and Norman Long, 112–26. London: Routledge.

———. 2004. "Checkpoint: Anthropology, Identity, and the State." In *Anthropology in the Margins of the State,* edited by Veena Das and Deborah Poole, 67–80. Santa Fe, N.M.: School of American Research.

Johnson, Charles. 1992. *Dab Neeg Hmoob: Myths, Legends, and Folk Tales from the Hmong of Laos.* Saint Paul, Minn.: Macalaster College.

Julian, Roberta. 2004. "Living Locally, Dreaming Globally: Transnational Cultural Imaginings and Practices in the Hmong Diaspora." In *The Hmong of Australia: Culture and Diaspora,* edited by Nicholas Tapp and Gary Yia Lee, 25–58. Canberra: Pandanus Books.

Kalab, Milada. 1994. "Cambodian Buddhist Monasteries in Paris: Continuing Tradition and Changing Patterns." In *Cambodian Culture since 1975: Homeland and Exile,* edited by May Ebihara, Carol A. Mortland, and Judy Ledgerwood, 57–71. Ithaca: Cornell University Press.

Kalish, Richard A. 1980. *Death and Dying: Views from Many Cultures.* Farmingdale, N.Y.: Baywood.

Kaufman, Sharon R. 2000. "In the Shadow of 'Death with Dignity': Medicine and Cultural Quandaries of the Vegetative State." *American Anthropologist* 102 (1):69–83.

———. 2005. *. . . And a Time to Die: How American Hospitals Shape the End of Life.* Chicago: University of Chicago Press.

Keane, Webb. 2006. "Epilogue: Anxious Transcendence." In Cannell 2006a, 308–23.

———. 2007. *Christian Moderns: Freedom and Fetish in the Mission Encounter.* Berkeley: University of California Press.

Keyes, Charles F. 1982. "Death of Two Buddhist Saints in Thailand." In *Charisma and Sacred Biography,* edited by Michael A. Williams, Journal of the American Academy of Religion, Thematic Studies Series 48 (3–4), 149–80. Chico, Calif.: Scholars Press.

———. 1983. "Merit-Transference in the Kammic Theory of Popular Theravada Buddhism." In *Karma: An Anthropological Inquiry,* edited by Charles F. Keyes and E. Valentine Daniel, 261–86. Berkeley: University of California Press.

———. 1994. "Communist Revolution and the Buddhist Past in Cambodia." In *Asian Visions of Authority: Religion and the Modern States of East and Southeast Asia,* edited by Charles F. Keyes, Laurel Kendall, and Helen Hardacre, 43–73. Honolulu: University of Hawai'i Press.

———. 2002. "National Heroine or Local Spirit? The Struggle over Memory in the

Case of Thao Suranari of Nakhon Ratchasima." In *Cultural Crisis and Social Memory: Modernity and Identity in Thailand and Laos,* edited by Shigeharu Tanabe and Charles F. Keyes, 113–36. Honolulu: University of Hawai'i Press.

Kiernan, Ben. 1993a. "The Inclusion of the Khmer Rouge in the Cambodian Peace Process: Causes and Consequences." In *Genocide and Democracy in Cambodia: The Khmer Rouge, the United Nations, and the International Community,* edited by Ben Kiernan, 191–272. New Haven: Yale University Southeast Asian Studies.

———. 1993b. "Introduction." In *Genocide and Democracy in Cambodia: The Khmer Rouge, the United Nations, and the International Community,* edited by Ben Kiernan, 9–32. New Haven: Yale University Southeast Asian Studies.

———. 1996. *The Pol Pot Regime: Race, Power, and Genocide in Cambodia under the Khmer Rouge, 1975–1979.* New Haven: Yale University Press.

Kinzie, J. D. 1990. "The 'Concentration Camp Syndrome' among Cambodian Refugees." In *The Cambodian Agony,* edited by David A. Ablin and Marlowe Hood, 332–53. Armonk, N.Y.: M. E. Sharpe Publishers.

Kittler, Friedrich A. 1990. *Discourse Networks, 1800/1900.* Translated by Michael Metteer and Chris Cullens. Stanford: Stanford University Press.

Kleinman, Arthur. 1989. *The Illness Narratives: Suffering, Healing, and the Human Condition.* New York: Basic Books.

Klima, Alan. 2002. *The Funeral Casino: Meditation, Massacre, and Exchange with the Dead in Thailand.* Princeton: Princeton University Press.

———. 2004. "Thai Love Thai: Financing Emotion in Post-Crash Thailand." *Ethnos* 69 (4):445–64.

Koenig, Barbara A., and Jan Gates-Williams. 1995. "Understanding Cultural Difference in Caring for Dying Patients." *Western Journal of Medicine* 163 (3):244–49.

Kristeva, Julia. 1989. *Black Sun: Depression and Melancholia.* Translated by Leon S. Roudiez. New York: Columbia University.

Kübler-Ross, Elisabeth. 1969. *On Death and Dying.* New York: Macmillan.

———. 1974. *Questions and Answers on Death and Dying.* New York: Macmillan.

Kuriyama, Shigehisa. 1999. *The Expressiveness of the Body and the Divergence of Greek and Chinese Medicine.* New York: Zone Books.

Kwon, Heonik. 2008. *Ghosts of War in Vietnam.* Cambridge: Cambridge University Press.

LaCapra, Dominick. 2001. *Writing History, Writing Trauma.* Baltimore: Johns Hopkins University Press.

Ladwig, Patrice. 2012. "Visitors from Hell: Transformative Hospitality to Ghosts in a Lao Buddhist Festival." *Journal of the Royal Anthropological Institute* 18 (S1):S90–S102.

LaFreniere, Bree. 2000. *Music through the Dark: A Tale of Survival in Cambodia.* Honolulu: University of Hawai'i Press.

Langer, Lawrence. 1991. *Holocaust Testimonies: The Ruins of Memory.* New Haven: Yale University Press.

Langford, Jean M. 2002. *Fluent Bodies: Ayurvedic Remedies for Postcolonial Imbalance.* Durham, N.C.: Duke University Press.

———. 2003. "Traces of 'Folk Medicine' in Jaunpur." *Cultural Anthropology* 18 (3):271–303.

Laub, Dori. 1992. "Bearing Witness, or the Vicissitudes of Listening." In *Testimony: Crises of Witnessing in Literature, Psychoanalysis, and History,* edited by Shoshana Felman and Dori Laub, 57–74. New York: Routledge.

Law, John. 2004. *After Method: Mess in Social Science Research.* New York: Routledge.

Lawrence, Patricia. 1997. "Violence, Suffering, Amman: The Work of Oracles in Sri Lankan's Eastern War Zone." In *Violence and Subjectivity,* edited by Veena Das, Arthur Kleinman, Mamphela Ramphele, and Pamela Reynolds, 171–204. Berkeley: University of California Press.

Ledgerwood, Judy, and John Vijghen. 2002. "Decision-Making in Rural Khmer Villages." In *Cambodia Emerges from the Past: Eight Essays,* edited by Judy Ledgerwood and Kheang Un, 109–50. DeKalb: Southeast Asia Publications, Northern Illinois University.

Lee, Mai Na M. 2009. *A Culture in Peril: Hmong Grave Descration in Thailand.* Available from http://www.cce.umn.edu/media/headliners/lee/lee.mp3.

Lemoine, Jacques. 1979. "La mort et ses rites chez les Hmong." *Objets et Mondes* 19:196–207.

———. 1986. "The Constitution of a Hmong Shaman's Power of Healing and Folk Culture." *Shaman* 4 (1–2):143–65.

Levi, Primo. 1993. *Survival in Auschwitz: The Nazi Assault on Humanity.* Translated by Stuart Woolf. New York: Simon and Schuster.

Leys, Ruth. 2000. *Trauma: A Genealogy.* Chicago: University of Chicago Press.

Lindell, Kristina, Håkan Lundstrom, Jan-Olaf Svantesson, and Damrong Tayanin. 1982. *The Kammu Year: Its Lore and Music.* London: Curzon.

Lindell, Kristina, Jan-Ojvind Swahn, and Damrong Tayanin. 1977–95. *Folk Tales from Kammu.* 5 vols. London: Curzon.

Littlewood, Jane. 1992. *Aspects of Grief: Bereavement in Adult Life.* New York: Routledge.

Livo, Norma J., and Dia Cha. 1991. *Folk Stories of the Hmong Peoples of Laos, Thailand, and Vietnam.* Englewood, Colo.: Libraries Unlimited.

Lock, Margaret. 2001. *Twice Dead: Organ Transplants and the Reinvention of Death.* Berkeley: University of California Press.

Lowe, Celia. 2006. *Wild Profusion: Biodiversity Conservation in an Indonesian Archipelago.* Princton: Princeton University Press.

Ly, Boreth. 2008. "Of Performance and the Persistent Temporality of Trauma: Memory, Art, and Visions." *Positions* 16 (1):109–30.

Lyckholm, Laurie J. 2004. "Thirty Years Later: An Oncologist Reflects on Kübler-Ross's Work." *American Journal of Bioethics* 4 (4):W29–31.

Lynn, Joanne. 1996. "Caring for Those Who Die in Old Age." In *Facing Death: Where*

Culture, Religion, and Medicine Meet, edited by Howard M. Spiro, Mary G. McCrea Curnen, and Lee Palmer Wandel, 90–102. New Haven: Yale University Press.

Marston, John. 2002. "Democratic Kampuchea and the Idea of Modernity." In *Cambodia Emerges from the Past: Eight Essays,* edited by Judy Ledgerwood and Kheang Un, 38–59. DeKalb: Southeast Asia Publications, Northern Illinois University.

Mauss, Marcel. 1990. *The Gift: The Form and Reasons for Exchange in Archaic Societies.* Translated by W. D. Halls. New York: W. W. Norton.

May, Someth. 1986. *Cambodian Witness: The Autobiography of Someth May.* New York: Random House.

Mbembe, Achille. 2003. "Necropolitics." *Public Culture* 15 (1):11–40.

McCarthy, J. 2003. "Principlism or Narrative Ethics: Must We Choose between Them?" *Medical Humanities* 29 (2):65–71.

McClenon, James. 1991. "Near-Death Folklore in Medieval China and Japan: A Comparative Analysis." *Asian Folklore Studies* 50:319–42.

McLean, Stuart. 2004. *The Event and Its Terrors: Ireland, Famine, Modernity.* Stanford: Stanford University.

Men, Chean Rithy. 2002. "The Changing Religious Beliefs and Ritual Practices among Cambodians in Diaspora." *Journal of Refugee Studies* 15 (2):222–33.

Metcalf, Peter, and Richard Huntington. 1991. *Celebrations of Death: The Anthropology of Mortuary Ritual.* Cambridge: Cambridge University Press.

Mitford, Jessica. 1963. *The American Way of Death.* New York: Simon and Schuster.

———. 1998. *The American Way of Death Revisited.* London: Virago.

Moller, David Wendell. 1990. *On Death without Dignity: The Human Impact of Technological Dying.* Amityville, N.Y.: Baywood.

Morris, Rosalind. 2000. *In the Place of Origins: Modernity and Its Mediums in Northern Thailand.* Durham, N.C.: Duke University Press.

———. 2002. "Crises of the Modern in Northern Thailand: Ritual, Tradition, and the New Value of Pastness." In *Cultural Crisis and Social Memory: Modernity and Identity in Thailand and Laos,* edited by Shigeharu Tanabe and Charles F. Keyes, 68–94. Honolulu: University of Hawai'i Press.

———. 2008. "Giving Up Ghosts: Notes on Trauma and the Possibility of the Political from Southeast Asia." *Positions* 16 (1):229–58.

Morrison, Gayle L. 1997. "The Hmong *Qeej*: Speaking to the Spirit World." *Hmong Studies Journal* 2 (1): 1–17.

Moua, Mai Neng. 2002. *Bamboo among the Oaks: Contemporary Writing by Hmong Americans.* Saint Paul, Minn.: Minnesota Historical Society Press.

Mouanoutoua, Vang Leng. 2003. "Depression and Posttraumatic Stress Disorder: Prevailing Causes and Therapeutic Strategies with Hmong Clients." In Culhane-Pera et al. 2003, 216–21.

Mueggler, Erik. 2001. *The Age of Wild Ghosts: Memory, Violence, and Place in Southwest China.* Berkeley: University of California Press.

Munger, Ronald G., and Elizabeth A. Booton. 1998. "Bangungut in Manila: Sudden and Unexplained Death in Sleep of Adult Filipinos." *International Journal of Epidemiology* 27:677–84.

Murray, Stuart J. 2008. "Thanatopolitics: Reading in Agamben a Rejoinder to Biopolitical Life." *Communication and Critical/Cultural Studies* 5 (2):203–207.

Mystakidou, Kyriaki, Efi Parpa, Eleni Tsilila, Emmanuela Katsouda, and Lambros Vlahos. 2004. "Cancer Information Disclosure in Different Cultural Contexts." *Supportive Care in Cancer* 12 (3):147–54.

Nancy, Jean-Luc, and Richard Livingston. 1991. "The Unsacrificeable." In "Literature and the Ethical Question," edited by Claire Nouvet, special issue, *Yale French Studies* 79:20–38.

Naraindas, Harish. 2008. "Sacraments for the Dead? Still Births and the Science of Grieving in an American Hospital." Paper presented at a conference on "Ritual Dynamics and the Science of Ritual," Heidelberg, Germany, September 29–October 2.

Nelson, Christopher. 2008. *Dancing with the Dead: Memory, Performance, and Everyday Life in Postwar Okinawa.* Durham, N.C.: Duke University Press.

Nelson, Victoria. 2001. *The Secret Life of Puppets.* Cambridge, Mass.: Harvard University Press.

Ngor, Haing, and Roger Warner. 2003. *Survival in the Killing Fields* [1987]. New York: Carroll and Graf.

Nishii, Ryoko. 2002. "Social Memory as It Emerges: A Consideration of the Death of a Young Convert on the West Coast in Southern Thailand." In *Cultural Crisis and Social Memory: Modernity and Identity in Thailand and Laos,* edited by Shigeharu Tanabe and Charles F. Keyes, 231–42. Honolulu: University of Hawai'i Press.

North, Nicola H. 1995. "Crossing the Sea: Narratives of Exile and Illness among Cambodian Refugees in New Zealand." PhD Thesis, Massey University, Palmerston, New Zealand.

Ochoa, Todd Ramón. 2007. "Versions of the Dead: Kalunga, Cuban-Kongo Materiality, and Ethnography." *Cultural Anthropology* 22 (4):473–500.

———. 2010. *Society of the Dead: Quita Manaquita and Palo Praise in Cuba.* Berkeley: University of California Press.

Oeur, U Sam. 1998. *Sacred Vows.* Translated by Ken McCullough. Minneapolis: Coffee House Press.

Oeur, U Sam, and Ken McCullough. 2005. *Crossing Three Wildernesses: A Memoir.* Minneapolis: Coffee House Press.

Ong, Aihwa. 1987. *Spirits of Resistance and Capitalist Discipline: Factory Women in Malaysia.* Albany: State University of New York Press.

———. 2003. *Buddha Is Hiding: Refugees, Citizenship, the New America.* Berkeley: University of California Press.

Pandian, Anand. 2008. "Pastoral Power in the Postcolony: On the Biopolitics of the Criminal Animal in South India." *Cultural Anthropology* 23 (1):85–117.

Parkes, Colin Murray, Pittu Laungani, and Bill Young. 1997. *Death and Bereavement across Cultures.* New York: Routledge.

Parry, Jonathan. 1986. "The Gift, the Indian Gift, and the 'Indian Gift' of Death." *Man*, n.s. 21 (3):453–73.

———. 1995. *Death in Banares.* Cambridge: Cambridge University Press.

Pearson, Thomas. 2009. *Missions and Conversions: Creating the Montagnard-Dega Refugee Community.* New York: Palgrave Macmillan.

Pemberton, John. 1994. *On the Subject of "Java."* Ithaca: Cornell University Press.

Pereira, Peter. 2003. *Saying the World.* Port Townsend, Wash.: Copper Canyon Press.

———. 2007. *What's Written on the Body.* Port Townsend, Wash.: Copper Canyon Press.

Pigg, Stacy Leigh. 1996. "The Credible and the Credulous: The Question of 'Villagers' Beliefs' in Nepal." *Cultural Anthropology* 11 (2):160–201.

Pitt-Rivers, Julian. 2012. "The Law of Hospitality" [1977]. *Hau: Journal of Ethnographic Theory* 2 (1):501–17.

Ponn, Miech. 2001. *Komrong aiksaa sterbi propayni tumniem tumnoap kmae* [Writings about Khmer customs and traditions], *Part 1.* Phnom Penh: Buddhist Institute.

Povinelli, Elizabeth. 2002. *The Cunning of Recognition: Indigenous Alterities and the Making of Australian Multiculturalism.* Durham, N.C.: Duke University Press.

———. 2006. *The Empire of Love: Toward a Theory of Intimacy, Genealogy, and Carnality.* Durham, N.C.: Duke University Press.

Pran, Dith, and Kim DePaul. 1997. *Children of Cambodia's Killing Fields.* New Haven: Yale University Press.

Prigerson, Holly Gwen. 1992. "Socialization to Dying: Social Determinants of Death Acknowledgement and Treatment among Terminally Ill Geriatric Patients." *Journal of Health & Social Behavior* 33 (4):378–95.

Proschan, Frank. 1992. "Fieldwork and Social Work: Folklore as a Helping Profession." In *Public Folklore*, edited by Robert Baron and Nicholas R. Spitzer, 145–57. Washington, D.C.: Smithsonian Institution.

———. 1997. "'We Are All Kmhmu, Just the Same': Ethnonyms, Ethnic Identities, and Ethnic Groups." *American Ethnologist* 24 (1):91–113.

———. 2001. "People of the Gourd: Imagined Ethnicities in Highland Southeast Asia." *Journal of Asian Studies* 60 (4):999–1032.

Proudfoot, Robert. 1990. *Even the Birds Don't Sound the Same Here: The Laotian Refugees' Search for Heart in American Culture.* New York: Peter Lang.

Putsch, Robert W. 1988. "Ghost Illness: A Cross-Cultural Experience with the Expression of a Non-Western Tradition in Clinical Practice." *American Indian and Alaska Native Mental Health Research* no. 2 (2):6–26.

Quincy, Keith. 1988. *Hmong: History of a People*. Cheney: Eastern Washington University Press.

———. 2000. *Harvesting Pa Chay's Wheat: The Hmong and America's Secret War in Laos*. Spokane: Eastern Washington University Press.

Rajadhon, Phra Anuman. 1946. "The Khwan and its Ceremonies." *Journal of the Siam Society* 50 (2):119–64.

Rechtman, Richard, and Stéphanie Gée. 2009. *Interview with Richard Rechtman (2/2): "I Do Not Believe in a Deliverance Yielding Testimony."* Available from http://noko rkhmer.blogspot.com/2009/03/interview-with-richard-rechtman-22-i-do .html.

Rhodes, Lorna A. 1991. *Emptying Beds: The Work of an Emergency Psychiatric Unit*. Berkeley: University of California Press.

Robben, Antonius C. G. M. 2000. "State Terror in the Netherworld: Disappearance and Reburial in Argentina." In *Death Squad: The Anthropology of State Terror*, edited by Jeffrey A. Sluka, 91–113. Philadelphia: University of Pennsylvania Press.

Romanyshyn, Robert D. 1989. *Technology as Symptom and Dream*. New York: Routledge.

Rushdie, Salman. 1999. *The Ground Beneath Her Feet*. New York: Picador.

Saunders, Barry F. 2008. *CT Suites: The Work of Diagnosis in the Age of Non-Invasive Cutting*. Durham, N.C.: Duke University Press.

Scarry, Elaine. 1985. *The Body in Pain: The Making and Unmaking of the World*. New York: Oxford University Press.

Schein, Louisa. 1999. "Performing Modernity." *Cultural Anthropology* 14 (3):361–95.

Scheper-Hughes, Nancy. 2000. "The Global Traffic in Human Organs." *Current Anthropology* 41 (2):191–211.

———. 2005. "The Last Commodity: Post-Human Ethics and the Global Traffic in 'Fresh' Organs." In *Global Assemblages: Technology, Politics, and Ethics as Anthropological Problems*, edited by Aihwa Ong and Stephen Collier, 145–67. London: Basil Blackwell.

Scott, David. 2004. *Conscripts of Modernity: The Tragedy of Colonial Enlightenment*. Durham, N.C.: Duke University Press.

Seale, Clive. 1991. "Communication and Awareness about Death: A Study of a Random Sample of Dying People." *Social Science and Medicine* 32 (8):943–52.

Sebald, W. G. 1996. *The Emigrants*. Translated by Michael Hulse. New York: New Directions.

———. 1998. *The Rings of Saturn*. Translated by Michael Hulse. New York: New Directions.

Seremetakis, Nadia. 1991. *The Last Word: Women, Death, and Divination in Inner Mani*. Chicago: University of Chicago Press.

Serin, Ozge. 2012. *Life at the Limitlessness of the Limit: Ethics and Politics of the Death Fast in Turkish Prisons, 2000–2007*. PhD diss., Department of Anthropology, Columbia University.

Siegel, James 2006. *Naming the Witch.* Stanford: Stanford University Press.

———. 2011. *Objects and Objections of Ethnography.* New York: Fordham University Press.

Smith-Hefner, Nancy J. 1999. *Khmer American: Identity and Moral Education in a Diasporic Community.* Berkeley: University of California Press.

Song, Hoon. 2010. *Pigeon Trouble: Bestiary Biopolitics in a Deindustrialized America.* Philadelphia: University of Pennsylvania Press.

Spivak, Gayatri. 1988. "Can the Subaltern Speak?" In *Marxism and the Interpretation of Culture,* edited by Cary Nelson and Laurence Grossberg, 271–313. Chicago: University of Illinois Press.

Stanton, Gregory H. 1993. "The Khmer Rouge Genocide and International Law." In *Genocide and Democracy in Cambodia: The Khmer Rouge, the United Nations, and the International Community,* edited by Ben Kiernan, 141–61. New Haven: Yale University Southeast Asian Studies.

Steedly, Mary Margaret. 1993. *Hanging without a Rope: Narrative Experience in Colonial and Postcolonial Karoland.* Princeton: Princeton University Press.

Stengers, Isabelle. 2005. "The Cosmopolitical Proposal." In *Making Things Public: Atmospheres of Democracy,* edited by Bruno Latour and Peter Weibel, 994–1004. Cambridge, Mass.: MIT Press.

Stewart, Kathleen. 1996. *A Space on the Side of the Road: Cultural Poetics in an "Other" America.* Princeton: Princeton University Press.

Strathern, Marilyn. 1992. *After Nature.* Cambridge: Cambridge University Press.

Stuart-Fox, Martin. 1997. *A History of Laos.* Cambridge: Cambridge University Press.

Sturken, Marita. 1997. *Tangled Memories: The Vietnam War, the AIDS Epidemic, and the Politics of Remembering.* Berkeley: University of California Press.

Surbone, Antonella. 2004. "Persisting Differences in Truth Telling Throughout the World." *Supportive Care in Cancer* 12 (3):143–46.

Symonds, Patricia V. 2004. *Calling in the Soul: Gender and the Cycle of Life in a Hmong Village.* Seattle: University of Washington Press.

Szymusiak, Molyda. 1999. *The Stones Cry Out: A Cambodian Childhood, 1975–1980.* Translated by Linda Coverdale. Bloomington: Indiana University Press.

Tambiah, Stanley Jeyaraja. 1970. *Buddhism and the Spirit Cults in North-East Thailand.* Cambridge: Cambridge University Press.

———. 1984. *The Buddhist Saints of the Forest and the Cult of Amulets: A Study in Charisma, Hagiography, Sectarianism, and Millennial Buddhism.* Cambridge: Cambridge University Press.

Tapp, Nicholas. 1986. "Geomancy as an Aspect of Upland–Lowland Relationships." In *The Hmong in Transition,* edited by Glenn L. Hendricks, Bruce T. Downing, and Amos S. Deinard, 87–95. New York: Center for Migration Studies.

———. 1988. "Geomancy and Development: The Case of the White Hmong of North Thailand." *Ethnos* 53 (3–4):228–38.

————. 1989. "Hmong Religion." *Asian Folklore Studies* 48:59–94.

Taussig, Michael. 1987. *Shamanism, Colonialism, and the Wild Man: A Study in Terror and Healing.* Chicago: University of Chicago Press.

————. 1997. *The Magic of the State.* New York: Routledge.

————. 1999. *Defacement: Public Secrecy and the Labor of the Negative.* Stanford: Stanford University Press.

Tayanin, Damrong. 1994. *Being Kammu: My Village, My Life.* Ithaca: Cornell Southeast Asia Program.

Taylor, Charles. 1989. *Sources of the Self: The Making of Modern Identity.* Cambridge, Mass.: Harvard University Press.

Thao, Phillipe Nompus. 1993. "Between Two Worlds: Hmong Ethnography, Spirituality, and Ceremony for the Deceased." Master's thesis, Mankato State University, Mankato, Minnesota.

Thion, Serge. 1993. "Genocide as a Political Commodity." In *Genocide and Democracy in Cambodia: The Khmer Rouge, the United Nations, and the International Community,* edited by Ben Kiernan, 163–90. New Haven: Yale University Southeast Asian Studies.

Thipmuntali, Khampheng. 1999. "The Lue of Muang Sing." In *Laos: Culture and Society,* edited by Grant Evans, 148–60. Chiangmai, Thailand: Silkworm Books.

Thompson, Ashley. 1996. *The Calling of the Souls: A Study of the Khmer Ritual Hau Bralin.* Melbourne, Australia: Monash Asia Institute, Monash University.

Timmermans, Stefan. 1997. "High Touch in High Tech: The Presence of Relatives and Friends during Resuscitative Efforts." *Scholarly Inquiry for Nursing Practice: An International Journal* 11 (2):153–68.

————. 1999. *Sudden Death and the Myth of CPR.* Philadelphia: Temple University Press.

Tobin, Joseph Jay, and Joan Friedman. 1983. "Spirits, Shamans, and Nightmare Death: Survivor Stress in a Hmong Refugee." *American Journal of Orthopsychiatry* 53 (3):439–48.

Trankell, Ing-Britt. 1999. "Royal Relics: Ritual and Social Memory in Louang Prabang." In *Laos: Culture and Society,* edited by Grant Evans, 191–213. Chiangmai, Thailand: Silkworm Books.

Trawick, Margaret. 1992. *Notes on Love in a Tamil Family.* Berkeley: University of California Press.

Tsing, Anna Lowenhaupt. 2005. *Friction: An Ethnography of Global Connection.* Princeton: Princeton University Press.

Tuckett, Anthony G. 2004. "Truth-Telling in Clinical Practice and the Arguments For and Against: A Review of the Literature." *Nursing Ethics: An International Journal for Health Care Professionals* 11 (5):500–13.

Ung, Loung. 2000. *First They Killed My Father: A Daughter of Cambodia Remembers.* New York: HarperCollins.

Van Alphen, Ernst. 1999. "Symptoms of Discursivity: Experience, Memory, and Trauma." In *Acts of Memory: Cultural Recall in the Present,* edited by Mieke Bal, Jonathan Crewe, and Leo Spitzer, 24–38. Hanover, N.H.: University of New England Press.

Van Esterik, Penny. 1992. *Taking Refuge: Lao Buddhists in North America.* Tempe: Program for Southeast Asian Studies, Arizona State University.

Venkatsan, Soumhya, Jeanette Edwards, Rane Willerslev, Elizabeth Povinelli, and Perveez Mody. 2011. "The Anthropological Fixation with Reciprocity Leaves No Room for Love: 2009 Meeting of the Group for Debates in Anthropological Theory." *Critique of Anthropology* 31 (3):210–50.

Verdery, Katherine. 1999. *The Political Lives of Dead Bodies: Reburial and Postsocialist Change.* New York: Columbia University Press.

Vickery, Michael. 1990. "Refugee Politics: The Khmer Camp System in Thailand." In *The Cambodian Agony,* edited by David A. Ablin and Marlowe Hood, 293–331. Armonk, N.Y.: M. E. Sharpe Publishers.

Wall, Thomas Carl. 2005. "Au Hasard." In *Politics, Metaphysics, and Death: Essays on Giorgio Agamben's "Homo Sacer,"* edited by Andrew Norris, 31–48. Durham, N.C.: Duke University Press.

Watson, James L. 1982. "Of Flesh and Bones: The Management of Death Pollution in Cantonese Society." In *Death and the Regeneration of Life,* edited by Maurice Bloch and Jonathan Parry, 155–86. Cambridge: Cambridge University Press.

Watson, Matthew. 2012. "Newtons and Apes: Questioning Biocentrism and the Multispecies Turn." Paper presented at the Society for Cultural Anthropology Biennial Meeting, Providence, Rhode Island, May 11–12.

Webb, Marilyn. 1997. *The Good Death: The New American Search to Reshape the End of Life.* New York: Bantam.

White, Kenneth, and Jacques Lemoine. 1982. *Kr'ua Ke (Showing the Way): A Hmong Initiation of the Dead.* Bangkok: Pandora.

White, Stephen. 1997. "Hindu Cremations in Britain." In *The Changing Face of Death,* edited by Peter Jupp and Glennys Howarth, 135–48. New York: St. Martin's.

Willerslev, Rane. 2007. *Soul Hunters: Hunting, Animism, and Personhood among the Siberian Yukaghirs.* Berkeley: University of California Press.

———. 2009. "The Optimal Sacrifice: A Study of Voluntary Death among the Siberian Chukchi." *American Ethnologist* 36 (4):693–704.

Y, Ly. 2000. *Heaven Becomes Hell: A Survivor's Story of Life under the Khmer Rouge.* New Haven: Yale University Southeast Asian Studies.

Yang, Cziasarh Neng. 2002. "Cultural Capital: Old Hmong Culture in Modern Times." PhD diss., University of St. Thomas, St. Paul, Minn.

Yathay, Pin. 1987. *Stay Alive, My Son.* New York: Simon and Schuster.

Yoneyama, Lisa. 1999. *Hiroshima Traces: Time, Space, and the Dialectics of Memory.* Berkeley: University of California Press.

Young, Allan. 1995. *The Harmony of Illusions: Inventing Post-Traumatic Stress Disorder.* Princeton: Princeton University Press.

Zussman, R. 1997. "Sociological Perspectives on Medical Ethics and Decision-Making." *Annual Review of Sociology* 23:171–89.

Index

advance directives, 82, 84, 88, 99, 132, 228n11, 229n2

Agamben, Giorgio, 4, 28, 69, 164–65, 205, 206, 207

Alphen, Ernst Van, 225n6

American War in Vietnam (1961–1975), 31, 81–82

ancestors: as distinguished from ghosts, 213. *See also* dead

animality, 29, 151, 165, 205–6; figures of, 65–71; sea serpents, 69–70; souls, 67–68; in Southeast Asian folklore, 66–67, 68; tiger husband, 68–70

animism, 12, 15, 165, 166, 215

Antelme, Robert, 29

Aquinas, Thomas, 205–6

Ariès, Philippe, 82–83, 115–16, 128

Armstrong, David, 115, 116, 117

Asad, Talal, 76

Austin, John, 129

autology, 7, 93, 177, 181

autonomy. *See* patient autonomy

autopsy, 195

bad death: defined, 16–17, 32–33; and engagement with dead, 27; haunting of, 16–17, 26, 32–33, 39–40, 43; and imminent death, 36–37;

language of, 41–42; living person as ghost, 33–36; as ordinary, 35, 40–41; practices for, 30, 39, 48; and survival, 36

Bang Fai festival, 70

bangsukol, 173–74

Barley, Nigel, 106

Bataille, Georges, 181, 193

Battin, Margaret Pabst, 83

Benjamin, Walter, 18, 19, 20, 81

Benveniste, Emile, 28

bereavement support, 103–4. *See also* grief and mourning

Berger, Jeffrey, 119

Beste, Jennifer, 80

bioethics, 5, 6; and cultural practices, 120; latent Christianity in, 151; and personal narrative, 126; sovereignty of, 97–98; on spirits, 215–16; on truth-telling, 118–19, 130–31, 151; and uncanny, 120–21

biomedicine, 6, 91–93, 143–44, 147. *See also* medicine and medical technology

biopolitics, 4, 68, 91, 165, 215

Bonanno, George, 235n6

Boun Khau Padab Din, 170–71

Bourdieu, Pierre, 234n10

Jean M. Langford is associate professor of anthropology at the University of Minnesota. She is the author of *Fluent Bodies: Ayurvedic Remedies for Post-colonial Imbalance.*